The Tears that Made the Clyde

The Tears
that made the Clyde

Well-being in Glasgow

CAROL CRAIG

ARGYLL ✤ PUBLISHING

© Carol Craig 2010

First published in 2010 by
Argyll Publishing
Glendaruel
Argyll PA22 3AE
Scotland
www.argyllpublishing.com

The author has asserted her moral rights.

**British Library Cataloguing-in-
Publication Data.**

**A catalogue record for this book is
available from the British Library.**

ISBN 978 1 906134 47 1

Printing: Bell & Bain Ltd, Glasgow

In memory of my two
Glaswegian grandmothers

Mary Craig
(née McCondichie) 1894–1958

Helen Earlie
(née Haugh) 1900–1924

Contents

ACKNOWLEDGEMENTS

MUCH of this book could not have been written without the prior work of a large number of historians and other scholars who have deliberated on Glasgow's, or Scotland's, past. I fully acknowledge my debt to them. I also want to express my gratitude to the various people who grew up in Glasgow or the west of Scotland and who have written accounts of their lives in personal memoirs or literature. Many have courageously exposed aspects of their past and in so doing have contributed enormously to our understanding of family and personal life.

One historian has played a particularly large part in this book – Professor Tom Devine. His work on Scotland's past is not only scholarly, insightful and authoritative but also accessible to a wide audience. At various points in the book it was Devine's work which helped shape my analysis. I am flattered that Professor Devine was willing not only to look at an early draft and comment on it but also to write the foreword.

I am particularly grateful to Professor Phil Hanlon not just for writing an afterword but also for his contribution to my analysis. His thinking on culture and health, and the need for an integral approach, has had a major influence on my thinking on well-being.

I would also like to thank Alan Sinclair, Professor John Frank and Dr. Harry Burns for helping me to reach my main conclusion on the importance of the early years. I would also like to thank the following for their willing-ness to discuss aspects of my analysis or providing me with information: Jean Barr, John Carnochan, Jim Dixon, Elaine Duncan, Derek Goldman, Gerry Hassan, Bill Hunter, Rod Hunter, Andrew Lyon, Isobel MacNaughtan, John Matthews, Andrea Nove, Fabio Sani, Ronnie Scott, Alex Smith, Jim Sweeney, David Walsh, David Webster, Diana Wernisch and Zoe Van Zwanenberg.

I am indebted to Board members at the Centre for Confidence and Well-being for their practical and moral support: Charlie Miller, Ian McKay, Hazel Black, Kate Dunlop, Martin Stepek, Phil Hanlon and particularly the Chair, Fred Shedden. It was Fred's desire that the Centre should make a contribution to an understanding of Glasgow's health and social challenges which encouraged me to think seriously about the topic. Thanks too are due to other Centre staff for their help and support: Archie Dalrymple, Anna Wilson, Emily Cutts and Pete Fletcher.

I would also like to thank my family for their interest and support during the writing of the book – Alf and our two sons Ewan and Jamie and the new girls in our lives – Merlin and Rhiannon – as well as my sisters Marianne and Janice. Particular thanks go to my parents who were happy to talk to me at length about Glasgow in the old days while I was working on the book.

I would like to thank Archie Fisher for permission to quote from 'The Fairfield Crane' – the song which includes the line 'it was tears that made the Clyde'. Thanks for permission to quote are also due to Michael Marra for the lines from 'Mother Glasgow', Alasdair Gray for use of some verses from *Old Negatives*, Eric Bogle for 'The Glasgow Lullaby' and Kirsteen Stokes for the use of lines by her father, Maurice Lindsay. Unfortunately we were not able to trace Neil McLellan whose poem 'This Unrung Bell' is used in the last chapter in ways which I think are in tune with its theme.

When deciding the cover for this book the publisher and I were in total agreement that we wanted an image which was both completely fresh and sufficiently abstract to allow readers to interpret it for themselves. Michael Scott's beguiling painting, 'Night Magic', is perfect on both counts. Indeed in discussing the influences on his work, Mick once wrote: 'Analysis would tell you why these things interest me. I don't know. Please make of them what you will.' Sadly Mick died in 2006. This image is used courtesy of the artist's estate and I would like to thank his widow Gill Scott for her help.

Finally, I want to thank Derek Rodger of Argyll Publishing. Derek has been everything I wanted from a publisher and editor – a pleasure to work with, supportive yet challenging, and completely committed to the book and its objectives.

Carol Craig
February 2010

G LASGOW, Scotland's largest city, is an urban conundrum. From one perspective it has been widely praised as a modern success story. A new order has risen, phoenix-like, from the ruins of past economic dereliction and social decay. After the long drawn-out agony of deindustrialisation, which scarred its history for much of the late twentieth century, the city has emerged at the start of the new millennium as the reinvented 'Scotland with style', the second biggest shopping centre in the UK after London with its vibrant main streets crammed with new restaurants, bistros and clubs. *National Geographic* magazine has gone so far as to dub it 'Capital of Cool' and the city's international reputation has flourished to such an extent that it now draws tourists from far and wide.

This is the Glasgow of the glossy journals and the marketing hype. But it is not a myth or a figment born simply out of exaggerated spin and advertising display. Much of the city core has indeed been transformed beyond recognition by new forms of employment and economic diversification which have underpinned a veritable urban renaissance in which Glaswegians have a right to take considerable pride. The visitor can sense a spirit of confidence among the citizenry. With its magnificent Victorian architecture, cleaned and restored public buildings, world-renowned museums and galleries, distinguished universities and dynamic cultural scene, Glasgow is, by any standards, an attractive urban space in which to live, work and enjoy life.

But this is only part of the story. Glasgow has a schizophrenic personality and, while the body might seem healthy on the surface, it conceals a diseased underbelly. The city's grave social problems in certain areas have stubbornly resisted improvement even as urban reinvention has gathered pace. Glasgow is therefore still near the top of those unenviable league tables in both the UK and Europe for poor life expectancy, incapacity, alcohol and drug addiction and obesity. Indeed, these problems are so acute that the 'Glasgow effect' has even had a strongly negative impact on Scotland's national health statistical record. Public and private interventions to confront these trends have been numerous and imaginative but success has been little better than partial and limited. Even more seriously, there is no intellectual consensus on the reasons for the distinctive health patterns in Glasgow, despite the fact that convincing explanation is the vital first step in pursuit of effective diagnosis and action.

This is the question that Carol Craig seeks to address in her wide-ranging analysis. She conclusively demonstrates at the start that common-sense reasoning will not easily work in this case. No one can doubt that the catastrophic collapse of the old industrial staples of Glasgow and the resulting alarmingly high levels of unemployment in the 1980s caused poverty and social misery. But these factors in themselves cannot explain the current Glasgow problems. The peoples of other great cities across Europe and North America also suffered much during those times of deindustrialisation and yet did not experience health crises on the scale, depth or duration of Glasgow's. As Dr. Craig argues, if we are to move closer to an intellectually satisfying explanation, we must dig deeper and wider.

This she does by building nothing less than a new model of

interpretation. A central contention in the book is that the real answers to the key questions lie far back in time. The social problems under consideration have a long lineage and so historical analysis of the Glaswegian past, she suggests, is an essential approach to them. Using many of the results of the recent revolution in Scottish history writing, Dr. Craig provides a total picture of Glaswegian life over the centuries which includes discussion of economy, male culture, drinking habits, urban modes of life, middle class ideologies and much else. It is an exhilarating brew.

To this, she then adds insights from modern social science and comparative examples to provide context for the evidence and enhance the impact of the overall argument. Not content with diagnosis, Dr. Craig concludes the book with a series of recommendations on how this particular urban patient might be treated and improvement assured over the longer term.

The 'Glasgow effect' is not simply a major challenge for the city. The nation as a whole must be moved to action by the plight of so many of our fellow citizens. Their condition is indeed a rebuke to the conscience of Scotland. How to act effectively is, nevertheless, the hard question. Carol Craig has unquestionably moved the debate on that forward. Even those who may disagree profoundly with her thesis in this stimulating, provocative and, yes, uncomfortable book, will now have to think, equally profoundly, of their own answers to the Glasgow conundrum.

T.M. Devine
Sir William Fraser Professor
of History and Palaeography,
University of Edinburgh

INTRODUCTION

T HE BEST place to get a sense of contemporary Glasgow is at the top of Buchanan Street, beside the statue of Donald Dewar, the political architect of the Scottish Parliament and Scotland's first First Minister. Once a residential thoroughfare, built with money from the tobacco lords, Buchanan Street now houses the city's most upmarket shops. In 2004 city marketeers rebranded Glasgow 'Scotland with style', eagerly selling the city as a shoppers' paradise. But as is usually the case in Scotland's largest city, a few eyebrows were raised. Shoppers' paradise? Glasgow was historically renowned for its production, not consumption; the city produced ships, engines and locomotives by the ton and internationally the term 'Clydebuilt' was synonymous with quality and workmanship. Standing at the top of Buchanan Street, one expects to catch at least a glimpse of the world-famous Clyde, but it is an elusive river and we cannot even see a crane in the small window of sky.

Glasgow is now the quintessential 'post industrial city'. In the 1980s and 90s the city, and the west of Scotland as a whole, haemorrhaged jobs from shipyards, steelworks, mines and even from the new industries which were supposed to take the place of the old heavy industries – such as the Linwood car plant. But the city rallied remarkably well from the shock to its economy – commerce, services, education and creative industries injected new life. Within ten miles of this spot there are four universities and countless colleges. Behind us is the Glasgow Concert Hall – not a great architectural statement perhaps but an important jewel in Glasgow's recent crowning as UNESCO City of Music. Glasgow is also noted for its art: not just its great municipal collection housed in the impressive, refurbished Kelvingrove Art Gallery, a couple of miles to the west, but also the work of one of the city's most creative citizens – Charles Rennie Mackintosh – the internationally renowned architect.

Indeed Glasgow has been a huge success story when it comes to 'culture-led regeneration'. The city has instigated a number of high-profile campaigns to project a different image for itself: prior to 'Scotland with style' there was the distinctive 'Glasgow's miles better' which successfully utilised the services of the 'Mr Happy' character. It has also been very effective at bidding for, and then organising, a number of high profile, feel-good initiatives – the 1988 Garden Festival, the City of Culture designation in 1990, the City of Architecture label in 1999, UNESCO City of Music in 2008, and more recently the successful capturing of the 2014 Commonwealth Games. These events, and the real transformation of the Merchant City and other areas into attractive places to live, work and shop, have made Glasgow a Mecca for other cities interested in tackling post-industrial decline. However, Glasgow's success on this front makes the story which unfolds in this book even more surprising.

I cannot claim to be a Glaswegian as I was brought up on the outskirts of the city and still do not live within its boundary. However, my parents and grandparents were born or lived here and it is this city's values and beliefs which are in my blood. What's more I studied, lived, gave birth to my two sons and have worked in various jobs in and around Glasgow for over thirty years. In 2005 I set up the Centre for Confidence and Well-being – a small charitable organisation housed a block or two away from Buchanan Street. As a result of the Centre's work on positive psychology I am only too aware of the power and the importance of appreciation; that when seeking to improve an organisation or develop an individual it can be more productive to look for the positives and build on these than to dwell on mistakes and problems.[1] So in this book on Glasgow I would love to tell readers what a wonderful city this is. I would dearly love to believe that somehow we could deal with some of the city's social problems not by focussing on them or being critical but by sidestepping them and accentuating the positive.

I still believe that an appreciative approach can solve problems and is a useful tool, but sometimes it is inappropriate. Many important societal changes have occurred not through appreciation, or enhancing the positive, but as a result of righteous anger and indignation – the extension of the franchise to working men, votes for women, factory legislation, the end of slavery.[2] These are all changes which came about because campaigners didn't like what they saw – they bridled at injustice, unfairness or outright barbarism. Glasgow's problems are deep-seated – they stretch back hundreds of years. Arguably one of the main reasons that problems have persisted is that Glasgow's citizens have not confronted them enough – huge cracks have been papered over; the city's politicians have reached for the gloss rather than being prepared to chip away to find the core of the problem and come up with innovative and radical solutions. Indeed one of the most remarkable aspects of Glaswegian culture is the way that truly negative aspects of the place are often ignored, played down or even laughed at. Scottish institutions too collude in denying Glasgow's problems. Since

2007 Scotland's official on-line gateway has been telling the world that the city shook off its violent image in the early 1980s:

> . . . and today the no-mean-city image of Glasgow is perhaps only still believed by a handful of elderly ladies in Hampstead, the kind who believe that civilisation ends at the top of the Northern Line. Nowadays, finally, the rest of the world is beginning to believe what the locals have known for some time now: that Glasgow is one of the most cultured, cosmopolitan and increasingly affluent cities in the world.[3]

At the end of the 1990s, a few feet away from the Donald Dewar statue, rival gangs of young teenagers battled one another and an innocent 27 year old man, walking his girlfriend to the bus, was stabbed to death by a boy, aged 15.[4] CCTV footage shows the teenager gesticulating triumphantly as he examines his knife and sees it is covered in blood. Of course, we can regard this incident as a random act of violence which could have occurred in any city in the world. Up to a point this is true, but we cannot escape the fact that murders in Glasgow are so frequent that it is the most violent city in Western Europe. Murders in London have received a great deal of publicity in recent times with widely reported youth-on-youth stabbings and shootings. They are on the rise but per head of the population Glasgow is twice as violent as London and has been for a long time.[5] Indeed death by stabbing has become so frequent in Glasgow that the Scottish press hardly reports it anymore. One particularly revealing fact is that in this violent city, facial injury is so common that surgeons in the local hospitals have become world experts in their fields. Another shocking fact is that one secondary school in this city can list seven pupils who have died in recent years from stab wounds.

One of the most remarkable aspects of the Buchanan Street murder is that it happened in the city centre in territory used by the city's middle classes. The vast majority of murders and serious assaults in Glasgow occur in the east end or in peripheral housing estates. This is a city which likes to espouse its egalitarian values but it is deeply divided by social class. Every so often a middle class lad or man gets caught up in street violence. Much more commonly it is young men from 'deprived' areas who are knifing each other and are victims or perpetrators of the killings.

Even when we look at death by natural causes we see the heavy imprint of social class. In this city, there are areas where the life expectancy for men is 55 – lower than in many third world countries. In some leafy neighbouring communities their male counterparts can expect to live 23 years longer. For women, the gap in life expectancy figures between rich and poor is not quite so stark but nonetheless women in the west of Scotland die younger than their sisters in most of Europe, including Eastern Europe.

At the top of Buchanan Street, on the wall of the Concert Hall, we can find the ubiquitous Glasgow coat of arms featuring St. Mungo, and the symbols with which he is associated – a bell, tree, fish and bird – as well as the city's motto 'Let Glasgow Flourish'. But no-one can look at the evidence on Glasgow's health, social problems and record of violent crime and conclude that this is a flourishing city. The victims and perpetrators of violent crime are not flourishing; neither are the young people committing suicide, the drug addicts, the neglected and abused children, the alcoholics, the men in their fifties too incapacitated to work, the battered women, the drunks. Of course, Glasgow has no monopoly on these social problems, and we can find them in cities right round the world, but per head of the population Glasgow has a higher incidence of many of them than other European cities. Why?

This book tries to respond to that question. The easy answer is deprivation and, of course, this is a hugely significant factor. But recent comparative research, outlined in the next chapter, rules this out as a comprehensive explanation on its own. My own deliberations suggest that the problems can only be understood in a historical context which is why this book takes a new look at Glasgow's past.

The first chapter provides the evidence on Glasgow's record on health, violence, poverty and so forth. It also outlines the ideas of Professor Richard Wilkinson, an epidemiologist who argues that health inequalities, and a clutch of other problems such as violence, prejudice, drinking and domestic abuse are linked to pronounced income inequality. If analysts only look at current numerical data then Glasgow does not seem to suffer from excessive income inequality. However, the picture which Wilkinson paints of what happens with pronounced inequality is so redolent of Glasgow that his thesis demands further inspection. One of the main purposes of this book is to ask whether historically there was so much inequality in Glasgow that it has created a culture which produces the effects Wilkinson describes. The following chapter gives an overview of the relevant aspects of Glasgow's history from early times to its height as an industrial centre.

Chapters 3 and 4 look at Glasgow's history through the lens of Wilkinson's dominance hierarchy. The first of these focusses on the behaviour and attitudes of wealthy Glaswegians to money-making and to the poor. The second looks at the same issue but from the perspective of the workers themselves. The focus is on whether there was a pronounced 'pecking order' within Glasgow's working class.

Chapter 5 then looks at why alcohol came to play such an important part in the lives of poor people in Glasgow. Chapter 6 take a historical look at violence within the city including routine violence between men, gangs and domestic abuse. Chapter 7 specifically looks at women's lives and how they were often blighted not just by poverty but the actions of men more intent on their own pleasures than playing a positive role within the family. We also look here at women's attitude to money and their 'great escape' to the cinema.

Chapter 8 looks at the extent to which Glaswegians flourished in the period under review. To help us evaluate this we look at 'flourishing' through the fulfilment of three basic psychological needs – the need for autonomy, competence and relatedness. Chapter 9 then looks at the positive vision of flourishing and well-being promoted by figures like James Maxton but, sadly, also shows how so much of this socialist idealism ended by creating a dependency culture. Chapter 10 looks at the role of education in the city.

Chapters 2 through to 10 focus on Glasgow's history prior to the 1950s and 60s. Where relevant I may refer to the later period but only when it helps to illuminate an aspect of Glasgow's past. Chapter 11 begins to shift our thinking towards more contemporary times. It examines the importance and themes of Archie Hind's seminal Glasgow novel, *The Dear Green Place* – most notably Glasgwegians' attitudes to culture and self-expression. Chapter 12 looks at the importance of love not just to child development but later health and happiness. With this in mind we look at the verbal aggression inherent in Glasgow's culture. Chapter 13 looks at how some of these themes play out in the lives of creative people like the author and artist Alasdair Gray, the author of *Lanark,* and the novelist Janice Galloway.

Chapter 14 then considers the creation of the peripheral housing estates and high rise blocks and the impact this new housing had on tenants. It also looks at the hugely negative impact of unemployment in the 1980s and 90s. Chapter 15 examines how many of the problems poor people face in the city are not just due to material deprivation but also to materialist values, poor family life, depression and lack of hope. Chapter 16, the penultimate chapter, discusses the controversial issue of self-esteem. The final chapter draws some of the disparate threads together and considers the weight, and merit of the various arguments presented in the previous chapters to the questions posed at the beginning of the book. It also outlines what I believe to be some solutions to these deep-seated problems.

It is important to point out that I am not trying to come up with a definitive analysis of the cause of Glasgow's current social problems. I say little about diet, or exercise, nothing about the lack of sunshine and I'm sure that I don't give adequate attention to language issues or religion. I don't spend time on these topics simply to be practical – these are all enormous subjects in their own right and to do them justice would have required more than one volume.

It is also appropriate for me to say something about method-ology and sources. Professor T.C. Smout is a celebrated social historian who has written extensively on Scotland. He once wrote that 'There is nothing more difficult for historians to explore than the personal and sexual lives of a past age.' [6] Given that much of what I write about here concerns intimate aspects of family life, finding appropriate evidence has been a challenge. This is why I have outlined where I have found most of my material and explained the justification for the weight I place on these sources. [7]

There are two ways in which this book is unashamedly one-sided. It is primarily interested in what historians would call 'the lower orders'. This means that in the historical chapters you will find little about the city's upper or middle classes unless their activities and beliefs have some bearing on the lives of the less fortunate. Secondly, it emphasises the problems and the difficulties at the expense of the positive aspects of the culture. Over the years there have been numerous celebratory books about Glasgow both historical and fictional – books such as *The Second City* by C.A. Oakley, *Dancing in the Streets* by Cliff Hanley or the various anthologies or books of photographs. The most recent offering is *Our Glasgow*, based on reminiscences collected by the English writer Piers Dudgeon, and intentionally written as a celebration of Glasgow's working class history. However, by definition, if we are going to find the roots of Glasgow's current social problems we are less likely to trace them back to the shiny, positive aspects of Glasgow's story. We have to dig underground and unearth the less pleasant aspects of the city's culture both in the past and the present. Much of what we have to consider does not even have to be dug up – it is staring us in the face if we are prepared to confront it for what it is and not try to put a positive spin on it or make excuses. Of course, what we uncover or give prominence to will not be unique to Glasgow. But the question we need to keep asking is this: **did the conditions and culture in Glasgow provide a particularly fertile seedbed for the development of various health and social problems and did these problems envelop a greater percentage of the city's citizens?**

After all the boys who ran amok in Buchanan Street wielding knives, the men dying years before their time, the countless drunks and the drug addicts have not landed here from another planet; they are creatures of this city. However, the point of this book is not about pointing the finger or attributing blame. It is about finding the root causes of problems which as a community we need to confront, discuss and, more importantly, discover the capacity, energy and motivation to solve.

CHAPTER 1

Glasgow – no picture of health

IN 2004 a group of concerned professionals working in the city, including Sir John Arbuthnott, successfully lobbied a range of organisations for investment in a research and development organisation which would explore the heart of Glasgow's health problems. The Glasgow Centre for Population Health (GCPH) was born. Since its inception the organisation has undertaken extensive empirical research to help explain the origins of Glasgow's poor health. In 2006 it published its first large report *Let Glasgow Flourish: A comprehensive report on health and its determinants in Glasgow and West Central Scotland*, written by Phil Hanlon, David Walsh and Bruce Whyte.[1] Other large reports have followed.[2]

Historically, at least since the Industrial Revolution, Glasgow was predominantly a working class city with a very small middle and upper class. One of the main themes reinforced by GCPH's research is that Glasgow has become 'more affluent and middle class'. Since 1981 the proportion of Glasgow's population in the top two social classes has more than doubled. This means that four out of ten of Glasgow's citizens are now classified as Social Class 1 or 2. In consequence Glasgow is now much more similar to other cities in the UK. Nonetheless, large health problems remain:

There is a 'Glasgow effect' – that is, an excess of

mortality beyond that which can be explained by current indices of deprivation. The result is that Glasgow's health status remains worse than that of comparable English cities like Liverpool. [3]

On the positive side, Hanlon *et al.* point out that general life expectancy across the area is increasing. Indeed life expectancy has doubled in the last 100 years. Children's dental health is slowly improving. Smoking has gone down substantially as have some medical conditions such as heart disease and stroke. Indeed Glasgow is no longer 'the coronary capital of the world'. However, the GCPH reports shows that there are a number of worrying trends in the opposite direction. For brevity, I summarise the most important of these below, with some additional or updated data where relevant.[4]

Life expectancy

- Male life expectancy at birth in Glasgow is 69.1 – four years less than the Scottish average and eight years less than the East Dunbartonshire figure, the best in Scotland. Glasgow women fare slightly better. Their life expectancy at birth is 76.4, 2.5 years less than the Scottish average and 4.5 years lower than the best figure – East Renfrewshire at 81.1 years.

- There is a fifteen year age gap between male life expectancy in the poor areas of the city (Bridgeton and Dennistoun) and more affluent areas (Anniesland, Bearsden and Milngavie). In some Glasgow postcodes life expectancy is as low as 55 years, making a 23 year gap between these areas and the prosperous district of Lenzie only a few miles away. For women the equivalent comparisons are better but still show a difference of seven to eight years of life expectancy between rich and poor areas.

- The gap in male life expectancy in Greater Glasgow has widened in the last 20 years from 6.9 years to 11.8 years.

- In the last twenty years life expectancy for men in the most affluent areas of Glasgow has increased by around four years whereas it has dropped by almost one year for those in the most deprived areas.

- More than one fifth of Glasgow's population die before their 65th birthday. The rate for men is one in four.

- Glasgow's mortality rate is not reducing at the same rate as Scotland's.

General health

- *Obesity* rates in Glasgow are among the highest in the world and 'show no signs of levelling'. This is increasing diabetes rates to worrying levels. More than half of men and women in Glasgow are considered 'overweight'. 20 per cent of Glasgow's children are also considered overweight, including 8 per cent who are classed as 'obese'.

- The incidence of *heart disease and strokes* has improved in Glasgow, and in Scotland as a whole. However, Glasgow's figure for these conditions used to be the same as the Scottish average but is now worse for both men and women.

- The average age at which people in Glasgow are likely to be affected by a *long-term illness* is seven years younger for men, and five years younger for women, than the Scottish average. This means that Glasgow men, on average, are affected by long-term illness as early as 47 years.

- In Glasgow 15 per cent of people describe their *health as 'not good'*, the figure for Scotland is 10 per cent. In Edinburgh and Aberdeen the equivalent figure is around 8 per cent. In some poor areas of Glasgow the figure rises to 26-29 per cent.

- The *self-rated health* of people in deprived areas is lower for white Scots than for people living there from black and ethnic minority backgrounds.

- In Glasgow's poorest areas, the number of elderly claiming *Attendance Allowance* is 28-34 per cent. The equivalent figure for Scotland as a whole is 15 per cent.

Unemployment and incapacity

- In the last decade Glasgow's *worklessness* figure has improved. Nonetheless 24.3 per cent of the working age population is on benefit compared to 16.5 per cent across Scotland.

- Research conducted in 2007 found that one fifth of the Glasgow working age population was on *incapacity benefit* – the highest level in any British city. [5] 35 per cent of 55-59 year olds in Glasgow claim incapacity benefit. [6]

- In 2001 36 per cent of children in Glasgow were *living in households where no-one was employed*. The equivalent Scottish figure is 18 per cent. In some areas of Glasgow (Bridgeton and Dennistoun, Maryhill/Woodside and North Glasgow) the figure is nearer 50 per cent.

Income and poverty

- 15 per cent of Scotland's population is considered *'income deprived'*. The equivalent Glasgow figure is 28 per cent – 160,000 people.

- In Glasgow 42 per cent of school pupils are eligible for *free school meals* – this is double the national figure.

Alcohol and drugs

- Glasgow has higher *levels of drinking* (for men and women) than the Scottish average. It also has higher figures for drink driving offences and alcohol-related/attributable hospitalisations – mainly people from poor areas. 'By 2003, 17 per cent of all premature deaths among males in Greater Glasgow were related to alcohol, while liver cirrhosis mortality rates among males exceeded the maximum national figure in Western Europe'. [7]

- The west of Scotland as a whole, but particularly Glasgow City, has the highest rates of *'problem drug users'* in Scotland. These problems are particularly concentrated in deprived areas. Bridgeton and Dennistoun have more than seven times the national rate for drug-related deaths. It is estimated that there are more than 11,000 'problem drug users' in Glasgow alone and around 25,000 in the west of Scotland.

Sex and sexual relationships

- In Scotland as a whole the number of *acute sexually transmitted infections* (STI) increased by 71 per cent in the eight years between 1996-2004. In Greater Glasgow it rose by 93 per cent during this period. (Though this may be due to better screening in Greater Glasgow.)

- Glasgow has a significantly higher rate of *teenage pregnancy* than Scotland as a whole. Indeed ten post code areas in Glasgow had a rate which was twice the Scottish average.

These areas tend to be the most deprived. There is a 'strong association' between teenage pregnancy and deprivation. *Teenage abortion rates* were also higher in poorer Glasgow areas.

- At the last census (2001) the percentage of *one parent families* in Scotland was 28 per cent of all families with dependent children whereas the figure for Glasgow was 46.4 per cent – the highest in Scotland and the fourth highest in the UK. The average figure for Great Britain is 25.6 per cent and it is one of the highest in the world. [8]

- *Domestic abuse figures* mainly involve a man abusing a woman (88 per cent). The Glasgow rate is the second highest in Scotland and is 56 per cent higher than the Scottish average. The only higher figure is for West Dunbartonshire (64 per cent higher than the Scottish figure), an area that takes in Clydebank and Dumbarton on the Clyde.

Children

- Scotland has one of the lowest rates of *breast-feeding* in Europe and the Scottish Government has set a target of 50 per cent of babies being breast-fed at 6–8 weeks. The Scottish figure is currently around 28 per cent. The Glasgow figure is 22 per cent and in deprived areas it is only 14 percent.

- It is estimated that around 6,000 children growing up in Glasgow are living with at least one *parent with 'a substance abuse problem'* – that is around one in twenty children.

- In Scotland as a whole the rate per thousand of 10-17 year olds being *'looked after'* is 10.3. In the west of Scotland it is 12.3 and in Glasgow it is twice the Scottish rate at 20.8.

- It is estimated that in Glasgow at least 30 per cent of children who are 'looked after' are there because of '*lack of parental care/desertion/abandonment*, and at least 20 per cent as a result of drug and/or alcohol abuse by the carer.' [9] Glasgow also has the highest percentage of children in Scotland on the *child protection register*.

Mental health

- *Mental health problems* account for around 50 per cent of incapacity benefit claims in Glasgow.

- Scotland as a whole has a very high level of *suicide* for young men (twice the international average, and England's average). Research has identified that one of the worst areas for suicide of young adults in Scotland is east Glasgow. [10]

- Glasgow's most deprived communities record much higher levels of *psychiatric hospital admissions* than the average for Scotland. Indeed some poor areas have two to three times more admissions than better off areas in Greater Glasgow.

Possible explanations

So what is at the heart of these health and social problems? At first glance the answer seems deceptively simple. Deprivation and unemployment have undermined the health of poor people in Glasgow. Some of this may be historical – many of Glasgow's citizens suffered from terrible living conditions and even up to the 1960s overcrowding was a serious problem. Glasgow also suffered acutely from industrial collapse and restructuring during the 1960s, 70s and 80s. In short, Glasgow's health problem is simply a particularly acute case of 'deindustrialisation' which 'decimated traditional communities'.

However Hanlon *et al.* point out 'the central paradox' in all this. For decades now massive amounts of money have been invested in Glasgow in an attempt to improve health and social problems. The housing stock has been given numerous facelifts and millions spent to transform and improve communities in a myriad of initiatives. Also, investment in the city has led to a growing middle class, a rise in median earnings, higher levels of employment – developments which ostensibly create the opportunities for social mobility. Nonetheless 'commensurate improvements in (the city's) health have not yet followed.' [11]

But if the problem is that Glasgow has not managed to recover from the economic dislocation caused by the decline of its traditional industries it must be asked how other cities and regions have coped with similar problems. After all, Glasgow is not the only place to have suffered this fate. So in 2008 David Walsh, Martin Taulbut and Phil Hanlon produced another GCPH report *The Aftershock of Deindustrialisation: Trends in mortality in Scotland and other parts of post-industrial Europe.* This aims to examine health in the west of Scotland in the context of how 'other post-industrial areas in Europe have fared in respect of recent health trends'.[12] They analysed twenty of these areas including English regions such as Greater Manchester and Merseyside; Swansea and the South Wales coalfields; Northern Ireland; and post-industrial areas in Germany, France, Belgium, Netherlands, Poland and the Czech Republic.

This study confirmed that in each of these regions health was worse than it was in the parent countries overall. However, the west of Scotland figures are much worse than these other regions. Here is the summary of the two most important findings:

1. West of Scotland females currently have lower life expectancy than every selected region.

2. West of Scotland males have lower life expectancy than every region except Poland and the Czech Republic. However, projections suggest that these regions will overtake the west of Scotland in around 10 years time given current trends. [13]

Walsh *et al.* then look at a number of possible explanations. Four are most important for our purposes. The first is that the west of Scotland has greater income inequalities than other regions. As we shall see more fully below, some experts argue that the more pronounced income inequality is in a population, the greater the health inequalities. At the time of writing Walsh and his co-researchers did not have numerical data for the west of Scotland to ascertain exactly where the region ranked in terms of inequality. However, their comparison of Scotland as a whole with that of other European countries suggests that Scotland's inequality is in the middle of the spectrum. Recent comparisons of Glasgow with Liverpool and Manchester suggest very similar levels of inequality in the three cities, yet much worse health outcomes in Glasgow.[14]

The second possible explanation is that people in the west of Scotland are more likely to behave in ways which are injurious to their health. For a variety of reasons, mainly due to the availability of data, they found this difficult 'to prove or disprove'. Follow up research published by GCPH, which looked in part at health behaviours in the west of Scotland and other European regions (not exactly the same regions as the Deindustrialisation study), found that the results were mixed.[15] For example, physical activity levels were better than other places in the UK, female smoking rates were higher than most regions in the study and male rates higher than other UK areas but lower than many European countries. However, even if research proved conclusively that people from the west of Scotland have worse health habits this would still beg the question – why?

The third possible explanation of the west of Scotland's particular health problems is that 'deindustrialisation was more severe than in the other regions'. What the authors mean by this includes factors such as the total jobs lost through industrial restructuring and the number of industrial, as opposed to service sector, jobs which remained. On this measurement, the west of Scotland was one of the most severely hit. Walsh *et al.* write:

> The west of Scotland has transformed itself from
> an industrial to a post-industrial economy but the
> process of transformation appears to have been
> more far reaching than in comparable European
> regions and may, as a result, have caused greater
> social trauma and adverse health outcomes. . . the
> west of Scotland may have experienced a more
> severe dose of deindustrialisation than the majority
> of the other regions.[16]

As the authors themselves admit, however, the idea that the extent of 'deindustrialisation' accounts for the west of Scotland's problems is still more speculation than fact.

A fourth possible explanation is that 'the west of Scotland is more deprived than the other areas'. This is the explanation that Scots are most likely to advance. However, having looked at the figures, Walsh *et al.* are not convinced by this argument. They point out that unemployment is usually an 'important element in many deprivation indices'[17] but is not a particular issue in the west of Scotland. Indeed some of the regions in the survey have unemployment rates three to four times higher than in the west of Scotland. What's more, while it can be difficult to compare deprivation in Scotland with continental countries, UK data allowing comparisons with English regions show that poor health in Glasgow and the west of Scotland cannot be accounted for by deprivation. So Walsh *et al.* are clear that it would be 'unwise' to attribute the west of Scotland's health problems to 'deprivation', since all these areas have problems with deprivation, some much greater than Scotland's, yet this does not translate into such poor health outcomes.

In reaching this conclusion, Walsh *et al.* have helped the debate on poor health in Scotland enormously by forcing us out of the automatic assumption that the problem is primarily about material resources. This is not to say that economic deprivation is irrelevant – simply that it is not the whole story and that we must continue to search for explanations.

Violence and prejudice

In *The Aftershock of Deindustrialisation* Walsh *et al.* mainly examine mortality trends in the selected regions together with some socio-economic data. They do not look at violence. Glasgow's health record puts it at the bottom of the European division but it is violence that puts it in a league of its own. Glasgow has the highest rate of murder per head of population in Western Europe. Its violence record makes it much more like an American or South American city than a European one. Sadly Glasgow's violence figures cannot be attributed to a fad or fashion which may subside. It is estimated that Glasgow's violence record may stretch back to the 1930s, razor gangs and Glasgow's notoriety as 'no mean city'.[18] Fortunately, there is no longer the same denial about the problem and in 2005 a Violence Reduction Unit was established within Strathclyde Police.

In 2002 the World Health Organisation reported that Scotland's homicide rate was 5.3 per 100,000 population in males aged between 10 and 29. The overall rate for Scotland is 3.1. This puts Glasgow in the same league as Argentina, Costa Rica and Lithuania. England and Wales have a rate of 1.0 per 100,000. The Violence Reduction Unit point out that the Glasgow figure is 'the tip of the iceberg; underneath lie an increasing volume of attempted murders, serious and simple assaults and a culture of knife carrying'. They are also aware that there is significant under-reporting of assaults. Research into admissions in three Glasgow hospitals in 2004 suggests that serious assaults are under-reported by 50-70 per cent.[19] In short, many injured people access medical care without the police ever being aware of the incidents in which they have been involved.

Glasgow has a reputation for being a bigoted and sectarian city. In recent years there have been various debates about the actual extent of the problem. In 2001 Glasgow City Council commissioned research to determine 'the scale, nature and impact of sectarianism in the city.'[20] The report found that people believe that 'a culture of prejudice' exists in the city and that two thirds of those surveyed did not think that sectarianism is a 'thing of the past'. 12 per cent of respondents agreed that 'sectarianism affects me personally'[21] but the report found that less than one per cent of those asked reported that they had been personally attacked or discriminated against because of their religion.

It is difficult to draw much comfort from this report as it

threw up worrying levels of prejudice against homosexuals and people from other races and cultures: around 31 per cent expressed concern about living next door to 'homosexuals' and 15 per cent said they would be concerned if 'Muslims' or 'people from a different race' moved next door to them. 'Skin colour, race and country of origin were all commonly mentioned as reasons for crime and discrimination.'[22] As there were only small numbers of people from different ethnic backgrounds participating in the survey the researchers were not able to draw 'definitive conclusions' about the actual prevalence of the problem. However, recent data show that the bulk of recorded hate crimes in Scotland occur in the Strathclyde Police area and most involve racism.[23]

The role of family life and drink

Leaving aside the issue of racism and prejudice for the moment to return to the list of health and social problems, we need to start looking at what might be going on, not from the point of view of the economy or deprivation, but in terms of other human needs. One of the most striking features of Glasgow's figures concerns relationships. Glasgow's poor areas have high figures for domestic violence and single parent families – a combination which does not suggest positive relationships between the sexes. High figures for acute sexually transmitted infections also add to this picture of poor sexual relationships.

Family life and the nurturing of children does not look good either. The UNICEF report 'Child Well-being in Rich Nations' demonstrated that the UK has one of the highest percentages of children living in single parent families and in step-families (17 per cent).[24] The only higher figure for single parent families in this survey is the USA (21 per cent). However, the Scottish figure is 23 per cent – significantly higher than the UK figure – and the Glasgow figure a staggering 37 per cent. The UNICEF report authors admit that it seems 'insensitive and unfair' to use family structure as an indicator of child well-being: after all some children are brought up badly in two-parent families and children of single parents can be raised well. Nonetheless the report states:

> . . . at the statistical level there is evidence to associate growing up in single-parent families and step-families with greater risk to well-being – including a greater risk of dropping out of school, of leaving home early, of poorer health, of low skills, and of low pay. Furthermore such risks appear to persist even when the substantial effect of increased poverty levels in single-parent and step-families have been taken into account. . .[25]

Glasgow's deprived areas also have high levels of teenage pregnancy which suggests that sizeable number of babies have mothers who are immature, come from challenging backgrounds and are unlikely to have the psychological resources to give their children the best start in life. Glasgow also has twice Scotland's average for the number of looked-after children and most of these have been the result of abandonment, neglect and abuse of some kind. In the past few years, research has shown conclusively that poor parenting and neglect has huge impact on young people's ability to empathise, a key ingredient in building positive relationships, as well as cognitive skills. This is an important topic to be considered in a later chapter.

We are used to seeing all these types of problems as the result of deprivation but this on its own does not help us to account for poor health. Should we not begin to ask if it is the breakdown of so many families and relationships in Glasgow which may be a causal factor? Could it be the case that these personal relationships in Glasgow were poor anyway and that deindustrialisation undermined them even more?

The second theme we need to explore further is inequality. Walsh *et al.* may have eliminated it, on the grounds that the west of Scotland's inequality did not look too bad in comparison with some other regions with better health. Nonetheless there are very good reasons for exploring inequality further.

Another theme which emerges from the data is the tendency in Glasgow to seek oblivion and escape, presumably from problems and negative feelings, in drink, drugs or, for young men, suicide. Given the level of obesity, turning to food for comfort may also be a part of this pattern. Has there been a particularly Glaswegian tendency to cope with problems in this way which may have been exacerbated by large-scale economic changes?

The inequality thesis

Professor Richard Wilkinson is an epidemiologist and public health expert based at the University of Nottingham Medical School. In 2005 he published an important book *The Impact of Inequality: how to make sick societies healthier*.[26] These insights have now been marketed to a wider audience in a highly influential book called *The Spirit Level*, co-authored with Professor Kate Pickett.[27]

Wilkinson and Pickett demonstrate that although class differences appear to be disappearing in contemporary societies, as is 'absolute material want', poor people have, on average, lower life expectancy than their richer neighbours. They also show that social problems and various aspects of unhappiness are much more common in the poorest areas. This does not mean to say that affluence or low income necessarily lead to specific health outcomes. In American states, for example, there is little or no relation between longevity and income. What matters, they argue, is not so much the amount of money we have but our 'socioeconomic status'. In other words, it is not spending power as such which matters but what Wilkinson and Pickett call 'psychosocial factors'.

Wilkinson and Pickett present international evidence which shows that in societies where income differences between rich and poor are not too pronounced then the quality of social relations is better. These better social relations can be seen, they argue, in data which show that more equal societies have higher levels of trust, enhanced social capital and social cohesion, and lower levels of homicide and violence. But why should equality have an effect on the quality of community life? To help find an answer we need to understand something about Wilkinson's basic thesis about human society and psychology.

Wilkinson argues that one of the most difficult aspects of life, not just for humans, is that members of the same species compete for scarce resources. This means that the potential for competition and conflict is high. 'How human societies deal with this problem,' writes Wilkinson, 'provides the basis of their social structure.' [28] Early human life appears to have been similar to many primate species, such as baboons, and based on dominance hierarchies. In this environment fear dominates and those in lower status positions have to be submissive or risk being attacked. Wilkinson claims that during the 'hunter gatherer' period which followed, people had equal access to resources and the social structure became more egalitarian. Hunter gatherer societies emphasised reciprocity as well as the exchange of gifts. This type of social order can be seen in many of the great apes where support and reciprocity dominate and mutual grooming underpins social relationships. For human beings this egalitarian social order was eroded by farming ('settled agriculture'). Scarcity, in the form of famines, as well as surpluses, resulted in the evolution of a pronounced social hierarchy or class system and unequal access to resources. All modern societies, claims Wilkinson, lie between the two extremes of pronounced dominance and inequality and co-operation and affiliation. As human beings, we have the capacity to operate in either type of social system. He writes:

> Human beings are. . . programmed for both kinds of social interaction and tend to make sharp distinctions between dominance behaviour up and down the social hierarchy and affiliative behaviour between equals. . . These two forms of social interaction are merely the two opposite extremes of the ways in which we can conduct social relations: at one pole they are a matter of power and self-interest and, at the other a matter of social investments, trust and reciprocity. In practice, social life involves varying mixtures of the two.[29]

Citing researchers such as Robin Dunbar, Wilkinson also argues that human beings' large brains, and speech, have evolved to allow us to interact socially with others and that we have great powers to empathise and identify with others' predicament and feelings.[30] While we are capable of acting in ways to exclude and discriminate against others, thus reinforcing our own status, our psychological make-up leads us to experience real shame and embarrassment if others treat us as inferiors or if we even think we are being judged as unequal in their eyes.

As the Scottish thinker Willa Muir once wrote: 'It is relatively easy to be proud and poor when everybody of consequence is poor; it is far from easy when money begins to spread itself.'[31] She wrote this decades ago but recent data are proving her right: surveys show that these negative experiences have a detrimental affect on health.

Wilkinson cites studies of non-human primates where hierarchies are central to the social structure which show that animals who have been forced into submission by a higher ranking animal then turn and attack others lower in the pecking order. Primatologists call this the 'bicycling reaction' because 'animals show their back to the top while kicking towards the bottom'. R.M. Sapolsky describes how this plays out in baboons:

> Such third-party displaced aggression accounts for a huge percentage of baboon violence. A middle ranking male gets trounced in a fight, turns and chases a subadult male, who lunges at an adult female, who bites a juvenile, who slaps an infant.[32]

The term (*Radfahrer-Reaktion*) originally came from Theodor Adorno's work *The Authoritarian Personality*, written in an attempt to understand why the Jews had been scapegoated in Nazi Germany.[33] Wilkinson asserts that the 'bicycling reaction' can be seen in the increased number of racist attacks during periods of unemployment and economic hardship. He also cites data which show that the worst problems of racism in the USA are in states with the most pronounced income inequality.

This bicycling reaction can also be seen in men's relationships with women. Research into 16 non-patriarchal, pre-industrial societies showed there was no domestic violence. Modern societies, particularly those with pronounced inequality and strong macho values, seem to encourage domestic violence. Indeed the domestic violence researchers, Russell and Becky Dobash, argue that women are much less likely to be beaten up in societies where there is relative equality of the sexes. Conversely, research in the USA shows that women married to men employed in hierarchical settings, such as the armed forces, are twice as likely to be beaten by their husbands as other women in their society. Wilkinson claims that women's position in general is prejudiced in societies with pronounced income inequality and strong dominance hierarchy among men: 'In a more aggressive culture, where male power is what counts, women will be more subordinated and have lower status relative to men,' writes Wilkinson.[34]

It is important to realise that in societies with a pronounced dominance hierarchy, it is not just women who suffer – men do as well:

> The costs are shown in their increased levels of violence, more risk-taking behaviour (from car crashes to sexually transmitted diseases), excessive drinking, and cardiovascular diseases. . . there is a 'culture of inequality' that is not only more violent and aggressive, but more macho.[35]

Wilkinson claims that 'there have now been over fifty studies showing a clear tendency for violence to be more common in societies where income differences are larger.' [36] This violence manifests itself in homicide figures or in violent attacks. The argument here is that men at the bottom of the dominance hierarchy feel bad about themselves but are not likely to tackle the dominant males. Instead they are more likely to attack one another in an attempt to achieve some respect. Indeed Wilkinson argues that 'the most frequent trigger of violence is people feeling they are disrespected and dishonoured.'[37] To support this contention Wilkinson quotes James Gilligan, a prison psychiatrist and Director for the Study of Violence at Harvard:

> I have yet to see a serious act of violence that was not provoked by the experience of feeling shamed and humiliated, disrespected and ridiculed, and that did not represent the attempt to prevent or undo this 'loss of face' – no matter how severe the punishment, even if it includes death.[38]

Everything Wilkinson writes in *The Impact of Inequality* and later in *The Spirit Level* about what happens in societies with pronounced dominance hierarchies relates powerfully to Glasgow: male violence, macho culture, heavy drinking, wife beating, racism, sectarianism, suicide, teenage pregnancies and poor health outcomes. However, as we have seen, Walsh *et al.* could not substantiate the thesis that the west of Scotland had particularly bad health simply because the region had extreme inequality. Wilkinson presents data on 'income inequality and death rates of working-age men in 528 cities in five countries'. Glasgow's inequality is better than average for the cities studied, yet has one of the highest death rates – much higher than cities such as Toronto or Sydney which have similar inequality yet fewer deaths for this group of men.[39]

The similarities between Wilkinson's description of the effects of inequality and what is happening in Glasgow is uncannily suggestive and needs further investigation. Wilkinson and Pickett argue that societies do not have to be perfectly equal to foster good health and social relationships. Indeed they point out that Scandinavian countries and some American states cannot be said to be equal but they have less profound inequality than some of their neighbours and this translates into very beneficial social and health outcomes. But there is no formula here – it is not possible to say that a given level of equality is generally supportive of health and that achieving a particular level of inequality automatically tips the scales in an adverse direction. There must be lots of different contributing factors. Wilkinson concentrates on the idea of dominance and respect, linked to economic inequality. Given the lack of supporting evidence that the west of Scotland's health problems are due to excessive inequality we need to consider if a modified version of Wilkinson's thesis may be applicable. This involves looking at whether Glasgow (or the west of Scotland in general) *historically* suffered from such extreme inequality that the type of mentality Wilkinson describes has become deeply embedded over a long period of time in the local culture.

So simply from the examination of the data presented in this chapter, some important questions need to be answered. First, has dominance and inequality played an important part in Glasgow's history? Second, has Glasgow traditionally had strained relationships between the sexes and poor family relationships? Thirdly have Glaswegians traditionally been particularly drawn to addictive behaviour and to the feeling of oblivion? These, and other questions and themes, related to well-being, form the backbone of this book.

The Glasgow Centre for Population Health has done a sterling job in helping to understand how Glasgow's health compares with similar industrial regions in Europe. However, they are soon to publish another study which throws an even more worrying light on the problem. They have now compared Glasgow's health figures with those of Liverpool and Manchester. All three cities are remarkably similar in terms of unemployment, deprivation and inequality yet Glasgow has significantly higher mortality and not just for those in lower socio-economic groups – even middle-class Glaswegians have poorer health and die earlier than those in Liverpool and Manchester.[40] So what is it about the culture and lifestyle in this city which undermines health and well-being?

CHAPTER 2
The making of industrial Glasgow

O NE OF my favourite pictures of old Glasgow is an etching of the city in the eighteenth century. Viewed from the south side of the river it shows an attractive city, not unlike Florence, approached by an ancient and elegant eight pier bridge. Majestic steeples dominate the city's skyline. In the foreground figures stroll along the waterside and the natural shallowness of the Clyde is illustrated by the horse drawn cart splashing through the river.[1]

Glasgow's appeal in this picture is not the work of a romantic artist. In the seventeenth and eighteenth centuries Glasgow was reputed to be a beautiful city. One of Cromwell's soldiers described Glasgow as 'not so big or rich yet. . . a much sweeter and more delightful place than Edinburgh.' John Macky described it as 'the beautifullest little city I have seen in Britain' – a considered opinion from a man who wrote letters about his travels throughout the country.[2] In 1726 the novelist and journalist, Daniel Defoe, described Glasgow as 'one of the cleanliest, most beautiful, and best-built cities in Great Britain.'[3] Tobias Smollett, Edward Burt and others all made similar pronouncements on Glasgow's charms. Within a hundred years, for most of its inhabitants, Glasgow was a living hell.

The city's foundations

The story of Glasgow begins with the city's patron, St. Mungo (Kentigern) who was supposedly born and educated in Culross. Legend has it that he arrived in Glasgow in the sixth century, founding a monastery near the Molendinar burn, on the same spot St. Ninian consecrated a cemetery and St. Mungo buried St. Fergus. This latterly became the site of Glasgow Cathedral. Mungo was consecrated Bishop of Strathclyde. Glasgow's development over the next millennium was largely as a religious site. Its early streets were laid out in the shape of a cross.

One of Glasgow's great advantages is its position. It had grown up on the banks of the Clyde, at a point on the river where it was a mere 15 inches deep. This meant that people crossing from north to south could easily ford. The eight pier bridge ('the old Glasgow bridge') was built at 'Stockwell shallows' c.1350. Glasgow's location on a shallow river ultimately presented enormous difficulties but historically it had been an advantage. Being situated on a river unsuited for the ships used by Norse raiders gave the city a good defensive position. The River Clyde was also abundant in fish, notably trout and salmon. Today we consider Glasgow's climate to be foul but this is not how it was seen by some in earlier times. Glasgow was hailed for its mild climate and noted for its orchards and gardens.

Glasgow's growing wealth permitted urban expansion and improvement. In the seventeenth century the university acquired new buildings to the east of the High Street. A new market cross and Merchants House, Tron Church and Hutcheson's Hospital were important additions to the city. Wealthy merchants also built fine new houses. One of the city's most attractive features was the colonnaded walks in Glasgow

Cross. These were covered pavements inaccurately termed 'piazzas'. The city was also enhanced by its copious gardens and surrounding pastures. Many citizens kept beehives on their rooftops.

In 1720 there were only eight streets – High Street, Drygate, Rottenrow, Gallowgate, Saltmarket, Bridgegate, Stockwell and Trongate. As trade and wealth increased the city changed substantially. Around the middle of the eighteenth century there was development towards the west and also to the south of the river. Streets were laid out on a grid and Glasgow took on the feel of a 'new town'. Fashionable suburbs appeared and many of the rich moved from the old part to large, elegant, tenements or townhouses. Buchanan Street became one of the most prestigious streets in Britain. In his tour of Scotland in 1832 William Cobbett claimed Glasgow to be as fine as anything he has ever seen, with the exception of Edinburgh's New Town. He wrote of Glasgow:

> The whole is built of beautiful white stone; and
> doors, windows, and everything bespeak solid
> worth, without any taste for ostentation or show. . .
> By the side of the river, above the bridges, there is
> a place modestly called Glasgow Green, containing
> about a hundred English acres of land, which is in
> very fine green sward, and is at all times open for
> the citizens to go for their recreation.[4]

Cobbett also noted that Glasgow was a clean, smoke-free city as the industry was confined to the outskirts. Glasgow was also noted for its university. The buildings created in the High Street in 1539 and 1658, with four quadrangular courts and a high steeple, were considered particularly fine examples of Scots architecture and at least as attractive as those at Oxford and Cambridge. The university was also an important seat of learning not only in Scotland but internationally. Francis Hutcheson, considered the father of the Scottish Enlightenment, lectured in Moral Philosophy. Other important Enlightenment figures, Adam Smith, John Millar, Dugald Stewart, Joseph Black and William Cullen, to name but a few, also gave lectures and played a part in university life.

The rise of commerce and industry

Situated on the west of Scotland, Glasgow's position originally afforded good links with Ireland. This was an advantage in ancient times but Glasgow began to lose out politically as trade developed with Scandinavia and the Low countries. Edinburgh became Scotland's capital city. St. Andrews developed into a more important ecclesiastical centre, gaining a university fifty years before Glasgow. In 1600 Glasgow had a population of 7,500 and was only the eleventh biggest town in Scotland. By the latter part of the seventeenth century Glasgow, however, was in the ascendancy and had become the second biggest city in Scotland. The rise in her fortunes is attributable to trade. Some rival burghs, such as Dumbarton – situated near the mouth of the river – were in a better geographical position than Glasgow. But in the mid-seventeenth century the problem of the shallow river was navigated by the creation of a new harbour at Newark (later Port Glasgow), further down the Clyde.

With the creation of American colonies Glasgow businessmen sensed they had an advantage over ports, like Leith, on the east coast. There was one serious barrier, however; the English Government's Navigation Acts prevented Scots from openly trading with their new colonies though smuggling was endemic. Scotland was soon to plan for its own trading colony on the Isthmus of Darien in Panama. This ended in spectacular failure, almost bankrupting Scotland in the process. One of the consequences of the 'Darien Disaster' was that it helped to force a reluctant Scottish Parliament into a union with England. Glaswegians were particularly opposed to the loss of Scottish sovereignty. However, city merchants were soon to see that this dark cloud in Scottish history had not just a silver but a golden lining. One benefit of the Union was that Scotland gained legal trading access to English colonies. Glasgow merchants immediately used their geographical position, investing in ships and beginning to trade in plantation commodities – tobacco, sugar and cotton. By 1735 Glasgow had become 'Scotland's urban window to the Atlantic economy'.[5]

At first the Clyde merchants made healthy profits from the tobacco trade as they undercut English rivals by extensive smuggling. By the mid-eighteenth century a series of reforms put an end to these illegal practices. Glasgow merchants (men such as John Glassford) were soon to steal another march on their English counterparts – this time reducing prices by cutting time off sea crossings and establishing sound commercial practices. 'The tobacco lords', the name usually given by posterity to these elite merchants, amassed huge fortunes during the good days but did not reign for long. Their dominance, like their business disappeared in a puff of smoke in 1776 with the advent of American independence. More importantly, for the city's economy, the tobacco trade had stimulated other manufacturers. Whole industries developed to provide goods to export to the American colonies: linen, woollen cloth, boots, furniture, pottery, rope and other saleable items. Fortunately for Glasgow businessmen as the tobacco trade waned another new product came into vogue – cotton. Glasgow had both the capital and the skilled labour resources for textile production. Indeed Glasgow was ideally placed to become a major producer of cotton – her damp climate provided the humid atmosphere needed for manufacturing the cloth. There were 134 cotton factories in Scotland in 1834 and almost all were within 25 miles of Glasgow's city centre. The industry remained prosperous until the middle of the nineteenth century when the American Civil War disrupted cotton supplies.

Cotton manufacture, like the production of many goods, became increasingly mechanised. The inventions which underpinned the new technology for cotton spinning came from England but Scotland was good at utilising them and was soon to put its own spoke in the great wheel of industrial improvement. James Watt, from Greenock, was working at the University of Glasgow when he devised a way to refine the 'separate condenser' for the steam engine. This meant that the power for factories and mills no longer had to come from rivers thus allowing them to be sited anywhere – a development which was critical to urbanisation and the Industrial Revolution. Other Glasgow inventions, such as Henry Bell's *Comet* (steam propulsion for ships), and J.B. Neilson's 'hot-blast process' were also key to the new industrial technology. From 1830 on shipbuilding became Glasgow's forte.

Glasgow's ready access to fuels and raw materials meant she was particularly well-placed for heavy engineering and manufacturing. Investment capital was easily available and so too, as we shall see shortly, was her access to copious amounts of skilled but cheap labour. The term 'Clydebuilt' was soon used internationally to mean an engineered product of quality.

As other commentators have observed, it is impossible to write about Glasgow without using numbers: the city's history is a rich seam of impressive statistics. For example, in 1870 there were 40 shipyards on the Clyde and their capacity, both in tonnage and engine power, outstripped that of all German shipyards combined. By the outbreak of World War I in 1914 Glasgow and its industrial environs produced 'one-half of British marine-engine horsepower, one third of the railway locomotives and rolling stock, one third of the shipping tonnage and about a fifth of the steel.'[6] Nineteenth century Glasgow also boasted the tallest building in the world – Tennant's stalk, the chimney at the St. Rollox chemical works – which towered over the city.

The skill of the Glasgow engineer was not only to be seen in the ships and other goods he produced but also in the construction of the Clyde itself. The Clyde was naturally a shallow river at low tide with numerous sandbanks allowing only small boats and barges to sail up to Glasgow. As early as 1566 improvers had attempted unsuccessfully to cut a channel through one of the worst sandbanks at Dumbuck near Dumbarton Rock. With lucrative trade beckoning, the Clyde was not going to be left in a 'state of nature': various engineers, including James Watt, put their minds to work to define the full extent of the problem and devise solutions. Engineers ultimately made a series of improvements, such as removing stones and gravel from the riverbed and contracting the channel where it had become too wide.

Many commentators on Glasgow remark that it was a hard culture made by hard men but the economy they created became increasingly fragile: the city's economy was too interconnected and overly specialised in 'skills, capital, equipment and markets'. It was also heavily dependent on exporting to international markets which were notoriously volatile. What's more, early industrialisation had been one of Glasgow's advantages but other countries were beginning to industrialise and catch up. This foreign competition would have cast a much longer shadow over the yards, leading to the eclipse of a greater number in the early twentieth century, if it had not been for World Wars. The Clyde became a major supplier not only of warships for the British Navy, but also fuses, shells, guns and other military artefacts. This importance to the war effort helped to protect Glasgow's economy until the late 1950s. It was then that the full problem of Glasgow's economy was felt. Many of the yards were obsolete and those still in production were hopelessly uncompetitive and struggling to stay alive. The post-war period also saw the demise of locomotive building and chemicals. Even the iconic Dixon's Blazes, which had been erected in 1839 and had lit up the Glasgow night sky for well over a century, finally closed and the site covered by high-rise housing.

The human tragedy

> The new wealth gleamed before the eyes of men. Scotland had the coal and iron they needed. And suddenly. . . a belt across the middle of Scotland was reeking with smoke, and men were pouring in from the hills and pastures and glens, and from oversees, to dig their living from the earth, to scarify miles of loveliness, to make new towns and railways and canals – and slums.[7]

Until the early part of the eighteenth century the vast majority of Scots lived in rural areas and Scotland was 'one of the least "urbanised" in Western Europe in the seventeenth century.'[8] However, in the hundred years between 1750 and 1850 Scotland rose to second in the urban league table for Europe, only below that of England and Wales. People from all over Scotland, highlands and lowlands, went to Glasgow to secure employment in the new textile industries or the range of jobs required in a burgeoning city. The development of industry in the west of Scotland acted like a magnet for poor Irish people. By 1851, 7.2 per cent of people living in Scotland were Irish compared with only 2.9 per cent of the population in England. Many of these were from Ulster – both Protestants and Catholics. The Irish made a substantial contribution to the Scottish economy in the first half of the nineteenth century, operating as a mobile force of unskilled and semi-skilled labour. This first wave of Irish immigrants assimilated easily, often marrying Scots and losing their Catholic faith. The second wave of immigration resulted from the potato famines of 1845 and 46. In a very short period of time huge numbers of destitute Irish Catholics flooded into Scotland – many of them in poor condition. Within six years there were over 207,000 people in Scotland who were Irish-born – most of them in the west of Scotland. As we shall see later, this wave of immigration created more hostility.

In the nineteenth century most workers in Glasgow, as elsewhere in urban Britain, endured horrific working conditions: the hours were long, the work hard and the conditions appalling. It was not only men who suffered but also women and children. In his *History of the Working Classes in Scotland*, Tom Johnston writes:

> In 1859 the child serfs in the west of Scotland
> bleachfields were being worked from 11 to 18

> hours daily in stoves heated from 80 to 100
> degrees; at Pollokshaws children were occasionally
> worked 'two and three days and nights
> consecutively'; when the Bleachfields Bill of 1860
> was before the House of Commons, Roebuck
> declared that these children led 'the life of the
> damned; the children's hands are often blistered
> and the skin torn off their feet, and yet they are
> thus obliged to work, the persons who overlook
> them being sometimes forced to keep them awake
> by beating on the table with large boards'. . . The
> Convener of the Education Committee of the
> Glasgow School Board told the Factory Acts
> Commissioners in 1875 that the employers were
> defying the Education Acts; Dr. Ebenezer Watson
> testified to the steady physical deterioration that
> was going on; and Dr. Irvine declared that without
> continual recruitment from the country the town
> populations would soon die out.[9]

So, as a result of 'push-pull factors' – expanding economic opportunities in Glasgow and changes in the rural economy – the city's population exploded. In 1830 there were more than a quarter of a million Glaswegians. This doubled by 1871 and doubled again by 1914, though this figure of a million was reached partly as a result of changes in the city's boundaries. By the turn of the twentieth century 70 per cent of those employed in Glasgow were working in manufacturing of some kind. Glasgow was truly 'the workshop of the world', with a high proportion of her workforce in skilled or semi-skilled jobs.

Glasgow's housing crisis

Traditionally Glasgow, like Edinburgh and other areas of Scotland, had followed the housing style, not of England, but Europe. On the continent tenements – multi-storied, flatted buildings where tenants utilised a common entrance or close – were common. The walled cities in France and Italy, for example, had been forced to adopt this building style due to problems of space. Holland too favoured this type of development. Tenements became a common type of urban housing in Scotland, including Glasgow. They were occupied by various classes of people, merchants and craftsmen, for example, and would often have shops occupying the ground floor. Some of the reasons advanced for the Scots' liking for tenements include the availability of stone; the fact they were easy to heat (important given Scotland's climate); and the shortage of space in some old Scottish cities. The early tenements built in the heart of Glasgow were usually four storeys or more in height, with thick walls. They were mainly large rectangular buildings with back greens for drying or bleaching clothes and growing flowers and herbs. These tenements had mixed occupants but the poor in Glasgow were mainly confined to decrepit wooden hovels.

As wealth increased the rich, and the middle classes, moved out of the city centre to town houses, terraces or new elegant tenements in the west and south of the city. The tenements vacated by the well-to-do were soon occupied by the hordes flooding into the city to take up jobs available as a result of Glasgow's economic expansion. The demand for housing, and the limited amount of space, meant that the back-greens were now used for new tenement blocks. The 'backlands' development, as it was called, immediately created wretched living conditions for everyone. The in-fill tenements were erected so close to the original building that people from different tenements could shake hands. This cramming meant that many of the tenements lacked ventilation and light. It also created a warren of dank, stinking wynds. Even without the backlands the old tenements were built for overcrowding – many were 'single-ends' or 'room and kitchens'. In other words, one- or two-roomed dwellings. They lacked their own toilet facilities (privies or dry toilets) which were shared with dozens of other families in the tenement.

As early as 1840 it was clear that Glasgow had a severe housing problem and that for many of its citizens living conditions were squalid, if not inhuman. The UK sanitary reformer, Edwin Chadwick, declared that the Glasgow wynds were the worst he ever saw. By 1914 a staggering 700,000 people (almost the current size of the city's population) lived in three square miles. Even in 1940, 700,000 people lived in 1800 acres in the city centre. These figures meant that Glasgow was the heaviest populated area of Europe. Around 85 per cent of Glasgow folk were born, raised and died in tenements. Over-crowding was a problem throughout Scotland but particularly acute in this city: the number of people per acre in Glasgow was twice that of Dundee and Edinburgh. In 1886 a third of Glasgow families lived in one room. Even though the single end could be as small as 14 feet by 11 feet, one in ten families took in lodgers. In his angry book, *Cancer of Empire*, published in 1925, the English journalist, William Bolitho, reported that 40,000 Glasgow families lived in one room; and that it was not uncommon for eight people to share a bed. 'The majority of the working families of Glasgow live and die in a misery which no passing calamity, war or earthquake, could surpass.'[10]

For many migrants to the city, their loss of contact with the land or with the natural world was palpable and painful. A journalist attending a meeting of a labourers' union in 1889 reported:

> In rather a flowery speech one of the orators contrasted the scenes amidst which they had passed the years of their childhood with the squalid misery to which they were now condemned. He pointed out that whilst they had been formerly accustomed to view the green fields and smiling valleys in their boyhood, to hear the singing of the birds, and listen to the gentle murmurs of the wind among the trees, that they had been forced by the greed of the capitalists to leave these beloved scenes. . . They were compelled, he said, to live in hovels where their employers would not keep their dogs. . . It was plain from the applause with which this speech was greeted that the large audience sympathised with his sentiments, and looked back with longing eyes to the happy times which he had so glowingly described.[11]

In the days of the backlands, the proximity of the buildings to one another meant that thousands of residents lived with no natural light. Even out on the street it was difficult to see the sky. Contact with the green world would have been minimal for most inhabitants in their daily lives – confined to daisies and dandelions growing on waste ground. A number of philanthropic organisations sprang up to subsidise or pay for poor children to have holidays at the seaside or in the country. They were (rightly) deemed to be good for the young folks' health. One scheme was called 'Fresh Air Fortnights' – a term still used in Glasgow today. By the late nineteenth century the City Fathers responded as best they could by creating parks and gardens. Indeed Glasgow was reputed to have more parkland per head of the population than any other city. However, some historians argue that the impact of parks was limited in Glasgow as most of them 'were too far from the most overcrowded areas' to be used by the inhabitants who needed them most.[12]

Given these conditions it is unsurprising that slum dwellers' daily disassociation from a green environment underlay so many negative observations on Glasgow and so too did the brutalisation of the natural world which made Glasgow a dark and forbidding place. For example, Lewis Grassic Gibbon, following a passage in which he describes the beauty of Loch Lomondside, near to Glasgow, asks: 'Why? Why did men ever allow themselves to become enslaved to a thing so obscene and so foul when there was *this* awaiting them here. . .?'[13] One writer likened the Clyde to 'a great artery' swelling to 'an ugly and unwholesome aneurism among Glasgow streets.'[14] Archie Hind contrasts the old Glasgow with its contemporary filth:

> . . . we come to the idyllic spot where the gentle
> oxen crossed and the little Molendinar burn
> flowed into the broad shallows of the river; the
> spot which the Gaels named *Gles Chu*. . . The little
> valley of the Molendinar is now stopped with two
> centuries of refuse – soap, tallow, cotton waste,
> slag, soda, bits of leather, broken pottery, tar and
> caoutchouc – the waste products of a dozen
> industries and a million lives. . .[15]

Insanitary, overcrowded living conditions are closely related to ill-health. Abysmal living conditions undermined the health of generations of Glaswegians; rickets was common as was tuberculosis. Infanticide and infant mortality were high, stature was not. Many turned to drink as an escape. Living conditions were so bad that numerous cholera and typhus epidemics broke out in the first half of the nineteenth century, prompting a campaign for sanitary reform and energetic municipal activity to cleanse and improve the city. By the 1890s Glasgow – with its public water supply, baths, public lighting, gas supply, libraries, trams and so forth – had more municipal services than any other city of its size.

Given the atrocious housing conditions it is understandable why T.C. Smout should write on the topic of deprivation in Scotland in the nineteenth century:

> It was Glasgow, however, growing in population and in wealth as no city in Scotland had ever done before, that remained the most dramatic and squalid example of urban deprivation. Everyone wanted to reform it – evangelist, temperance crusader, socialist, municipal activist.[16]

There were various official attempts to tackle the housing problem. The 1866 Glasgow Police Act, for example, gave the Town Council the power to inspect and if necessary 'ticket' houses which were three apartments or less. The ticket on the front door gave the cubic capacity of the dwelling and the number of people who could legally sleep in it. The Town Council also acquired powers to clear out insanitary areas, widen streets, make new streets and so forth. Often these powers led to the demolition of properties which were seen as a public health or public order hazard but not to the rehousing of the poor tenants who were thereby displaced. Indeed the poor were often seen as the *cause* of the slums – not the victims.

These moralistic attitudes started to change by the end of the nineteenth century. A Royal Commission on Housing in Scotland reported in 1917. Unsurprisingly it described atrocious conditions in Scotland's cities, particularly Glasgow, referring to 'clotted classes of slums in the great cities'.[17] It stipulated that no more single room dwellings should be built, tenements should be limited to three storeys high and terraced housing would be preferable to give more ventilation and light. This, together with the successful rent strike organised during World War I by Glasgow women, committed Lloyd George's coalition Government to talk about a programme of 'homes fit for heroes'. Legislation followed allowing for state subsidies for housing and granting local councils more power.

These are some of the bare facts in the making of industrial Glasgow. It is now time to add some detail to the story and look at what happened in the light of what we now know about well-being.

CHAPTER 3

The tiers that made the Clyde

A Welcome to the Waters of Loch Katrine

Thou comest to a city where men untimely die,
Where hearts in grief are swelling, and cheeks are seldom dry-
A city where merchant princes to Mammon basely kneel,
While those that drag the idol's car are crushed beneath the wheel.

James Nicholson (1822-1897)

SCOTLAND is a country which loves to proclaim its commitment to equality – it is the land of Robert Burns' 'a man's a man', and the democratic Presbyterian Church; a country that fulfilled John Knox's vision for a 'school in every parish', educating the poor alongside the middling classes. Undoubtedly there were, and still are, deep democratic instincts within Scotland but this is by no means the full picture. Between 1750 and 1830 huge changes took place in rural Scotland which are an essential part of our understanding of the Glasgow story. These changes did not simply create slums and overcrowding but also reinforced inequality and an ethos of dominance.

The Lowland clearances

From 1500 Lowland Scotland had five main social orders: landowners, tenant farmers, cottars, servants and labourers. Until the 1760s farmers were usually part of a group with a multiple tenancy from a landlord. Cottars did not own land and had no legal rights but they were allocated a tiny parcel of land from farmers in return for various types of labour, thus allowing them to grow their own food. Historians estimate that in 1500 around half of all Scotland's land consisted of 'commonties' – land surrounding private estates that people could use for rough grazing or for sources of peat, turf and so forth. In rural areas communal work practices were also standard for building houses, cutting peat and managing the system of 'outfields'. Indeed co-operation was a major, though declining, aspect of the old system of land use. This system of agriculture managed to feed Scotland's population reasonably well from c.1660, except in some years in the 1690s when Scotland, like most European countries, suffered serious crop failures.

In 1750 only one Scot in eight lived in a town and the land was hugely significant for the mass of the population. But Scotland's traditional patterns of rural life changed dramatically in the eighteenth century. Landlords replaced the remnants of collective endeavour and social ties with individualism, the market and self-interest: multiple farm tenancies were replaced by tenancies for individual, enterprising farmers and commonty land was allocated to big estates. By the 1820s there were virtually no cottars left and much of Scotland had been transformed. By 1850 one in three Scots inhabited large towns. According to Tom Devine what is most remarkable about Scotland's urbanisation was its speed. England became the most urbanised country in Europe as a result of 'a continuous and protracted process of steadily intensifying urban expansion'.[1] Scotland's urbanisation, by contrast was 'abrupt and fast'.

But where did the drive behind such rapid change come

from and why was Scotland able to urbanise so quickly? The motivation came in part from Scottish landowners. By the eighteenth century they no longer saw their land only as a source of inherited wealth or position but also as a way to make money to spend on large houses and ostentatious lifestyles. Secondly, thanks to the Scottish Enlightenment, and the thinking of men like Adam Smith, an improvement ethic had gripped Scottish elites. They considered the old ways of farming inefficient and desperately in need of reform and rationalisation. By the 1830s when the transformation of rural areas was more or less complete, Scotland even looked different: for the first time her countryside had a managed, tidy look with 'trim fields and compact farms, separated by hedges and ditches' in place of the 'strips, rigs and open fields of the old order'.[2] Many of the people who had once lived there had also gone.

Ironically, for a country which likes to pride itself on its egalitarianism and fairness, Scotland 'had probably the most concentrated pattern of land ownership in Europe.' For example, by 1870 a mere 1500 proprietors owned 90 per cent of Scotland's land. Landowners in Scotland also had considerable 'social and political authority'.[3] Since voting rights were linked to property it was the landowners who controlled elections and, along with the Kirk, had power over poor relief and education.

In Scotland there was virtually no peasant class with legal rights which helped the hegemony of the landed class. Indeed those living in the country had very few rights at all, as was observed in 1521 by the Scottish historian John Major:

> In Scotland, the houses of the country people are
> small, as it were, cottages, and the reason is this:

> they have not permanent holdings, but hired only,
> or in lease for four or five years, at the pleasure of
> the lord of the soil; therefore do they not dare to
> build good houses, though stone abound, neither
> do they plant trees or hedges for their orchards,
> nor do they dung their land; and this no small loss
> and damage to the whole realm.[4]

The landed class was able to bring about rapid agricultural improvements, involving changes in land usage partly because they had the power to remove tenants at the end of a lease. These rights were not common in other countries. In most parts of Europe landlords were often constricted by the prevalence of peasant ownership and the legal traditions which buttressed rights to land. Effectively, this meant landlords' room for maneouvre was limited. Not so in Scotland. Indeed the Scottish Parliament was dominated by landed interests and in 1695 passed two Acts making the type of agricultural changes outlined above possible. Scottish landlords also had 'considerable seigniorial authority. Their feudal rights and privileges were maintained until well into the eighteenth century, long after they had been abandoned elsewhere in Britain.'[5]

One of the most remarkable features of Scotland's agricultural revolution is that, outside the Highlands, it has attracted little attention from historians.[6] Another remarkable fact about these changes is that (again outside the Highlands and unlike France or Ireland) they were accomplished with very few popular protests or uprisings. This may be because this was a period when Scotland's rural and urban industries were growing, so as cottars and agricultural workers lost their livelihood on the land they obtained new work. In short, displaced agricultural workers were able to find new ways to put food on the table and maintain a roof over their heads.

Indeed this rapid transformation of life for poor people in Scotland raises an important point about power in the old Scotland. Professor Devine maintains: 'Scottish landowners as a class were used to being obeyed and their tenants were long accustomed to the firm hand of proprietorial authority'.[7] Indeed one of the main arguments advanced by the 'Scottophobe' and English rights activist, John Wilkes, was that 'The principal part of the Scottish nobility are tyrants and the whole of the common people are slaves.'[8]

It is worth asking if there was anything about Scotland which suggested that it was a particularly top down society? Some scholars think so, arguing that the concentration of power in Scotland may have predisposed Scots to be efficient policemen or managers of the British Empire. It is certainly the case that many of the sons of the landed classes in Scotland ended up administering Britain's colonies. In her celebrated work *Britons* Linda Colley argues that while undoubtedly men like Wilkes put forward odious opinions about the Scots there may well be some truth in the idea that the Scots had authoritarian tendencies; that they 'found the business of presiding over thousands of unrepresented subjects in the colonies neither very uncongenial nor particularly unfamiliar.'[9] She argues that this tendency was cultivated by concentrated land ownership and electoral power as well as a 'strong military tradition' within the Scottish landed classes.

Tom Devine speculates that a tendency to authoritarianism may be apparent in Scotland's particular involvement with slavery. Scottish thinkers may have put forward a compelling case for the abolition of slavery but 'enormous vested interests integral to the slave economy won over abstract theory'.[10] Unlike Liverpool, Glasgow did not play an active part in the transportation of slaves but the Scots were heavily involved in plantation crops – cotton, tobacco and sugar – and many owned and ran numerous plantations, particularly in the Caribbean. By all accounts the Caribbean plantations were the most inhumane; the owners preferring 'salt water slaves' – straight from the ship – who they would work to death before buying a new consignment. The horrible truth is that much of the money made through the work of slaves financed the making of Glasgow as a major industrial centre. Undoubtedly many were not content with this fact and Glasgow played a significant role in the UK's fight against slavery. Nonetheless if we are interested in 'the tears that made the Clyde' we must not forget those shed by African slaves and their families.

The Scots whose way of life was transformed were well aware where power lay – with the landed classes. The countless thousands who moved to Glasgow soon knew their new lords and masters. The new entrepreneurial elite which emerged from trading with the American colonies certainly did not act as if they were great upholders of equality. Indeed they were quick to display their status. Glasgow's tobacco lords, for example, erected opulent mansions to the west of the Old Town: Buchanan, Dunlop, Ingram, Oswald and Glassford are a few of the 'lords' whose names live on in Glasgow streets. More importantly for our purposes these men acted like aristocrats:

> They assumed important airs and the deportment
> of very superior persons, looking down upon their
> fellow tradesmen and dependants with a supercil-
> iousness that would be laughed at in these days.
> They considered themselves princes, and strutted

about on the Plainstanes as if they were the rulers of the destinies of Glasgow. They were (like the merchants of Venice) distinguished by a particular garb, being attired in scarlet cloaks, curled wigs, cocked hats, and bearing gold-headed canes.[11]

By the end of the eighteenth century many of Glasgow's tobacco and sugar lords had emulated Scotland's landed classes and bought estates. Indeed by 1815 'the counties around Glasgow were ringed by the estates' of merchant families.[12]

Money, money, money

Glasgow became 'the Second City of the Empire' because it was an industrial and commercial hub – an entrepôt. It was money, in the form of capital and investments, which fuelled the rapid expansion of Glasgow's commercial and industrial activities and money, in terms of profits, which provided the motivation for the expansion. Some successful west of Scotland families such as the Tennants, Bairds, Weirs and Coats were among the wealthiest in Britain.

In commentaries on Glasgow's history what typically emerges is the view that 'the dear green place', once a spiritual centre full of herbs, orchards and pleasant smells, was transformed into a stinking cess-pit of unbelievable human degradation. In short, a beautiful and well-endowed town was 'scarified' by massive industrial expansion which oppressed the majority of its inhabitants. It is also common for commentators to argue that the people responsible for this calamity were ruthless entrepreneurs. For example, the late Sydney Checkland, a great admirer of the sheer energy and productivity of Glasgow's economic past, was nonetheless appalled at what was done in the name of progress. He asserts that 'the fate of the mass of Glaswegians derives from the exploitation and short-sightedness of the men of business who built the place'; that they were content to allow huge numbers of people to gather and set them to work 'without regard to dignity or suffering.'[13]

In 1936, the novelist Willa Muir wrote:

> '. . . the Lowland Scots, by nature more logical, followed the logic of capitalism more unswervingly than the English. . . they did not disrupt the logic of capitalism by any consideration for the social welfare of their country.' [14]

Indeed it has been commonplace for commentators on Glasgow to talk about its rampant, 'me first', individualism. The idea that Scotland's economic engine – Glasgow – was dominated by ruthless, money-oriented capitalists is at odds with the story we often tell ourselves in contemporary Scotland. The historian T.C. Smout too says he is 'astounded' by the fact that Scotland – a country which prided itself on 'high moral standards' – would have tolerated such 'appalling social deprivation', adding: 'What was the point of all those triumphs of the great Victorian age of industry if so many people were unspeakably oppressed by its operations?' [15]

The point of these economic activities was simple: the industrial elite's personal aggrandisement, acquisition of wealth and overarching belief in 'improvement'. What should be shocking for modern day Scots' sense of themselves is that as money was amassed in nineteenth century Scotland little was done to improve the terrible living conditions of the masses. 'Material progress was being maintained while social dereliction was widespread'.[16]

Of course, the logic of capitalism helps explain this. For Scots with money to invest, a much greater return was likely from various projects in the New World, such as the construction of railways or factories, than from investing in local housing. Indeed Scotland invested more money per capita abroad than England or most other developed nations. This was of great benefit to the Scottish banks and those with money to invest in risky, but potentially profitable, overseas ventures but did little for the poor Glaswegian or for the Scottish people as a whole.

The tobacco lords paved the way for Glasgow to become a money-making centre and they were particularly noted for their conspicuous consumption so it is hardly surprising that Glasgow spawned a particular type of money-oriented industrial elite.

'The ambition of the Glasgow man is ample money, a big house in Kelvinside or Pollokshields, and all the other outward signs that he is a man of wealth,' writes Edwin Muir, adding 'The Edinburgh vices are snobbery and gentility; the Glasgow ones tasteless ostentation and materialism.'[17] It is impossible to look at the City Chambers in Glasgow, many of the buildings in the commercial quarter of the town or some of the prestigious residential streets and not be convinced that, not only was this a rich city, it was given to ostentatious spending.

There's little doubt that Glasgow was an opulent, elegant city for the rich and powerful. The American writer Nathaniel Hawthorne visited Glasgow in the mid nineteenth century and was impressed by the new city centre: 'I am inclined to think it the stateliest city I ever beheld,' he writes. 'The Exchange, the other public buildings and the shops, especially in Buchanan-street, are very magnificent: the latter, especially excelling those of London.' But Hawthorne's visit to the High Street and the

73

Saltmarket told a different story. He could see that some of these buildings had been 'stately and handsome in their day' but he was appalled at the numbers and condition of 'the lower orders'. Indeed Hawthorne wrote in his notebook:

> I think the poorer classes of Glasgow excel even those of Liverpool in the bad eminence of filth, uncombed and unwashed children, disorderly deportment, evil smell and all that makes city-poverty disgusting.'[18]

In Glasgow's early history people from all walks of life lived side by side. Indeed they often lived in the same tenements. Partly as a result of accumulating wealth and partly fear of contamination of disease from the slums, from the 1820s on, the wealthy and the middle classes moved out of the Old Town into new houses mainly to the west and south. Those who could afford it went further afield. This geographical segregation was not simply about housing but also about recreational use of the city: the wealthy would parade along Great Western Road while the poor would walk to Glasgow Green. So even use of the city was predicated on social class. It was only in some streets in the city centre that the classes ever mingled and met.

The poet Maurice Lindsay grew up in the 1920s in the leafy west-end and recounts how aware he was of 'dichotomies' – particularly class: the contrast of tea time in the elegant Copland and Lye's and the shabby men he could spy from the tram, hanging about Dumbarton Road.[19] In some areas of Glasgow, tenement living allowed for mixed tenancies: doctors, for example, could live near their working class patients. There was a strong, collective sense of being a Glaswegian and a certain pride in the city's achievement. However, what was more powerful than this cohesion was strong social division – a division partly based on 'geographical segregation on a class basis'.[20] It is unsurprising that the poor should feel neglected by the better off. A verse from 'A Lament on Glasgow Green' complains:

> The rich maun ha'e their West End Park,
> Wi pure and caller air
> But tho' the poor should choke in smoke
> The great folk dinna care. [21]

Of course, Glasgow was not alone in having a city split geographically on class grounds. The west-end, east-end dichotomy can be found in many Western European cities. However, one of the reasons why this division into rich and poor appeared so stark in Glasgow is that the city had a very small middle and professional class, in comparison with Edinburgh, for example. Glasgow was a working class city with a huge number of very poorly paid and housed workers. In nineteenth century Britain industrialism wore a particularly ugly face everywhere it appeared but, as we shall see more fully below, its visage was particularly hideous in Glasgow. Of course some of this was structural and beyond individuals' control but it is difficult to read the history of Glasgow and not be shocked by the callousness and avarice of many landlords who were willing to treat their tenants worse than cattle. In *The History of the Working Classes In Scotland* (1946), Tom Johnston quotes from an 1869 newspaper exposé of conditions in Glasgow which illustrates the involvement of the middle classes:

> Hovels with earthen floors earned rents of six
> shillings a month. In Oakbank Street there were
> tenanted cellars that never enjoyed daylight. . . At

St. Andrew's Lane there were no conveniences, and the human excreta was thrown over the windows, so that the window sills, the walls and the bottom of the court were 'covered with human ordure'. At Creilly's Crescent the children are 'quite dwarfed and attenuated to mere skeletons, their crooked limbs and wasted bodies and little claw-like hands all combine to give them a weird appearance.' The proprietor of Creilly's desirable mansions was a Sauchiehall Street banker who called personally for the rents, and was 'very civil to those who pay promptly, but sharper than a serpent's tooth to unfortunates who may not be able at the moment to pay up.' In 102 Main Street, Gorbals, were 46 houses, the tenants of which were all apparently liable to pay poor's rate, for we read of raids by Sheriff's officers for the poor's rate 'with expenses added'. In one house the sole article of furniture, a chest valued at 4s. 10d is seized; in another case a woman complains that 'they cam' an' took my pot aff the fire wi' a penny-worth o' liver in't for poor's rates.'[22]

Blaming the poor for their misfortunes

In the west of Scotland there was some real interest in tackling poverty and improving the lives of industrial workers and their families. One internationally renowned project to improve lives was New Lanark on the Clyde set up by Robert Owen on utopian socialist principles. Owen showed that industrialists could house and employ their workers properly and still make a profit. There was also a network of churches in the west of Scotland committed to the Chartist movement. One of the main exponents of this approach was the Reverend Patrick Brewster from Paisley.

Nonetheless, despite these reformers' views and despite the

terrible conditions, mortality rates and outbreaks of epidemics within the city, virtually nothing was done to tackle Glasgow's housing problems until the 1840s and much of what happened in the following decades was motivated as much by self-interest as by a genuine concern for the poor. There are a variety of different reasons why the better-off as a whole did not act to ensure that Glasgow's working classes were housed properly. Enid Gauldie, an expert on 'the middle class and working-class housing in the nineteenth century', argues that the reformers were 'confused'. Their actions and views were driven by competing motives – fear of their own vulnerability to disease and genuine compassion for the slum dwellers. They also found it difficult to decide the direction of causality – was poverty the problem or was it diseases; did the poor become undermined by their conditions or was their own immorality the cause of the problems; and to what extent should concern for others' welfare interfere with the operation of the free market? Gauldie is clear that this confusion was a godsend for those with straight-forward ideas about making money. She writes:

> Those who speculated in land, those who drew rents from overcrowded insanitary property, those who put up jerry-built workers' rows, could benefit from the reformers' confusion.' [23]

Many of those who owned the slum dwellings were members of the Kirk and from the well-to-do middle classes.

Dr. Stana Nenadic, an expert on the gentry in Scotland, argues that in the early part of the eighteenth century the middle ranks gave charitable support to poor people who were generally known to them. This was often based on the view that the poor were unfortunates or elderly people who needed help. Sometimes the poor were people who had once been of middling rank themselves and had fallen on hard times. In this respect, charitable giving was almost like an insurance policy. However, Nenadic argues that as the century progressed in Glasgow social relationships broke down and the poor became anonymous. The middle ranks also felt their position more solid. These changes, together with the idea that all problems are 'amenable to reform', led to a different basis for charitable giving. Nenadic's research into charitable income in Glasgow in 1815 reveals these changes and 'the anxieties that haunted the middle-rank attitudes towards the poor':

> Half of these charities, and a majority of donations, were directed towards the reform or amelioration of problems that were held to threaten the well-being of the community; ill-health and disease, of both the body and the mind; moral corruption and dissolute behaviour; cultural deviance and ignorance; idleness and irreligion. . . Not only did they target particular social ills; a second and striking characteristic of many of these organisations is that they sought to resolve the problem they had identified through the institutional incarceration of individuals in special-ised hospitals, prisons, asylums or schools. Problem people, in effect, were to be analysed, categorised and removed from the community to be treated by professionals, in the hope that by their removal and treatment they would be reformed and the community would be saved from further pollution.[24]

In short, the better-off perceived the problem as 'character deficiency' of some kind.[25] So rather than simply helping the poor or targeting the unspeakable conditions – child labour, long working hours, poor wages, foul living conditions – which were the root of the problem, the middle classes in Glasgow primarily sought to change the people or remove those who were unproductive and undesirable. As Tom Devine says, 'There was an urge to cleanse the moral world rather than the physical environment.' [26] No wonder the poor often saw themselves as 'victims', resenting the various types of interference in their lives.[27]

Nonetheless it is also true that many better-off folk in Glasgow had a Christian conscience and believed that they had a duty to help those in trouble. As the nineteenth century progressed we can find an impressive number of philanthropic societies organising do-gooding activities such as soup kitchens. It was this generosity of spirit which allowed these Glaswegians to accept the influx of poor, starving Irish immigrants even when there was little work for them. But well-to-do Christians were also totally opposed to the idea of being compelled to pay tax to improve social problems until much later. Poor relief in Scotland was the lowest in the whole of the UK and was generally below what was needed for basic subsistence; even in the early twentieth century 'the annual cost of relieving paupers per head of population in Scotland was a full 50 per cent lower than in England.' [28] The Scottish Kirk was responsible for poor relief and firmly believed that people would not work if they were given money for nothing. Evangelicals, like the charismatic preacher Dr. Thomas Chalmers – one of the most influential figures in nineteenth century Scotland – argued strongly that the rich had a responsibility to support the poor but was firmly of the view that the existing economic order had been ordained by God. Dr. Chalmers set up an experiment in the Tron parish in Glasgow: poor relief was suspended in the area and money gathered from voluntary donations. Only the poor who passed a character test were awarded monetary benefits. This and other similar projects initiated by Chalmers were finally judged to be failures.

The desire for voluntarism is complicated by the fact that while evangelicals like Dr. Chalmers opposed state intervention, the City Fathers were active in improving living conditions for all citizens and these improvements were carried out on the rates. For example, water was piped into the city from Loch Katrine in 1859. This was the first in a long line of municipal services – gas, trams, baths, swimming pools, laundries, hospitals, libraries, art galleries, markets, refuse collection, public parks and more. Glasgow became one of the first cities in the world to provide a network of such services. They were never devised as money-making ventures and aimed to provide all citizens with good services and value for money. Of course, the poor benefited from clean water, for example, but many still lived in properties with no running water and inadequate sanitation.

Government commissions and medical officers continually exposed the depravity of the slums and the extent of social problems yet the well-to-do resisted having to foot the bill to eradicate them. For example in 1901, the newspaper for Glasgow's middle class, *The Glasgow Herald*, ran an editorial strongly opposing the proposal advanced by the Corporation to borrow money and impose a rate increase largely to build council housing: 'We are to pledge the credit of the city in order to borrow £750,000 for this vague and indefinite purpose, and we are to burden the rates with interest and sinking fund on the debt. Where is this kind of thing to end?' it proclaims. [29]

Clearing the slums and providing good housing on the rates

was a massive step too far. Ultimately it was central Government in London which legislated and provided state support for municipal housing.

A different class of being?

In the nineteenth century the English Roman Catholic Archbishop and Cardinal, Henry Edward Manning, claimed:

> . . . our streets are infested with miserable creatures, from whose faces almost everything human has been erased, whose very presence would put us to shame but for familiarity with the sight. Poor wretches! filthy in body, foul in speech, vile in spirit. Human vermin! Yes, but of our own manufacture, for every individual of this mass was once an innocent child.[30]

During this period it was common for the slum dwellers to be seen, throughout Britain, as 'human vermin'. However, Manning at least recognised their humanity. In other words, he saw them as the victims of circumstance. But this viewpoint was less common in Scotland. The ideology in Scotland, largely put forward by the Kirk, was that poverty and squalor were due to bad character, and not environmental circumstances. This is part of the essential Calvinist belief that God in his infinite wisdom has divided human beings into two groups – the elect who would find ultimate salvation and those who were damned for all eternity. Those leading good Christian lives, with the outward signs of success, were likely to be members of the elect while those living wretched lives demonstrated their abject worthlessness.[31] This is one reason why the Scottish Poor Law had a strong moralistic and judgemental character to it. Before the rise of industry it might have been possible to say that some poor people were feckless or lazy – that they could have worked to provide for themselves but did not. But with mass unemployment in Glasgow an inevitable consequence of trade cycles, how could it possibly make sense to see poor, unemployed people as morally responsible for their predicament?

The Scottish academic Allan McLaren argues that, while some individual doctors made contributions to medicine and the understanding of disease, the strong religious beliefs which dominated in Scotland meant that the country as a whole lagged behind England, by more than a generation, in the movement for public health. McLaren argues that strong Calvinist beliefs led to the widespread view in mid-nineteenth century Scotland that cholera, or other such happenings, were the result of God's divine intervention and should not be questioned let alone interfered with. This gave way to the notion that cholera was 'God's judgement against filth'. [32] These judgemental notions which rob people of human dignity and personal worth resounded throughout Scotland for centuries. So, as well as having to bear the most appalling housing and working conditions, the poor were also told they were worthless and to blame for their predicament. This cast a shadow over Scotland as a whole but, given Glasgow's history, the idea that poor people are worthless was planted in soil manured for generations.

McLaren argues that the notion that spiritual and economic destitution were inextricably linked and 'the incorporation' of 'these ideas into middle-class ideology might be seen as one essential distinguishing feature between the Scottish and English bourgeoisie of the nineteenth century.'[33] Ultimately, the challenge to such views came from secular society in the views of English social reformers like Charles Booth and Seebohm Rowntree as well as a host of Royal Commissions on various issues ranging from working conditions and wages, housing and Poor Law. These official reports illustrated the importance of environmental factors. Indeed they estimated that between 27-43 per cent of poverty could be traced to problems of old age, sickness, widowhood and family size.

This new sociological perspective ultimately led to the appeal of the new socialist parties and in the long run it was the state which largely paid for slums to be demolished and new houses built. The approach which portrayed the poor as victims of poverty and circumstance rather than responsible for their plight did ultimately triumph but up till 1917 enquiries in Glasgow on the slum problem still heard evidence from groups intent on blaming the poor for their own misfortunes.

Professor Richard Rodger is a social and economic historian who provides some of the most compelling evidence and analysis on Scottish cities. He takes the view that low wages were not only a problem for the welfare of Glasgow's working classes but also undermined the city's long-term economic prospects – stopping investment and keeping Glasgow trapped in low productivity and an overdependence on a few heavy industries. In an analysis of employment, wages and poverty in Scottish cities from 1841 to 1914 he concludes:

> Without a Booth or Rowntree for Glasgow, without empirical work on the west of Scotland labour market, English surveys of poverty could be pigeon-holed as inappropriate by a newly created, though largely impotent, Scottish Office whose officials, drawn from the middle-class milieu of the Edinburgh bourgeoisie, could point to intemperance and

improvidence as long-standing character deficiencies. In the context of the capital's counter-cyclical employment experience, insulated through its tertiary sector from the late Victorian squeeze on credit and profits visible in west central Scotland, any analysis of housing or wider social problems which identified inadequate incomes of the working class was heretical. An embryonic Scottish Office was therefore unlikely to recommend a fundamental shift of policy to its Whitehall superiors. No wonder then, that the Edinburgh-Glasgow axis, was, and remains, one of suspicion and antagonism. [34]

The link with inequality

Leaving politics aside, to help understand why it was so easy for the better-off to become callous in response to the less fortunate, let us return to Wilkinson's idea about why equality is necessary for good social relations. Prior to the Industrial Revolution, in Scotland at least, various classes in society lived side by side. The rich may have lived in better and bigger houses than the poor but they were still neighbours. However, as the rich felt compelled to move away from streets inhabited by the poor to escape contamination, they began to think of the people being crowded into fast-growing industrial cities as a separate class of individual, having different and less pressing human needs. Thus they were able to condone the deterioration of the inner urban area into slums. [35]

Ultimately the middle classes began to see the slum dwellers not just as different but as an *inferior* type of being. This is exactly Richard Wilkinson's argument. The more different people are in terms of status and income the less easy it is for the rich to identify with the predicament of the poor. This is the same idea advanced by the nineteenth century figure Alexis de Tocqueville – a Frenchman who wrote about his observations on American democracy. Tocqueville argues that in countries with pronounced hierarchies, such as aristocratic France prior to the Revolution, it is easy for the ruling elite to become blind to the suffering of the masses as they do not see them as human beings:

> When all men. . . are ranked in an irrevocable way according to their occupation, wealth, and birth. . . each caste has its opinions, its sentiments, its rights and moral habits, its separate existence. Thus the men who compose it bear no resemblance to any of the others; they do not have the same way of thinking or of feeling, and if they believe themselves to belong to the same humanity, they do so just barely. . . When the chroniclers of the Middle Ages, who all, by their birth or their habits, belonged to the aristocracy, report the tragic death of a noble, they express infinite sorrows; where they recount in one breath and without batting an eye the massacre and tortures of the common people. [36]

Glasgow was a city of extreme differences in wealth and living conditions and the gross insensitivity of the middle classes to the plight of fellow citizens seems to corroborate Tocqueville's argument. Even when they did not justify the conditions it was fairly common for the middle classes to believe that somehow the people who occupied the slums were a different type of human being – human beings with character deficiencies and defects, naturally disposed to criminal or destructive behaviour. Even those who wanted to see improvement in living conditions still had this view of the slum dwellers as a different type of being. For example, political economy professor William Smart advised that any new homes:

> . . . should be houses that the tenants cannot spoil –
> four bare walls, say of concrete, with an indestruct-
> ible fire place, and an indestructible bed-frame. So
> far as possible, no wood to hack or burn; no plaster
> to pull down; no paper to tear away; no fittings to
> carry off by the light of the moon, well-lit, that there
> be no concealment of evil-doing. . . [37]

The idea that the poor, and those with extreme social problems, are worthless and contemptible – scum or worms – crops up repeatedly in literature or commentaries on the city. The journalist and author Meg Henderson reports a shocking example in her autobiography about growing up in Glasgow. In 1959 she met with a doctor who had worked in Blackhill where she had lived as a child. He did not know her connection with the place and so is unguarded in his comments about the local inhabitants. He talked about it as 'a hell-hole, a den of thieves and murderers'. When she asked if there weren't any decent people there he replied: 'It must be difficult for someone like you to understand, but those people were barely human, the absolute dregs of humanity at the most.' [38]

However, rather than justifying the conditions of the lower orders it is even easier for the well-to-do to sidestep the problem or pretend it does not exist. A telling example is that of the University of Glasgow. The original building was housed at the top of the High Street and by the 1840s it was in the midst of Glasgow's unfolding human drama. Brian Dicks, in a chapter on segregation in nineteenth century Glasgow, quotes from contemporary sources before giving us his own perspective:

'The area round the College had become appallingly decayed and overcrowded. The evening law classes had been abandoned because of the nightly pandemonium of screams and policemen's rattles, and the inexpediency of bringing young men through the parade of women of the town in front of the college entrance.' The adjacent area, in which the students lodged, included the notorious Vennel and Havannah slums, 'inhabited by rag dealers, thieves, prostitutes and receivers of stolen goods.' In an era long before social sciences gained academic respectability, the University though engulfed by an authentic sociological laboratory, ultimately succumbed to middle class trends and moved to new premises in the West End.[39]

Glasgow University chose to turn its back on the problem. So too did most of Scotland's literati. One of the aspects of industrial life in Scotland, which has attracted much negative comment from literary commentators, is the fact that throughout the nineteenth century not one Scottish writer of note produced a novel about life in Glasgow or other Scottish industrial towns. In other words no figure, like Charles Dickens, recorded what life was like for the slum-living, labouring poor. There were a large number of stories on city life, including the slums, serialised in Scottish newspapers – so there was no literary blackout as such – but until the 1930s Glasgow's industrial fiction was relatively low-profile. What was fashionable was stories about rural or small town life – a genre of fiction usually referred to as 'the kailyard'.[40]

This changed in the 1930s. Edwin Muir, Lewis Grassic Gibbon, Neil Gunn and George Blake wrote powerful fiction, or non-fictional works, conveying the brutality of industrialisation and the daily horrors of the slums. The first truly industrial

Glasgow novel was *The Shipbuilders* (1935) by the Greenock-born journalist, George Blake. The novel tells the story of two men – Leslie Pagan, a shipyard owner, and Danny Shields, a riveter in his yard who had previously been Pagan's batman in the army. This is a gritty realistic novel about family and industrial life during the Depression and depicts an extremely hierarchical relationship between shipyard masters and craftsmen. Pagan is kindly, but patronising to Danny who knows his place. In a visit to the city Danny thinks of Pagan as 'the Boss, belonging by right to this secure and shining world.' [41]

Edwin Muir is much more savage about Glasgow in his travelogue of Scotland published as *Scottish Journey* (1935). One of the most moving sections of the book is his account of Glasgow during the Depression, though he also contributes his own observations as a former resident. Muir was born and raised in Orkney. He was an idealist, a mystic and poet, and he saw Glasgow through the eyes of a visitor from a green and distant land. Muir's observations are particularly relevant to our topic of the impact the slums had on the middle classes. He maintains that their faces carried the look of 'depraved knowledge'; that they cannot wash away the 'dirt and squalor' of the slums no matter how big and commodious their dwellings, and so they become 'blunted and dead' to their surroundings and to their part in the process. [42]

Given how bad the slums were it is hardly surprising that the middle class often dissociated from the problem, harbouring the fear that the slum dwellers would rise up in anger. William Bolitho was moved to write his account of the Glasgow slums as he was convinced that the appalling conditions were bound to lead to a socialist revolution. As a young man, the poet

Maurice Lindsay was on a bus pushed over by rioting Lanarkshire miners, an event which may have prompted the following poem about Glasgow, indicating profound middle-class guilt and fear of rightful reprisals:

the comfortable forgetfulness of the many
who lie in content's soft arms, and are safe and sure
in the fabled Grecian wanderer's lotus-land;
who forget the sullen glove of the wet grey skies,
and the lashing Northern wind that flicks the skin,
where hum-drum poverty's dull and listless eyes
are pressed to the window, hearing the friendly din
of the party, watching the lights and laughter within.

But oh! I cannot forget. so I wait and wonder:
how long will the thinly-dividing window hold?
how long will the dancing drown the terrible anger
of those, the unwanted, who peddle their grief in the cold,
wrapped in their own despair's thick and unkindly fold? [43]

The need for a step change

If the middle classes feared reprisals from the lower orders it is also true to say that the poor had good reason to fear their masters. This was due in part to the ferocity of their bosses, who like the Scottish landed aristocracy, were used to being obeyed:

They included such names as Colville, Baird, Yarrow,
Tennant, Lorimer, Elder, Pearce, Neilson and
Beardmore. . . They were autocrats, their decisions
were made, conveyed, and not discussed. They had a
strong desire to keep everything in their own hands.
A man like Beardmore, perhaps the greatest of them,
took his own authority over the concern to be
absolute and rightful: he and his peers were not

given to self-doubt and self-questioning. . . though the business might be slipping away or heading into a crisis, it would be a courageous junior who would raise his voice. . . The magnates of the Scottish basic industries at the end of the nineteenth century may perhaps be taken as a distillation of the Victorian ethic. It centred upon the dominant male of middle age or over, brooking no interference, speaking only with his equals so far as there was any conferring at all. . .[44]

In the mid-nineteenth century there had been some consultation with the workers in Scottish enterprises but, according to the Checklands, quoted above, this had disappeared by 1900 and they were given little information about the company. 'Labour had become in large measure merely a hired input,' they write, 'with an underlying fear of dismissal.'

Economic circumstances meant that this autocratic attitude had to change. As many of the industries these men, or their families, had created were dependent on world markets and vulnerable to foreign competition, by the end of the nineteenth century it became evident that Glasgow's industry was built on an increasingly shaky foundation. A major problem was that Scotland as a whole, but the west of Scotland in particular, was too dependent on heavy industry and had too few growth industries. The low wage economy was also a problem as it 'encouraged continued labour-intensive production methods' thereby keeping productivity and investment low. [45] Compared with England, Scotland had little indigenous demand for service jobs and consumer durables and a much smaller middle class.

So by the early twentieth century it was clear that Scotland in general, and Glasgow in particular, needed more economic diversity. In 1931 a group of leading industrialists, led by the influential Clyde shipbuilder Sir James Lithgow, set up a Development Council which aimed to attract new industries north of the border. At first they hoped to counter the Clyde's growing reputation for shop-floor militancy but, partly as a result of the activities of Tom Johnston, the Labour MP who was Secretary of State in Churchill's coalition Government from 1941 to 1945, they soon became passionate corporatists. The Development Council quickly became a strong advocate of the kind of powerful central planning of the economy that was to become such a feature of post-war Labour government strategy. Johnston then went on to create various organisations which finally became what is still known as the Scottish Council for Development and Industry (SCDI). Following its creation, post-war Scotland benefited from a number of significant inward investment projects from the rest of the UK and from the United States. By 1951, Ferranti, NCR, Honeywell and IBM had all set up in Scottish locations. Scotland also took state-led corporate planning to its heart with the Toothill Report on the Scottish economy, the creation of the first new towns and the establishment of the Highlands and Islands Development Board.

This step change was in tune with the growing desire for state provision and control – not just of the economy but also in welfare provision which though often inadequate and ill-conceived still made a huge difference to the lives of the poor people of Glasgow. It was much needed as the rich and middling classes in Glasgow had in the past simply failed to look after the interests of poor working people who they often viewed as a different class of being.

CHAPTER 4
The twin track city

ONE OF the questions I've repeatedly been asked about my research for this book is how different conditions were in Glasgow from other industrial centres such as London, Liverpool or Manchester and whether inequality wasn't simply a fact of life for all industrial workers and their families. Of course, it is true that urbanisation throughout the UK brought terrible living and working conditions for factory workers and urban dwellers and shocking extremes of wealth and poverty. But this is relative. On the one hand, as the second city of the Empire, Glasgow was an extremely wealthy city – wealthier than Manchester or Liverpool, for example. The well-to-do lived in handsome buildings and streets – indeed the city they inhabited was one of the finest in the UK and on a par with the best of Europe. On the other hand, it was often stated that the conditions in Glasgow for the poor were the worst in Europe.

Glasgow's overcrowding was particularly awful when compared with London's figures, or England's as a whole. In 1891 the London County Council defined overcrowding in terms of two or more persons per room. In the metropolis one-third fell below this standard but in Glasgow two-thirds, or twice London's number, of residents lived in overcrowded accommodation. In 1917 approximately 38 per cent of Glaswegians lived three or four people to a room; the equivalent figure in English cities was just over 2 per cent. Another major difference is that the predominance of tenements meant that Glasgow had virtually no working class suburbia – no rows or terraces of back-to-back housing commonly seen in England. This type of housing was spacious in comparison with old tenements. Indeed 'two up, two down' was common in England and such housing was roomy in comparison with the Glasgow worker's lot. Ironically, in Glasgow during the period of such incredible overcrowding, houses often stood empty. Sometimes they were simply built in the wrong locations – too far from places of work – but more often the builders wanted rents which were too high for people on low, unpredictable earnings. In Scotland Glasgow's rival for putrid conditions was Dundee yet that city never had anything like the overcrowding problem of Glasgow. Edinburgh slums were also notorious for their nauseating stench but a much smaller percentage of the city's population were housed in such conditions than was the case in Glasgow.

No, we cannot escape the fact that there was nothing as bad as the Glasgow wynds and no other city had the scale of Glasgow's problems. A Select Committee on the Health of Towns heard from one witness: 'I did not believe, until I witnessed the wynds of Glasgow, that so large an amount of filth, crime, misery and disease existed in one spot in any civilised country.'[1] Accounts like these, and historical records, show that Glasgow topped the bill when it came to the sordidness of the conditions, the extent of overcrowding, the sheer numbers living in slum conditions, infant mortality and other health problems.

As we have seen, these problems were due in part to the massive influx of migrants seeking employment – an influx so great that overcrowding on a grand scale was inevitable. But other factors were also at work: economic insecurity caused by frequent bouts of unemployment led workers to fear taking on the higher rents that better housing would entail. The problem was exacerbated by the fact that leases tended to be longer in Scotland than England, where short lets were more common. This meant that even skilled workers would only rent single-ends in case they lost their job and could not meet the payment demanded by a lease signed in more fortunate times.

The problems for Glasgow's workers were caused not just by poor housing but by low wages. One of the strategic cost advantages throughout the nineteenth century for Glasgow bosses was that wages were low in comparison to the average for the United Kingdom. Indeed in 1872 the United States Congress heard that the 'worldwide success of Clyde-built ships was to be explained in the final analysis by "the abundance of skilled workmen and the low wages paid to them".' [2] Even in 1912 the Board of Trade calculated that 'real wages (after taking into account living costs) were fully 10 per cent less in Scottish towns than their counterparts in England.' [3] It has also been estimated that people living in Glasgow during this period paid more for their food and rent than those living in Leeds, Salford and Nottingham. For example in 1911 the Board of Trade estimated that the retail price index, including rent, in Glasgow was 93 where it mainly ranged from 86 to 89 for equivalent English cities.[4] Some of this variation was accounted for by higher rents in Glasgow – a scandal given the overcrowding and conditions.

If this was not bad enough there was yet another challenge for the poor. 'For many Scottish city dwellers, even though the wage rates were below and the cost of living above national levels, the cause and course of poverty was determined by another consideration – irregular employment.'[5] Looking at the four Scottish cities this irregularity of employment was especially common for many Glasgow workers. Historians estimate that at the end of the nineteenth and beginning of the twentieth centuries, '20-23 per cent of male and 26-29 per cent of female employment was in occupations closely associated with seasonal variations.'[6] As far as the insecurity of workers was concerned this problem was compounded by the fact that many of Glasgow's jobs were also affected by international economic cycles. In Edinburgh, by contrast, those employed in industry were working often for 'small-scale consumer industries' which were catering for local demand from the middle and upper classes. This meant there was much more stability and security for the Edinburgh working class.

Another difference between Glasgow and Edinburgh was that the former had a very small professional class – the 1883 Census shows only 4 per cent of the workforce in this category against the capital's 12 per cent. This clearly had consequences for the economy with Edinburgh employing more domestic labour and allowing for indigenous consumer industries. This meant much better employment or business opportunities for builders, shopkeepers, craftsmen and others catering for the needs and desires of Edinburgh's middle classes. What's more, Glasgow's lack of professional jobs created a very divided city: without a thriving professional middle class, and labour aristocrats to cater for them, there were more extreme status differences between the wealthy commercial classes and the labourers. But did this inequality, uncertainty and abject poverty lead to divisions among the poor themselves and to the type of 'bicycling reaction' described by Wilkinson and Pickett whereby people kick out at those below them in the hierarchy in order to feel better about themselves?

The Poor's pecking order

One commentator on Glasgow recently concluded from interviews with ex-residents: 'There was a social ladder in tenement society.' [7] In old Glasgow, there were different types of accommodation and facilities for the lower orders – single ends, room and kitchens and two-room and kitchens – and the size and quality of the accommodation conferred status. Some houses had no sanitary facilities, others were shared. Some tenants, for a variety of reasons, ranging from amount of disposable income or energy and pride, kept their houses cleaner than others. This allowed for a distinct hierarchy to develop within the tenements themselves.

My father's family who lived in tenements in Maryhill from the 1920s to 1960s would jokingly say 'we might be poor but we're clean'. Or they would talk about the Craigs being 'top drawer' because they were finally housed in a two-room and kitchen with an indoor (private) lavatory. There were eight of them and so this was by no means salubrious but it was much better than many neighbours' houses. Of course, there were much better living conditions than my family's. The Craigs could easily be trumped by those living in a red-sandstone tenement, particularly if it had a 'wally' (tiled) close. That wasn't just a drawer above – it was a whole new tallboy.

The novelist Janice Galloway humorously reflects on the status divisions in her west of Scotland upbringing when she tells us her mother's family 'were a long line of miners and labourers' while her father's 'could boast a glove-maker or chauffeur, two car drivers and a chap who had, at least on one occasion, owned a van.' [8]

One of the perplexing aspects of writing on Glasgow is how much it contains extreme contradictions on the issue of equality. For example, in Meg Henderson's life story she paints her mother as a loving, big-hearted woman who believed passionately in human decency and desired to treat everyone equally. Nonetheless she also tells us that 'the most damning comment' her mother could make about people was to pronounce them 'common'. What's more in her family there is a strong division into two camps and it is partly on the basis of the value of 'decorum' and 'good manners'. [9]

This contradiction was brought to life in comic fashion by the Scots journalist and writer Cliff Hanley in an article aptly named 'Snobs and scruff'. Hanley begins the article writing: 'It is often asserted, even by me, that the class thing never got off the ground in Glasgow, and that we are all Jock Tamson's bairns.' He also refers to Glasgow as 'this savagely egalitarian city' yet he then fills several pages outlining how the 'snob-scruff system' operates in Glasgow and that he grew up 'infused with snobbery'. According to Hanley 'we all need to know that there's somebody worse off than we are, somebody we're entitled to sneer at. . .' So unlike the Hanleys, who were 'respectable', the Gilligans (near neighbours) were 'scruff'. They were scruff because they wore parish suits, 'heads shaved into the wid, with a cow's lick left at the front'. In fact, they were scruff because they were scruff.[10]

But it wasn't just personal characteristics that separated snobs and scruff. It was also where you lived and unfortunately, for the Hanleys, they lived on the other side of the tracks, even when they moved to a new Corporation housing scheme in Sandyhills.

> The stratification went on stratifying. People in semis were clearly a cut above those in terraces, and more so those in two-up-two-downs. Then another bizarre division arose.
>
> Sandyhills is bisected East to West by Shettleston Burn. . . We peasants on the north side could claim only to live in Shettleston. The houses were identical, but obviously there is an inherent superiority in the word Sandyhills, and any linguist will tell you the arrangement of letters in Shettleston is socially debased. [11]

This is all good knock-about stuff but it is also deadly accurate about the inherent social gradations in this supposedly egalitarian city.

Respectability was an important value in the nineteenth century for the professional and middle classes and they used this as a standard by which to judge the working classes. There is nothing exclusively Glaswegian about the concept of respectability and its importance was evident throughout Scotland and other parts of the UK. Victorians were particularly dominated by the pursuit of respectability. In Scotland, as elsewhere, respectability appears to have been of particular significance as the well-to-do cleaved to the notion that poverty and slum living resulted from bad and immoral character, not living conditions. It was 'respectability' which separated the moral and the immoral; the deserving and the undeserving. Middle class organisations set up to improve housing or living conditions 'excluded tenants who did not fulfil the requirements of respectability.' [12] Private landlords too often refused to house those they deemed 'unrespectable' or 'undeserving' and the new tenement houses were generally allocated to skilled workers and their families who had a modicum of respectability.

The term respectability was always ambiguous but for men it involved being thrifty, sober and financially independent. Given the importance attached to respectability – how it could literally make or break families – it is unsurprising that for women too 'respectability' became a much sought-after badge of honour, particularly in better off working class areas. For women respectability was conferred not only on the basis of sexual morality but also personal cleanliness; the appearance of offspring; a well-ordered home; and a clean washing pegged out neatly in the back green on the appointed days. Washing standards were often policed by older, bossy women who organised the rota for the communal wash house and decided on fair access to the washing lines. They would also make sure that everyone took a turn of washing the stairs.

Again Ralph Glasser, from a Jewish background, had the outsider's distance to pick up on aspects of the culture others may take for granted. He tells us how 'respectable' was an important word and how much it was used to limit and restrict the activities of girls. Even staying out past ten at night was not deemed respectable. Showing your underwear – particularly if it was needing washed or mended was a particular problem, with mothers warning of a possible calamity if the girl met an accident and had to be taken to hospital. 'What are they going to think?' [13] the girl's mother would warn, shuddering at the thought of nurses fingering dingy knickers or old, twisted straps.

Disunited we stand

What about the workplace in Glasgow? Did it also have pronoun-ced stratification? After World War I Glasgow was seen inter-nationally as a militant city – Red Clydeside was legendary. But in reality Glasgow had not been a stronghold of political radicalism. The Chartist movement was 'mild and moderate' in comparison with England. Those who were disgruntled were more likely to emigrate than put up a political fight. Indeed emigration is often seen as a 'safety valve', relieving pressure for radical reforms. There was also not much strength in trade unions, let alone union militancy, in the nineteenth century. The Glasgow cotton spinners strike had taken place in 1837 but was brutally put down by the authorities. The fact that Glasgow continued to attract new workers displaced from the land here as elsewhere meant that labour was abundant and therefore cheap – this gave employers a distinct advantage over workers. Indeed Glasgow employers generally took a strong anti-union view although, ironically, they themselves joined together in strong employers' alliances. From the mid 1850s England developed strong national unions, which exhibited a great deal of militancy, whereas Scotland tended to form federations of small, independent unions supported by Trades Councils. A motivating factor for leaders was a strong sense of local autonomy and independence. It is hardly surprising that when Beatrice Webb visited Scotland in 1892 she was distinctly unimpressed by Glasgow trade unionists, noting, in her diary, their divisiveness: 'The Scottish nature does not lend itself to combination; the strong men seek to rise and push for themselves and not serve others.' [14]

Indeed one of the reasons why Glasgow workers did not form strong unions is that there was considerable division in the workplace. Demarcation disputes, between various occupational specialisms, were common. Skilled men jealously guarded their position by fighting to continue wage differentials between themselves and semi or unskilled workers. In the shipyards, for example, there was a decided hierarchy with engineers at the top. They saw themselves as labour aristocrats and even dressed differently from other workers – they wore bowler hats at the weekend. Boilermakers and patternmakers were also at the top of the tree in the shipyards. In the middle were blacksmiths, joiners, hammermen, riggers and so forth. The unskilled workers were at the bottom of the pecking order.

In the Upper Clyde Shipbuilders work-in of 1971-72 these sectional interests were so evident that they became an issue for the leaders. Thus Jimmy Airlie openly rebuked the boilermakers for 'rowing their own canoe' and claimed that the disunity of the unions in the industry 'left a bad taste in the movement's mouth'.[15] This hierarchy was not only of the workers' making but was part of the very structure of the heavy industries. This can be seen in the fact that shipyards could have six canteens catering for different grades of managers and employees. However, the labourers, no matter how skilled, were lower in the pecking order than white collar staff.

Sectarianism

There are additional factors which suggest that Glasgow suffered from more division and status disputes than other cities. In his book on Glasgow, Sean Damer, a sociologist greatly sympathetic to the socialist cause and working class politics, argues that 'The class was fissured – more deeply than any other in Britain – by skill, gender, religion, and regularity of employment.[16] Ian

Hutchison, in a review of working class politics in Glasgow up to World War I, argues, 'The fragmentation of the city's working class, and in particular the persistence of ethnic and sectarian loyalties, meant that working-class unity was difficult to achieve and still more to maintain.' [17] Undoubtedly a strongly divisive feature within the Glasgow working class was religion. For example, it is claimed that the Amalgamated Society of Engineers did not have one Catholic member until 1931. Some higher status jobs such as train drivers or other railway jobs were more likely to go to Ulster Protestant Scots than the Catholic Irish. The same was true of the skilled jobs in the shipyards. Tom Devine asserts 'boys from unskilled Catholic families would be permanently excluded from the best jobs'. [18] Devine also writes about different types and waves of emigration from Ireland and different levels of assimilation but he still takes the view that:

> . . . sectarian conflict loomed over the Depression years. The Church of Scotland and the United Free Church led a public campaign to enforce rigorous controls on Irish immigration and denounced the 'Scoto-Irish' as an inferior race who could not be assimilated despite the fact the numbers of migrants had actually slowed to a trickle in the 1920s. Job discrimination on the basis of religion increased in the labour market as the number of workers was ruthlessly cut back and the authority of chargehands and foremen who were often Masonic and/or Orange background was consolidated.

Quoting John Cooney, Devine adds, 'For young unemployed Catholics, this was the era of What school did you go to? Were you in the Boys Brigade? and Who was your Sunday School teacher?' [19] This is exactly the mentality that Wilkinson argues underlies status hierarchies and the 'bicycling reaction' – kicking out at people lower than you in the pecking order. It is worth bearing in mind that Wilkinson asserts that the 'bicycling reaction' can be seen in the increased number of racist attacks during periods of unemployment and economic hardship. He also cites data which show that the worst problems of racism in the United States are in those with the most acute income inequality. As Neal Ascherson says: 'Race prejudice and sectarian prejudice are the same beast.' [20]

Sectarianism was not only an issue at work or in periods of high unemployment in Glasgow. Indeed as early as 1740 Professor Francis Hutcheson, who came to Glasgow from Northern Ireland, told an Irish friend that in Scotland 'there remains too much warmth and animosity about matters of no great consequence to real Religion.' [21] Sectarianism inevitably developed a life of its own through Catholic and Protestant organisations, such as the Ancient Order of the Hibernians and the Orange Order. It also became institutionalised in Glasgow's warring football teams – Rangers and Celtic. Religious tribalism could also divide families and cause acute emotional pain as it did in my own family. My maternal grandmother was from a Catholic Irish family. In the early 1920s she met and fell in love with a man who was Scottish Protestant. They married despite the bitter opposition of both families. Life was a strain for this young couple bereft of family support. My mother's younger brother died in infancy, her parents split up and her mother died of TB a few months later.

As many have observed, Glasgow is a city of dichotomies: toffs and keelies; snobs and scruff; east enders and west enders; Prods and left footers. In areas containing Jews they were often looked down on by the local inhabitants. A Jewish doctor remembering his childhood in the 1930s recalls being asked 'Are you a Billy or a Dan or an Old Tin Can?' [22] The last name applied to Jews who were beaten up by the two other sides. One of the shocking aspects of *The Shipbuilders* is how much latent hostility it contains to 'yids'. Nonetheless in Glasgow there was not widespread hostility to the Jews as they tended to stay in specific areas of the city and generally worked in Jewish-owned industries which meant they were not always in competition for jobs. Also, in comparison to what happened in some European cities, anti-Semitism was minor in Glasgow. In Glasgow kicking out at those below you in the pecking order may be seen more clearly in day-to-day violence figures which we shall examine in the next chapter.

Us and them

As discussed earlier, the well-to-do often saw the poor as architects of their own problems and much of their do-gooding was about clearing or managing the problem rather than improving life circumstances for the poor. It is hardly surprising that until the state began to show some compassion for their plight the poor were hostile to the state and those who executed its powers. This resentment extended well beyond the policymakers and the magistrates:

> The local state was the work of the Improvement Trust, which by its slum-clearance policies drove the slum dwellers from their homes into yet more crowded remaining houses. The local state was the new town hall, undoubtedly magnificent but on land gained at the cost of clearing the houses of

the poor. The local state was the parochial board
which treated the poor, in need or in sickness,
with a parsimonious disregard for basic needs. The
local state was the administrators of the Lord
Provost's relief fund who treated applicants with
what was intended as a deterring harshness. The
local state was the belt-happy teacher or the
truancy officer of school boards that had made
education compulsory but not free. [23]

Little wonder that one of the things which so aggrieved poor
people in Glasgow, and other Scottish cities, was the salaries
and superannuation and privileges of local officials and that
they resented having to make a contribution to such a privileged
lifestyle through the rates. Glasgow, as we saw earlier, had a
smaller professional class than was usual for cities in the UK
but nonetheless it employed significant numbers of police,
prison and municipal officials, 'the agents of environmental and
social control'. [24]

When we put the poor's dislike of state officials together
with the huge disparity between their terrible living conditions
and those of the wealthy we can see why Glasgow's working
class would have adopted a strong 'us and them' attitude. This
was further exacerbated by the aggressive management style of
their bosses. Checkland argues that by the twentieth century it
had become common for Clydeside workers to uphold 'the idea
that it is right to hate the boss, and through him the firm.' [25]
Checkland also reports the views of an American economist,
David Granick, who spent a year in Glasgow in the early 1960s
studying labour and management. Granick observed that in
Glasgow, as in other places where 'class conflict is sharpest',
'there often seems to be far more interest in the proportion
between the wage level and profits than in absolute wages.'

Essentially this means that workers are less interested in boosting their standard of living and more concerned about the gap between their income and the bosses. So Granick writes: 'A policy of rising wages which was accompanied by more rapidly rising profits would be interpreted as a trade union defeat.' [26]

As we saw earlier, a great deal of trade union effort went into defending sectional interests and this also was often concerned with differences between groups of workers rather than the spending power of wages. Contemporary psychological research undertaken internationally shows that it is common for people to want money, not for what it can buy, but for its status value. [27] So the issue here is not whether Glasgow's working class had a view of money which was unique; rather whether it was, as Granick observed, more intense since it was deeply rooted in the local culture.

Granick's study of Glasgow's industrial relations also led him to argue that incentive schemes were less motivational here for peculiarly local reasons. Checkland summarises his argument as follows:

> The workers concerned lived in the old slum parts of Glasgow, by far the worst in Britain. Their rent was negligible: there was little to be done with additional earnings without stepping beyond the community's accepted expenditure pattern: such social and residential mobility might even raise the dreaded question of 'Who does he think he is?' This attitude was especially strong among the older workers. Generalised, workers' attitudes towards additional income were related to the long-run aspirations of the family: in a culture where these values which require higher incomes for their realisation are at a discount, wage incentives are unlikely to promote a productivity response. [28]

Who do you think you are?

Granick's observations, made in the 1960s, suggest that the attitudes he detects are deeply rooted in the past. They certainly accord with the account I have outlined in my earlier book *The Scots' Crisis of Confidence*. [29] Scottish egalitarianism conveys the idea that if everyone is equal then no-one is better than anyone else. This type of egalitarian value system levels down, dampening aspirations. In Glasgow, this belief, together with the strong sense of solidarity against the rich, has led tradition-ally to a hostility to 'getting on'.

Ralph Glasser, grew up in the Gorbals, left school at 14 and won a scholarship to Oxford as a young man. In his autobiog-raphies he recounts the hostility he encountered as a result of his success: folk that got on were often considered 'class traitors'. He tells us that when he returned from Oxford for a visit 'in the streets and closes of the Gorbals I was shunned as a leper.' [30] In more recent times the hostility to successful folk was displayed in attitudes to Billy Connolly, or Sheena Easton, who were accused of forgetting where they had come from. For me the most significant aspect of Glasgow's so-called egalitarianism is the dislike of what is often seen as social pretension but is often simply a dislike of people for being different. There was, and still is, a great deal of reverse snobbery: folk who are successful, or who do not behave the same as everyone else, are criticised or ostracised; they become the butt of jokes because they talk 'posh' and so must be snobs. The historian Richard Finlay argues that Scotland as a whole 'was plagued by a small-town mentality in which "I kent his faither" was used to rubbish social mobility.' He attributes the problem in part to 'jealousy' of those who come from the same background but still manage to get on. [31]

It was not only this predominant belief system which worked against aspirations in Glasgow. The social and economic structure contributed as well. For example, the lack of entitlement to adequate poor relief in Scotland, during periods of unemployment or sickness, meant that workers felt vulnerable. Many Scottish jobs were heavily dependent on world markets and so were precarious.

As tenements were the principal type of housing in the urban areas, workers who managed to accumulate some savings were less likely to become owner occupiers than their counterparts in England because tenements, involving a system of factors and common repairs, were not attractive propositions for home ownership. This was one of the reasons why in the middle years of the twentieth century Glasgow had the highest level of council tenants in any city outside the old Soviet bloc. Of course, some workers scrimped and saved and bought their own homes but this was much less common than in England. My father recounts that the nickname for one of the engine drivers at his work was 'Bungalow Bertie'.

What Glasgow's, indeed Scotland's, history suggests is that those with serious aspirations found it easier to emigrate than try to improve themselves in their homeland – wages were low, opportunities for varied employment limited, housing and living conditions poor. Besides, as we've seen, folk that aspired to something better could easily be seen as a toff or a traitor. It is this combination of attitudinal and socio-economic factors which help us understand what we could term Scottish exceptionalism. As Tom Devine points out, countries with significant levels of economic expansion do not often see large numbers of outward migration. Yet Scotland (throughout the nineteenth century at least) had considerable economic growth but one of the highest emigration rates in the world – on a par with Ireland and Norway. In Scotland we often present our migration figures as due to the clearances but research shows that consistently the Scots who emigrated tended to be the most skilled and/or aspirational and from urban Scotland. Even some of Glasgow's incomers moved on to greener pastures. In my own family, my great grandparents from Catholic Ireland emigrated to Scotland and lived in the Butney, the worst area of Maryhill. But my great grandmother, an enterprising type, went round the doors selling items from a case and ran other small scale businesses. The family became wealthy enough to flit from Butney to a red sandstone tenement – a move that was considered pretentious by those who knew them. A few years later, they emigrated to Pittsburgh and steel-making and died believing that America was 'God's own country'.

Housing schemes and inequality

Once the state started to clear slums, build new houses and pay out a range of social benefits life began to improve for poor Glaswegians – developments we shall examine more fully in later chapters. But the culture of inequality and social divisions did not ease much. Sean Damer, who has studied Glasgow housing, argues that divisions were at the core of allocation policy for the new houses. Schemes like Mosspark, Knightswood and Riddrie were built under the provision of the 1919 Housing Act and were supposed to provide housing for the 'general needs' of the working class. However, he claims that Mosspark, built in 1924 was an 'elite scheme':

In terms of occupational structure, 16.2 per cent of

> the first tenants to move in to the new scheme were
> 'professionals', 30.7 per cent were 'intermediate'
> and 27.5 per cent were 'skilled non-manual'. Only 18
> per cent were 'skilled manual' while a miniscule 0.3
> per cent were 'unskilled'. [32]

Damer claims that this pattern was partly about high rents and partly about the informal allocation policy which favoured 'desirable' tenants – essentially 'respectable' types who were mainly Protestant. 'Intermediate schemes', such as West Drumoyne, south of Govan, were built in the 1930s and they were allocated to skilled and semi-skilled manual workers – the 'respectable poor'. In the 1930s a series of 'Slum Clearance' schemes were built, such as the notorious Blackhill. These houses mainly went to unskilled workers and 'the disreputable poor'. [33] Status divisions were thus built into the very fabric of Glasgow's housing schemes. Damer accepts that there was some variation to this pattern – for example, some skilled workers were housed in the slum clearance schemes. Nonetheless, from his early 1990s work he writes:

> . . . this three-tier system was certainly the public
> perception of the Glasgow schemes, and was even
> more certainly the way they were managed; the
> Corporation Housing Department was a prisoner of
> its own offensive ideology. To this day the
> distinctions between them are obvious to the
> professional who with one glance can normally tell
> under which Act a scheme was built. Mosspark is still
> a leafy paradise to which many tenants in lower
> status schemes aspire, while Blackhill is a barren
> gulag where only the most demoralised of tenants
> would accept a house. [34]

Much of this chapter has been about Glasgow's history but it could have been about today. The quality of housing has changed dramatically, overcrowding is largely a thing of the past, yet Glasgow is still a city divided by wealth and health. This is nowhere more evident than in the life expectancy figures outlined in a previous chapter. The geographical divisions are also still there: Pollok and Pollokshields, Castlemilk and Kelvinside. There are only a few streets in the city centre and a few housing areas where you will find a genuine mix of social classes. What's more the sectarian divide as represented by Rangers and Celtic is still there. So too are the gangs and the violence, increasingly fuelled by drink, drugs and dominance.

CHAPTER 5

The demon drink

IN 2008 Bruce K. Alexander, a Canadian psychologist, published a paradigm-shifting book called *The Globalisation of Addiction: a study in the poverty of the spirit*. Citing the work of Charles Darwin, and various psychologists, Alexander argues that human beings have a need for what Erik Erikson calls 'psychosocial integration'. What this means is that human beings simultaneously need to 'express their individuality' and feel free but at the same time feel they belong to a wider social group in which they can make a positive contribution. 'Dislocation' is the term Alexander uses to describe the negative feelings human beings experience when their need for psychosocial integration is not met.

Alexander does not romanticise primitive societies, accepting that they were often barbarous to outsiders or individuals within their tribe. Nonetheless he argues that so-called 'primitive' and peasant societies were able to fulfil their members' needs for psychosocial integration. 'The genius of a successful culture', writes Alexander, 'is that it provides adequately for individual autonomy and social belonging at the same time – a balancing act of great virtuosity, since the needs often conflict with one another.' [1] Viewed in this light we can see why socialist societies have often failed this test as they are too centralised to allow for individual expression. Free market capitalist society, with its emphasis on individual activity and weak social ties, is also poor at providing this balance and, in its extreme forms, often leads to 'mass dislocation'. [2]

According to this theory, dislocation is not only 'socially destructive' but is also painful for individuals. The dislocated individual feels empty and overwhelmed by 'the poverty of spirit' or the sense of his or her lost soul. To help fill this void dislocated individuals don't simply turn, but become addicted, to other things in life – alcohol, drugs, gambling, romantic love, work, shopping, sex – all can provide a diversion and/or numb the pain. What a dislocated individual chooses is dependent on his/her psychology and what is available in that society. These types of addictions can ruin people's lives to varying degrees yet Alexander asserts that they should be seen as 'adaptive' in the sense that they provide a way for the individual to cope with dislocation. 'Without addictions', writes Alexander, those who lack psychosocial integration would have 'terrifyingly little reason to live'. [3]

This perspective on addiction helps us to see why historically massive social change, such as colonisation or rapid urbanisation, had such a profound effect on people often leading not just to social breakdown but large-scale addiction to drink, drugs and gambling. As we know, this is what happened to many aboriginal people in Canada and Australasia. Forced from their traditional lands and dislocated from what had previously given them meaning it is hardly surprising that many turned to drink and drugs to escape the extreme pain.

Alexander also argues that in Western countries alcohol became a problem with the rise of capitalism and the breakdown of traditional social obligations. England was the first country to industrialise and really develop a free market economy. It was also the first to register alcohol addiction as 'a national problem'. He argues that drunkenness was not unusual in England in medieval times. Nonetheless, while individuals drank to excess on occasions they were not addicted. There simply was nothing like the drink problem which flowed from the 'gin palaces' and other drinking holes, established in the early nineteenth century cities, and described so well by Charles Dickens. According to the distinguished historian Eric Hobsbawm, in the 1800s uncontrolled industrialisation and urbanisation spread a 'pestilence of hard liquor' across Europe, resulting very often in 'mass alcoholism'.[4] In recent times, as Britain has become more influenced by extreme free market capitalist ideas, the country has witnessed a huge rise in binge drinking and drug taking.

Alexander dedicates a small section of his book to the Scottish Highlands. He reports that in traditional clan society people often drank copious amounts of alcohol but this was mainly part of clan rituals and ceremonies and there are no known examples of individual addiction. However, Highland life was wilfully destroyed both by the Clearances, where people were moved off the land to make way for sheep, and by the brutal repression of Highland culture by the British Government after the 1745 Jacobite rebellion. In the wake of these huge changes – changes of such a scale that they are similar to what happened to many colonised people – many Highlanders turned to alcohol as a form of escape or found it so 'troublesome' that they had to become ardent abstainers.

What about the rest of Scotland? In his book, *Stone Voices*, Neal Ascherson writes: 'The key to understanding Scottish modern history is to grasp the sheer force, violence and immensity of social change in the two centuries after about 1760.' [5] As we saw in a previous chapter Scotland urbanised much more quickly than England or other European countries. Another way to think about this is that many Scots were subject to dislocation – a breakdown in social ties and opportunities to express individual freedom. Life for poor agricultural workers was often back-breaking and precarious but nonetheless it was still founded on co-operation and support and backed by tradition. People's lives were also linked to the land and the seasons and so to a way of life which supports well-being.

All this changed with urbanisation. Many Scots, like plants in the fields they once tended, were uprooted. They went forcibly, or willingly, to the cities. When we add to this profound psychosocial disintegration the terrible working and living conditions and the continual feelings of insecurity that characterised their new lives then we can see why urbanisation created ideal conditions for addiction to alcohol – a substance well-known to numb pain and lead to a loss of consciousness. These changes did not just affect the poor labouring classes: even those who materially benefited from these huge economic changes could suffer from dislocation. They too could easily become dissociated individuals in a society which was increasingly breaking with tradition.

The whisky culture

John Dunlop was a magistrate in Greenock operating mainly in the first few decades of the nineteenth century and one of the first temperance reformers. He portrayed Scotland as a country where the middle and working classes alike used every occasion as an opportunity for drinking. For example, when people got jobs they had to buy drinks; when someone hadn't done something properly their fine would involve the purchase of drink; packing or moving house would lead to a customary drink; apprentices were treated to a 'launch-bowl' when the ship slipped into the water; births, deaths, funerals – every occasion had some alcohol consumption associated with it. Indeed Dunlop concluded that 'in no other country does spirituous liquor seem to have assumed so much the attitude of the authorised instrument of complement and kindness as in North Britain.' [6]

In many cultures alcohol has a social function and, as we've already seen, this does not necessarily lead to alcoholism. The question which needs to be asked is whether in Scotland the rapid breakdown of old co-operative agricultural life and intense urbanisation gave rise to the circumstances for dislocation on a grand scale. Certainly by the nineteenth century Scotland's love affair with drink seemed to be outstripping England's. One of James Hogg's observations about London in the 1830s was that 'the people here are all sober, there being no deep drinking here as in Scotland.' [7] A *Scotsman* leader in 1850 proclaimed:

> That Scotland is, pretty near at least, the most
> drunken nation on the face of the earth is a fact
> never quite capable of denial. It may seem strange
> that Edinburgh, the headquarters of the various
> sections of a clergy more powerful than any other
> save that of Ireland, should, in respect of drunken-
> ness, exhibit scenes and habits unparalleled in any
> other metropolis, and that Glasgow, where the clergy
> swarm, should be notoriously the most guilty and
> offensive city in Christendom. [8]

Drinking was not only a problem of the working classes: the middle classes got 'fuddled in the privacy of their own homes' and all-male heavy drinking sessions were commonplace in middle-class Glasgow until 1820. [9] Official statistics suggest that there was a particular problem in Glasgow. A report to Parliament on arrests for drunkenness between 1831 and 1851 showed that 'Glasgow is three times more drunken than Edinburgh and five times more drunken than London.' [10] In the 1830s Sir Archibald Alison, Glasgow's Sheriff maintained: 'There are 10,000 men in Glasgow who get drunk on Saturday night: who are drunk all day Sunday and are in a state of half intoxication on Monday and go to work on Tuesday.' [11]

Drink was undoubtedly very easy to obtain. In Glasgow and Edinburgh there were a huge number of public houses, or drink shops of some kind – one for every 130 people. By all accounts, scenes of drunkenness in cities like Edinburgh and Glasgow were appalling. People in rags would stagger about the streets, amid the vomit, shouting, swearing and spitting. One report from the 1870s talks about drunks at the cross of Glasgow wrangling and quarrelling 'amongst themselves like a pack of hungry curs.' [12] Drink consumption was so high – much higher than wages – that some contemporary estimates suggest that drinking at that level could only be funded by begging, prostitution and crime. In the nineteenth century some temperance reformers linked the rise in drink in Scotland to the 'striking increasing in insanity'. Independent evidence suggested that a quarter of all mental illness in Scotland was caused by alcoholism. [13]

One of the misleading facts about drinking in Scotland is that at face value the Scots actually drank less per capita per annum than the English. In 1852 the per capita figure for Scotland was '7.83 litres of absolute alcohol' and the equivalent figure for England 8.84 litres. But the type of drinking varied enormously: 'the Scots drank 2.36 gallons of proof spirits per capita and 7.2 gallons of beer while the English consumed 0.57 gallons of spirits and 30.6 gallons of beer.' [14] Another issue is that per capital consumption figures mask the fact that drinking is uneven – a substantial part of the population may have drunk nothing in Scotland with hardened drinkers consuming much more than their fair share.

As the above figures suggest whisky didn't replace beer, as it continued to play an important role in Scotland's drink culture. It is more accurate to say that whisky was added – thus the penchant for a half and a half. What's more, unlike England where in 1830 beer-houses were not allowed to sell spirits, hard drink was freely available in Scotland. Public houses weren't licensed in Scotland till 1828 but this did not immediately bring about a reduction in drinking establishments. In cities like Glasgow there was a network of illegal drinking dens and 'shebeens'. Some of these were 'wee shebeens' set up within closes, often on the stair head, where a 'drunken old hag' would serve whisky mixed with methylated spirits. [15]

Dunlop made his remarks on the extent of drinking in Scotland in 1839. This was seen as drink's high water mark and consumption fell over the next few decades as a result of a variety of factors such as control of premises, doubling of spirit duty, elimination of illicit distillation and control of licensing hours. The Forbes-Mackenzie Act of 1853 closed Scottish pubs on a Sunday, and only allowed hotels to serve drink to *bona fide* travellers'.

The extent of the drink problem encouraged the development of a vigorous temperance movement in Scotland. Many prominent socialists, like Keir Hardie, were ardent teetotallers. Smout argues that while their message may have helped some individuals turn away from the demon drink and lead more wholesome, and successful lives, the effect of the temperance movement was minimal. He writes: 'after two decades of the most fervent campaigning, per capita consumption of duty-paid spirits was about 2 per cent more than it had been in the later 1820s.' [16]

Quite simply, it was the control and pricing of drink which caused consumption to fall dramatically. But even though there was a fall, drink continued to cast a particularly black shadow across Glasgow's tenements. In the words of George Gladstone Robertson, a Gorbals doctor recounting the 1920s and 30s, 'This was humanity living at its lowest level. . . drunks strewn in untidy heaps, many of them lying in their own vomit' [17]

Glasgow's love affair with drink

Glasgow was able to expand so rapidly in the first instance because it was able to attract large numbers of former agricultural workers from the Scottish lowlands, Irish peasants and dispossessed Highlanders to work in the new industries. In short, at the heart of Glasgow's expansion were people dislocated from more traditional ways of life. This on its own was likely to encourage 'deep drinking' and addiction. Becoming addicted to drink is often ruinous and self-defeating but nonetheless, as Bruce Alexander helps us see, it can provide meaning in life and help numb the pain of existence. Indeed many historical commentators on Glasgow's besottedness with drink point out that Glaswegians liked their drink to be 'anaesthetic'. In other words, drink in Glasgow was not so much about savouring, enjoyment, socialising or pleasure; it was much more about release and oblivion.

There may be additional, structural reasons why drinking in pubs, and getting out of the house, became particularly attractive to the Glasgow working man. George Blake claimed that drink played an important part in industrial Scotland because men had 'the sheer need for escape, by whatever means, from an almost intolerable environment'.[18] This too is the opinion of medical experts. Dr. Archibald Campbell was the Medical Officer of Health for Renfrewshire. In 1903 he gave evidence to the Glasgow Municipal Commission on the Housing of the Poor. In it he blamed the inadequate housing for much of the drink and social problems:

> The man has finished his day's work and has had his ill-cooked tea. . . His education has stopped short of making reading a pleasure to him. The children are noisy, as children are apt to be. There is little room to move. Perhaps there is washing hanging around to dry. This might do now and then. He might talk to his wife. Or he might play with the children. But for every day, all the year round it is impossible. He puts on his hat and goes out. . . The public house is warm and bright – where else is he to go? [19]

Drink allowed the Glasgow man to adapt to his hellish life through escape. This escape was not just from the pain engendered by dislocation or from terrible working conditions (conditions he shared with many English and European brothers) but also from his terrible living conditions: conditions which were objectively worse than those of other European workers. Remember the problem wasn't just about stinking closes and wynds but also the degree of overcrowding; a third of families lived in single ends and this could mean as many as eight staying in a room no larger than 10 feet by 14 feet often with lodgers. Even in 1914 75 per cent of all new houses built consisted of one or two rooms.

Comments made by Will Fyffe, the popular entertainer and composer of the song 'I Belong to Glasgow', indicate how the pronounced pecking order, and inequality, may also have fuelled drinking in the city. Apparently when Fyffe performed the song he used to pause between choruses for some gallus working-class patter. 'When you're teetotal,' he explained, 'you've got a rotten feeling that everybody's your boss.' [20] Indeed the song as a whole suggests that drink is a way for men to deal with being low in the pecking order as it goes:

> I'm only a common old working chap,
> As anyone here can see,
> But when I get a couple of drinks on a Saturday
> Glasgow belongs to me.

Other, paradoxical, factors may well have fortified the Glasgow man's love affair with drink. The temperance movement was not particularly successful in getting many working men to stop drinking but they undoubtedly helped to create a culture in which it was not considered 'respectable' to drink. This meant that the middle class and women stopped frequenting public houses leaving them 'to the less respectable male working classes'.[21] Devine reports that 'Women were increasingly excluded, both as drinkers and as barmaids, and the Scottish pub now became the male domain which it long remained down to the 1960s.' [22] What's important about this for our purposes is that Scotland as a whole developed a drink culture which was male and almost clandestine. An astute social commentator, George Blake writes:

> France, and to a lesser extent, England achieve reasonable temperance precisely because the pleasures of drinking are shared and openly indulged. In Scotland it is quite otherwise. There may be not a drop of drink in the true drunkard's household. The drunkard is likely to know shame on being seen to enter a public-house. Women patronising public places of refreshment are immediately suspect, and in houses of any pretensions it will sometimes be clearly indicated that their presence is unwelcome. [23]

Blake argues that this hypocrisy round drink, which he puts down to Calvinist repression, meant that the natural inclination to enjoy the pleasures of drink, and its social nature, were made 'furtive' – driving the instinct 'underground'. This difference between the traditional English and Scottish attitude towards drinking is often seen in comparisons of unattractive Scottish pubs, frequented mainly by men, and the more attractive English inns. While there were many handsome city centre pubs in Glasgow, such as the Horseshoe Bar, 'neighbourhood bars were often cheerless and functional dives' which were not at all attractive to women. Even if they had wanted to go they were actively prevented. Indeed some bars in the West End, like Tennants, would not allow women in the public bar, 'only the lounge where they would not be served a pint'.[24] Many even in the early 1970s would not admit women at all and it was the Sex Discrimination of Act of 1975 which forced many to provide women's toilets. Scotland did ultimately witness a rise of cocktail bars and more modern establishments, where both sexes were welcome, but Hugh MacDiarmid was clear that these were 'de-Scotticised resorts'. In 'The Dour Drinkers of Glasgow' (1952) he claims:

> Now, I am not a misogynist by any means. I simply believe there is a time and a place for everything – yes, literally, everything. And like a high proportion of my country's regular and purposive drinkers I greatly prefer a complete absence of women on occasions of libation. I also prefer a complete absence of music and very little illumination. I am therefore a strong supporter of the lower – or lowest – type of 'dive' where drinking is the principal purpose. . . [25]

Contrast MacDiarmid's ideal with the cafés on the continent where men can drink happily alongside women and members of their family. MacDiarmid claims that he is not being a misogynist. It is tempting to reply to this 'aye right'. But even if his views do not confirm misogyny as such they do not suggest a healthy attitude to alcohol or to family life.

Of course, conditions objectively improved and drink was not needed in the same way to escape the problems of inadequate housing and brutal working conditions. But a culture had grown up round men and drink and, once established, cultures develop a life of their own and are able to reproduce themselves. There are countless anecdotes, and photographs, of pubs near shipyards or other large industrial complexes, pre-pouring huge trays of drink, to cater for the large volumes of men who would squeeze into them during lunch breaks and the end of shifts. In many of these industries heavy drinking was always a part of the culture.

However, it is also true to say that throughout the UK it was common for working men to drink in pubs and it is not difficult to explain the attraction. Social anthropologist Daniel Wight carried out a study of an ex-mining community in central Scotland, published as *Workers Not Wasters: Masculine respectability, consumption & employment in central Scotland*.[26] Wight carried out this study in the 1980s but since it is about deep-seated attitudes in Scottish industrial males, its findings are pertinent here. To protect the community he uses the pseudonym 'Cauldmoss'. This study showed how drinking was 'intrinsic' to men's social life and motivation and how they liked to drink, at least some of the time, in largely all-male pubs. From his own and other studies of men in the UK, Wight argues that drink is often seen as having a 'restorative' effect on working men – a way of helping them regain the physical strength they have expended on work. Drinking in pubs is often the way that men also solidify their relationships with other men, out of the influence and control of women. Wight also noted how it is only when drinking in the pub that 'Cauldmoss' men were likely to show each other physical affection and risk being emotionally open with one another.

Obviously a huge part of the attraction of pubs for men is that they can go there and have a good time with their mates. This in part is about being able to talk about areas of mutual interest – the goings on at work, football, betting, hobbies. As an anthropologist Wight is good at explaining how public drinking also provides a way for men to affirm their identities as members of the community and how buying drinks and sharing cigarettes can reinforce reciprocal bonds and equality between men.

But we must be careful to put the positive, social effects of alcohol in perspective. As we shall see in the next chapter, this type of all-male drinking reinforces a particularly hard type of masculine identity which easily splinters and causes injury. What's more, men's drinking not only damages health but is often hugely destructive of marriages and family life.

'His' money

There's nothing in keeping your money,
And saving a shilling or two;
If you've nothing to spend, then you've nothing to lend,
Why that's all the better for you;
There's no harm in taking a drappie;
It ends all your trouble and strife;
It gives ye the feeling that when you get home,
You don't give a hang for the wife!

(Final verse of 'I Belong to Glasgow ' by Will Fyffe)

Autobiographical and oral history accounts suggest that in Glasgow men commonly drank a great deal of their wages. For example, 'the Gorbals Doctor' reports that 'there were many cases where the husband was completely irresponsible and was likely to spend a considerable proportion of his wages in the pub before arriving home on the Friday night.'[27] A former worker at Lithgow's shipyard recalls:

There's a different attitude to drink altogether
[nowadays]. In the old days I put a lot of it down
to the way we were paid by the squad. All the
money went into one big poke, and the men
always adjourned to a pub to pay out. The money
was divided on the table and a lot of it was in the
publican's pocket before they went home. It stood
to reason. Even the man that didn't want a drink
was more or less forced to have one. [28]

When men routinely drank a substantial amount of their wages, many women tried to take matters into their own hands. Until many of the new housing schemes were sited too far away from places of work, it was commonplace in Glasgow for women to line up outside workplaces, waiting for their men to come out, hoping to get at least some of the money which otherwise would literally go down the pan. Sometimes the women waited outside pubs to catch the man as he moved from one drinking hole to another. Bashir Maan, a former Glasgow councillor, came to the city from Pakistan as a student and settled in the Gorbals in the early 1950s. He recounts being disappointed in what he saw as there was:

> . . .a public bar at every corner and on Fridays crowds of women and children congregated outside the bars waiting for their husbands to come out and give them wages, if there were any left, so that they could buy food for their children.[29]

In *Up Oor Close* a Glasgow woman recalls:

> Women had to meet their men at the factory gates to collect their wages before they went to the pub. It depended on the man, usually his wife got what was left of his wage after he had been to the pub.[30]

In the Glasgow volume of *The Third Statistical Account of Scotland*, a sociologist writes in detail about the subject of family money. He starts by quoting a foundryman in a 1953 radio programme 'Me and the Pay-packet':

> When I was serving my time and when my time was out my mother always impressed upon me that I should keep one thing to myself after I was married, and that was my wages – the amount of

my wages. . . Now I think this is the general
practice among Clydeside workers. On a Friday
night in the Govan Road you will see carried along
by the wind thousands and thousands of torn pay-
packets, strewing and littering the streets, which I
think is sufficient proof that every man tears up his
pay-packet, and segregates his earnings – something for himself and something for his wife. [31]

As a sociologist, J.A. Mack is right to point out that this
practice is:

. . . no doubt a prime source of secondary poverty.
The husband may be making more money than
before, with or without overtime, but the wife still
gets her £4 or whatever it is for housekeeping in
spite of rising prices. One particularly dull woman,
applying for a charitable grant to go on holiday, was
advised to spend her own money instead since her
husband was making £14 a week. But of this, she
said, she got only £4 as always. The extra money, as
she pointed out was 'his' money, not hers. [32]

One man I spoke to who grew up in a tenement in the city
centre in the 40s and 50s recounts that his community really
looked out for one another. One manifestation of this was that
older local 'heavies' warned publicans not to take more than
fifty per cent of the man's wages if he was in drinking on payday.
This was what they judged a 'fair' amount for a man to blow on
one heavy drinking session. The same man recounts that 'decent
men' he knew would only hand over half their money to their
wives to keep the household. (And that was at least better than
the poor woman mentioned above who got less than a third of
the pay packet.) In *Our Glasgow* one man remembers it was
common in his grandfather's day for men to give their wife two

shillings and for them to keep four for drinking money for the weekend. [33]

Self-centred men who gamble or drink money which should go to their families can be found the world over. While this may not have been the norm in Glasgow, it seems to have been much more common than other places in Scotland. Jim Dixon, a West Lothian councillor, who used to work in adult education, recounts that locals like him were shocked that the Glasgow men who moved to Bathgate to take up employment in British Leyland from the early 1960s did not generally give their pay packets to their wives, as had been the tradition for miners in the area: instead the Glasgow men commonly spent a high proportion of their wages on themselves in the pubs and bookies.

The West Lothian tradition of men giving their money to women is also picked up by Daniel Wight in his study of the Stirlingshire mining village, 'Cauldmoss'. His research shows that in this community, which still operated on very traditional lines, only a sixth of the couples interviewed said that the man was in charge of the money. In over half the man handed over his whole wage packet to the woman and she then gave him some 'spending money'. Wight comments:

> Handing over the wage packet was an act of considerable symbolic significance for men, being the culmination of the sacrifice they had made for their family through employment, and a few husbands took great pride in handing it over unopened. Men were also aware that to a large extent their wives judged them on their ability to ensure security for the household by providing a steady weekly income. [34]

This does not appear to have been the typical ethos for many Glasgow working men. In oral history accounts women from the west of Scotland report never seeing a pay packet in their lives. Others never knew what 'the man earned'. [35] Former Labour MP and councillor Maria Fyfe recounts that her father gladly handed over his pay packet to his wife but she also witnessed the Glasgow working man's belief that his wages were primarily 'his' money, rather than his family's. Maria was on the committee in Glasgow Council at the time they wanted to change from giving manual workers pay packets to paying wages directly into bank accounts. The male manual workers were up in arms about the proposal. Their argument? Simply that they didn't want their wives to know their earnings and that the new system would make concealment more difficult. Fortunately their trade union did not support them and the proposal was accepted.

Given that until the advent of the welfare state in the 1940s, most working families were, in everyday parlance, 'a wage away from the gutter', the fact that so many Glasgow men were often more intent on their own pleasures than looking after their family put an incredible strain on women. Remember, any problems caused by lack of money were primarily borne by mothers: they were the ones who had to try and soothe sick or hungry children or make a decent home out of a filthy hovel. The fact that men were often more focussed on their own pleasures than those of their wives and families can be seen in the figures which show that as men got paid more money, the consumption of whisky rose substantially. Sadly what rises with drink is the likelihood of violence and marital breakdown.

CHAPTER 6
Macho city

I sat and listened to my father tell
Of the days that he once knew
When you either sweated for a measly wage
Or you joined the parish queue
As times grew harder day by day
Along the riverside
I oft-times heard my mother say
It was tears that made the Clyde

Now I've sat in the school from nine till four
And I've dreamed of the world outside
Where the riveter and the plater watch
Their ships slid to the Clyde
I've served my time behind shipyard gates
And I've sometimes mourned my lot
But if any man tries to mess me about
I'll fight like my father fought
(From 'The Fairfield Crane' by Archie Fisher)

WHAT'S interesting about the last two verses quoted above is how they convey the struggle and sense of hopelessness characteristic of Clydeside workers, and their families, as a result of poverty and unemployment. But the last line is particularly telling – reminding us that this is a city where it doesn't take much to trigger violence. This is precisely Glasgow's reputation as an aggressive, macho city. This is why a head-butt is often referred to as 'a Glasgow kiss' and the term a 'Glasgow stare' warns us to tread warily as the slightest injury to men's pride in this city spells danger. Richard Wilkinson quotes large volumes of research which show that this type of aggression – this willingness to fight other men, usually within the peer group – emanates from pronounced income and status inequality. 'A culture of inequality' is 'not only more violent and aggressive, but also more macho. More unequal societies are tougher, more competitive, dog-eat-dog societies.'[1] Glasgow's predisposition to violence is not only likely as a result of inequality and divisions; it was intensified as a result of the city's prolonged and intense love affair with drink.

Violence – Glasgow's record

Glasgow is now the most violent city in Western Europe so it is reasonable to ask if violence has always been a challenge. If we take murder to be the most extreme expression of violence then it appears that before World War I Glasgow had no particular problem. In fifteen separate years between 1860-1914 not one murder was committed and the highest figure in any one year during this period was six. However, it is also true to say that four of the murders committed in Glasgow, including the case of Madeleine Smith, were particularly high profile cases. Edinburgh, the city of Burke and Hare, had a much more deserved reputation as Scotland's murder capital. Over the centuries Glasgow has also had its share of criminal hard men who used violence and intimidation to make a living: men like Glasgow's Jimmy Boyle, London's Kray Twins or, the daddy of them all, Chicago's Al Capone. However, it is also true to say that most big cities are likely to breed economic thugs and gangsters.

Glasgow's particular claim to fame lies in more mundane, but potentially more worrying, types of everyday aggression and violence – punch-ups, alcohol-fuelled social disorder, domestic violence and gangs.

A helpful way to think about violence is to see that some individuals, as a result of 'poor attachment' to their carers, childhood abuse and neglect or the failure to develop empathy, have a *propensity* to violence. This propensity is then triggered, and turned into physical violence, by real or imagined insults, for example, or by alcohol.[2] Given Glasgow's violence figures, it is useful to realise that for over a century it has not taken much to trigger violence in the city.

Reading through copious historical material for this book I've been struck by the amount of everyday aggressive, violent behaviour. Some of the most graphic scenes are portrayed in a book published in 1858 called *Midnight Scenes and Social Photographs, Being Sketches of Life in the Streets, Wynds and Dens of the City*.[3] Violence seems to have permeated so much of Glasgow life – at least for the working classes. It was common, for example, for 'ordinary workers' to 'unhesitatingly go out the back-court, take their jackets off and have a "square go" with whoever had offended them'.[4]

This is the type of everyday violence Ralph Glasser, raised in the Gorbals in the 20s and 30s, recounts in his autobiography. 'We grew up with violence,' he writes. 'It simmered and bubbled and boiled over in street and close, outside the pubs, at the dance halls. . . '[5] Of course, there was violence linked to business and gangs but Glasser remembers: 'More often, violence settled private accounts, transgression of codes, the spilling over of grievance and spleen.' This was the type of area where 'decent' men were those that simply used their fists, not bottles or knives. A recurrent theme in fiction and reminiscences of life in the west of Scotland is working men, and young boys, constantly needing to get the upper hand; to show who is dominant and one up in the pecking order. Ralph Glasser gives a great example of this in his second book when he recounts being introduced as an Oxford student to a 'high heid yin' in the Glasgow rag trade:

> . . . with an aggressive leer he said: 'An Oxford student, eh! I'm proud of you – but d'you know what's worrying me? I've got money coming out of my ears, now what d'you say to that?' He was putting me down with a vengeance, according to his lights. Why, I wondered, did people like him feel so defensive? [6]

Following a negative exchange, Glasser reports that it looked like the guy was going 'to lash out' at him physically. This was a man who had worked his way up through the ranks and was taking the opportunity to make sure everyone knew he was cock of the walk. There's little doubt many violent encounters in Glasgow, then and now, start out with this type of exchange. The riveter, Danny Shields of *The Shipbuilders* is this type of hardman. At one point Danny thinking of a slight says to himself: 'A good drink one of those days, and he would knock the face off somebody.' [7] He is the type of guy who gets into a punch-up if someone says something he doesn't like. He is even imprisoned for assault at one point. Yet Danny's type of violence is seen as routine and not a particular problem: 'A bit of a booze and a fight – good enough and all in the day's work,' writes George Blake. [8]

Time and time again in Glasgow novels or commentaries about Glasgow and the west of Scotland we see how aggression is presented simply as a normal part of life. Songwriter Matt McGinn, for example, recounted that in 'the Calton culture' where he grew up, 'the fighting men were the heroes' and that 'the highest hope of a boy in that culture was to become such an idiot'. [9]

It is interesting to note how Piers Dudgeon treats the topic of violence in his books recounting 'memories of life in disappearing Britain' – *Our East End*, on London and *Our Glasgow*. Of course, in both books we find all the elements that we're considering in this chapter – drink, wife-beating and violence – for they are the frequent companions of inequality and poverty around the globe. But nonetheless every place has its own story. In *Our East End* Dudgeon calls one of the chapters 'Violence and Respect'. The violence he reports is mainly racial violence and hatred, the lure of boxing and boxing clubs for boys to win 'respect' and criminal and gang-based behaviour where violence is used primarily for material ends. The violent figures in this scenario are often businessmen, like the Kray twins, who demand respect, and will ensure they get it with violence, but who more often swan about acting like 'real gents'. Apparently the Krays became friendly with some Glasgow gangsters and came to the city for a visit in the mid-1960s. The story goes that the they talked about setting up some sort of operation in Glasgow but 'they found that the locals were too aggressive, especially when they'd heard the brothers' English accents.' [10]

In *Our Glasgow* there are a number of chapters scarred by recollections of violent episodes – fights with razors in dance halls, gang feuds, men and boys just looking for a fight. Dudgeon portrays Glasgow's violence as fuelled by two things – drink and feelings of inferiority. Many of the working men, recalled in the book, knew they were the bottom of the pile and were fed up with a life of toil for very little reward. The young men revolted at the prospect of becoming menial wage slaves. They aimed to get the respect they craved, and enhance their self-image, by being tough. This is exactly the argument set out by Richard Wilkinson in his work on why inequality leads to violence. At times Dudgeon's portrayal of Glasgow is romanticised but nonetheless he is fully aware of the toll that the city's drunken, macho culture exacted on family life:

> Any night of the week, the streets were littered
> with men, blind drunk, staggering home. . .
> Tragically, because drink does not relieve
> humiliation, nor does it make a true hero of a man,
> and because the pub was a male preserve and
> drinking became bound up with the macho
> element of a man's character, it had a terrible effect
> on the community, and in particular on women.
> Pumped-up and indignant, a man would turn his
> resentment on his family. . . [11]

Domestic violence

Archie Hind's novel *The Dear Green Place* is considered the most important Glasgow novel ever written. Hind was born in 1928 and raised in Carntyne. By all accounts his father was a wife-beater and Hind himself had to avoid going to the public baths to hide his own bruises. No wonder Hind includes this passage in his novel:

> There was plenty of violence – beatings from tired
> and exasperated parents, and in the street he saw
> many a furious fist fight, real accomplished stuff,
> skilled punching and gouching and butting. There

were the women who got knocked on the head with tomato sauce bottles by their husbands. Occasionally Mat saw the razor being used or the broken bottle. Twice he had seen men being killed.[12]

Societies are notoriously bad at quantifying the extent of domestic violence. Part of the problem is that the crime is usually committed within the home and so in private space. Up to the last decade the police in Scotland did not identify domestic abuse as a separate category of crime but usually categorised it alongside breach of the peace or assault. What's more, victims rarely report the assault to the police. Even in today's environment where domestic violence is taken more seriously than in previous times experts estimate that victims have been assaulted more than thirty times before they are likely to call in the police. So in writing here about domestic abuse in Glasgow it is extremely difficult to quantify the extent of the problem or compare it with other places. However, there are good reasons to believe that the problem was substantial.

When I was undertaking research for the book I was taken aback at how domestic violence was evident almost everywhere I looked. Ralph Glasser tells us:

> In the Gorbals, the public 'marital' quarrel was common, on tenement landings, in closes, in the street. . . Men and women came to blows. Women were struck and fell down the stone stairs of tenements. Men bled from whatever weapon came to a woman's hand – kitchen knife, kettle, copper pan. [13]

Piers Dudgeon's research and recordings on the city convinced him that domestic violence was a sizeable, if hidden, problem in Glasgow. He writes, 'For years, women took domestic violence as part of the daily round, bottled it up and didn't complain.' [14] Dr. Annmarie Hughes also carried out some oral history research about the extent of domestic violence in the Clydeside era in the inter-war period and believed that there was 'an extremely high incidence of domestic violence'. [15] One of her interviewees recalls 'it was a normal thing for a man to abuse his wife.' Since it was 'an everyday fact of life' neighbours only interfered if they feared that the woman was being 'murdered'. Hughes's explanation for why there was so much tension between men and women on Clydeside will be examined in the following chapter.

The argument traditionally advanced by those involved in researching domestic violence or supporting victims is that its origins can be found in patriarchy – men abusing the power they have over women. In short, the more powerless women are the more likely they are to be abused. As we shall see, women in Scotland as a whole were more financially dependent on men than was the case in England.

Another piece of circumstantial evidence which suggests a particular problem with domestic violence was, and still is, the level of drinking. As Professor Smout argues about Scotland in the nineteenth century, 'the battered wife was part and parcel of the whisky culture'.[16] Of course, domestic violence is not caused by drink and many a man in the past, as now, punched or beat up his wife when he was stone cold sober. However, evidence shows that drink makes matters worse – either escalating problems or allowing men to let go of inhibitions. UK and international research shows that alcohol misuse can increase the frequency of violence and its severity. [17] Certainly people's personal reminiscences stress that 'the man getting over-loaded with drink' was a common factor.[18] 'The Gorbals Doctor' recounts in his memoirs that it was common for men to hit women when they were 'befuddled by drink'. After recounting one case where a man seriously attacked his pregnant wife for refusing to have sex with him, and the wife then died in labour, the doctor writes:

> In the final analysis she had been murdered by her husband, but like so many other thoughtless young men in the Gorbals he knew no better. No animal would ever have treated his mate like some of these young men treated their wives in the Gorbals tenements. [19]

In the past, male aggression in drink may have sometimes stemmed from earlier, negative experiences, particularly of the war. My mother, now in her 80s, lived with her grandparents. She remembers her grandfather as a warm, gentle man – except when he had been drinking. Then he could become aggressive turning his wife out into the street and she had to seek refuge at a neighbour's house to escape her husband's drunken rage. My great grandfather had been in the army for a long period of time and served in the Crimean War and so it may have been these terrible experiences which underlay his aggressive tendencies when drunk.

In World War I Scotland lost a much higher percentage of troops than most other countries involved in the combat. 'The main reason for the higher-than-average casualties among the Scottish soldiers was that they were regarded as excellent, aggressive shock troops who could be depended upon to lead the line in the first hours of battle,' writes Tom Devine.[20] The way in which war brutalised men was poignantly demonstrated in that classic Scottish novel *Sunset Song*. Richard Finlay writes that the brutalising effects of war is only now. . .

> . . . being addressed by historians. Supposedly, a stiff upper lip was all that was required to get through it. Scottish men were brought up to be the strong, silent type, and did not cry or express emotions. To do so was unmanly, and this lesson was beaten into children. Soldiers who witnessed unspeakable horrors went though their life mostly in silence, trying to forget what happened. [21]

Drink may have loosened these inhibitions for some. For others drink may have been a way to block out their unforgettable experiences.

Children too were regularly beaten by their parents. Richard Finlay is particularly perceptive on how Scottish children were often treated violently by parents:

> There was an unusually wide range of words associated with physical punishment. 'Leathering', 'battering', 'tanning', 'skelping', 'bleaching', 'whipping', 'hammering', 'roasting', 'hiding' and 'thrashing' were familiar expressions for most children, as was the term 'doing' – as in 'You'll get a doing'. Perhaps the most bizarre of all was the way that almost any part of speech could denote a threat of physical punishment. Question: 'Can I go out?' Answer: 'I'll 'out' you!' Question: 'Can I have a sweet?' Answer: 'I'll give you a sweet!' Skelps and clouts were usually confined to the ear or head, while leathering and tanning were directed at the backside. [22]

A recurrent theme of this book, borrowed from Richard Wilkinson, is that inequality and status hierarchies lead those who feel offended to lash out at those lower in the pecking order. So far we have seen how 'the bicycling reaction' in Glasgow may have led to sectarianism and intense status divisions at work as men took out their own feelings of powerlessness and humiliation on other people even lower in the hierarchy. The bicycling reaction is also at work in how men asserted, not just their difference, but their superiority over women. But women's behaviour can also be affected by their treatment and they can then take it out on children, who are even lower in the pecking order. Children in Scotland were regularly subjected to beatings and corporal punishment and this was often meted out by mothers, not just fathers.

In *The Shipbuilders,* on numerous occasions Agnes suddenly rounds on her baby daughter, shouting aggressively and even 'cuffed her' for simply dropping a piece of bread. In *The Clyde-siders*, the novelist Hugh Munro, son of a riveter, treats us to the following scene between mother and child:

> Unhurriedly Julia turned with the stirring fork in
> her hand. Without heat she said: 'I'll take my hand
> off your jaw if you speak to me like that. You eat
> up the soup and if you dribble any of it on that
> good frock I'll warm your behind for you.' [23]

Finlay also points out that it was commonplace in working class communities for neighbours, shopkeepers or the police to beat children publicly for any transgressions. This was often on top of beatings they would then get from their parents. As we'll see in a later chapter, Scottish schools too were places where children were routinely subjected to physical punishment. Finlay is also right to point out that there was nothing particularly working-class about the routine violence towards children in homes and schools. Scottish society as a whole firmly believed in physical discipline for children and could not imagine how children could be brought up without fear of physical reprisals not just for misdemeanours but also for failing to do well at academic work. England too used corporal punishment in schools, with canings in public schools a particularly barbaric form of violence against children. The armed forces also used corporal punishment. But it is worth reminding ourselves here that in organisations which are particularly hierarchical, such as schools and the armed forces, we are likely to see the bicycling reaction at work. For example, a school master, disciplined by the headmaster, may turn on a prefect who will then abuse younger pupils. In the case of Glasgow working class children, everywhere they turned they would be confronted with low, if not high, level aggression. Indeed it was probably so much part of life that it would have seemed unremarkable.

Before moving on it is worth pointing out that this is still a city scarred by male violence against women. Indeed in March 2009 Strathclyde Police revealed that domestic violence can increase by as much as 88 per cent following football matches between Celtic and Rangers. They also reported that 'serious and violent crimes' more than doubled in the area after the previous 'Old Firm' game. However, the problem is not confined to these two teams: domestic violence also increases following important international games. Strathclyde Police report that most of this violence is 'fuelled' by drink. Fortunately, the authorities in Scotland as elsewhere are now recognising the problem of domestic violence and are taking more action.[24]

Gang warfare

Glasgow's penchant for aggression and violence became more prevalent and notorious in the late 1920s and 1930s as a result of mass unemployment and depression. Gangs were particularly rife in the poorer areas of the city, namely in Gorbals, Calton, and Bridgeton. In 1928 boys aged between 15 and 17 stabbed another young man to death in a large battle between rival gangs. Many of the gangs evoked 'ancient loyalties' – one of the 1930s gangs was called the Billy Boys and led by William Fullerton:

> In 1924 a tough football team, the Kent Star from Calton, had the misfortune to lose to a scratch Bridgeton team in a game on the Glasgow Green. Fullerton, then aged 18, scored the winning goal. For this he was marked down by some Kent Star supporters, who later made a mass attack on him. He was literally 'given the hammer'! Deciding on reprisals, he organised a small gang of his own, and hit on the name 'Billy Boys'. A significant feature was the general enthusiasm throughout Bridgeton for this new gang among many who were not gangster-minded but who had Orange sympathies. The Billy Boys quickly flourished until they numbered 800 at their peak. . . [25]

The Billy Boys went into battle with a Catholic gang called 'the Norman Conks'. A former police chief recalled that these rival gangs used swords, hatchets and sharpened bicycle chains and were brought into the battle by their 'queens'.

George Blake, a journalist as well as novelist, argued that the sectarian element to the gangs obscured the real problem which he saw as being boredom and lack of purpose caused by unemployment. In *The Shipbuilders* Blake portrays the problem of gang violence as an inevitable result of the Depression and so in this respect it is an 'economic crime'. Robbed of the opportunity to learn a trade and gain the pride which working brings, 'the world of men has denied Danny Shield's son every decent means of expression,' Blake writes. [26]

This sounds exactly like the problem Wilkinson is alluding to. However, we must also remember that other cities also suffered from the Depression but their communities did not degenerate so quickly into violence. Perhaps 'the Gorbals Doctor' was right to maintain: 'The seeds of hate that had been planted in so many immature bodies were now being allowed to blossom forth as the restless men, with time on their hands, faced a bleak and uncertain future.' [27]

The Glasgow police, through concerted campaigns of action, managed to contain the problems of gangs and by the 1950s many thought it had disappeared as a social problem. However, gangs and violence have grown substantially in Glasgow since the mid 1960s and are one of the major reasons why the city has such a high murder rate.

Glasgow's reputation for violence became inevitable given the publicity and sales of *No Mean City* – a novel on gang warfare in the city published in 1935. The book was the collective endeavour of Alexander McArthur, an unemployed worker from the city and a London journalist, Kingsley Long. It was an instant success. *The Times Literary Supplement* even gave it a good review praising 'the sheer weight of its sincerity' and, while acknowledging its literary failings, still claimed the book to have 'artistic value'. This has not been the view of the Scottish literary community who usually ignore or pan it for being 'sensationalist'. The city's libraries refused to stock it for years and it was not openly displayed in bookshops.[28]

Male dominance

In many ways Glasgow is the template for the archetypal macho city. As almost every commentator on Glasgow has observed, and as we have already witnessed, Glasgow is a hard city. Hard is a word we use in different contexts and has various meanings: firm and unyielding, challenging, vigorous or violent, oppress-ive, austere, harsh, severe, unsentimental and lacking delicacy to list only a few. Hard is a word which not only suggests male sexual power but also unyielding masculine authority. Its opposite is soft, gentle, yielding, tender, smooth, soothing, delicate, lenient – all feminine rather than masculine terms.

It is not difficult to see why Glasgow would become a hard city. It was dominated by dirty, heavy industry. The bulk of its jobs required grit, muscle, tenacity and strength. Living conditions for the masses were not simply austere but harsh and punitive. The culture men evolved reflected this harshness – they didn't just gulp back hard spirits, they became hardened drinkers. The culture also started to separate men from women – increasingly at work because of the preponderance of heavy industries and also, as we saw above, in the pub and leisure time. The city's pronounced pecking order meant that men were primed to be on the look-out for slights and put-downs – hence violence was never far from the surface.

Richard Wilkinson points out that women's overall social position is prejudiced in societies with pronounced income inequality and a strong dominance hierarchy among men. 'In a more aggressive culture, where male power is what counts, women will be more subordinated and have lower status relative to men,' writes Wilkinson.[29] Glasgow is undoubtedly a city where women's contribution has been ignored or downplayed.

Elspeth King, one of the few chroniclers of women's role in Glasgow, reports that apart from Queen Victoria there are only two statues of women in the city: in Elder Park there's one of Isobella Elder who was noted for her generosity to the people of Govan. The second is on the banks of the Clyde to La Passionara, a Spanish civil war leader. That's it. Of course, women have been involved in the shaping of Glasgow but they have largely been ignored and uncelebrated.[30]

It is not difficult to see why the type of male violence outlined above leads to extreme sexism and oppression of women. In a culture where men have to assert their position in the pecking order and are always on the look-out for disrespect it is really important for men to act tough and to display hard, 'masculine' qualities such as strength, physical skill, and endurance. This leads men to overvalue masculinity and to distance themselves from anything that may appear feminine. (This is why men often have to be drunk to be intimate with other men.) In such an environment anything which suggests men are effeminate or homosexual is a gross insult. When Ralph Glasser finally got to Oxford and realised that at parties there was a lot of homosexual activity going on he recalled how this would be seen in the Gorbals:

> Homosexuals were thought of as less than manly –
> the demotic use of the word 'pansy' conveying
> effeminacy, the opposite of aggressive, muscular
> masculinity, the only proper kind. For a 'normal'
> man to be approached – made a pass at – by a
> pansy was a terrible affront to which the proper
> response must be violence, incontrovertible proof
> that he was not 'so'. [31]

Richard Finlay reminds us of the number of epithets applied to any boy who was ambiguous 'in his display of masculine attributes'.[32] They include terms such as sissy, Jessie, Big Jessie, Nancy boy, big girl's blouse and so forth. Even small things, like wearing gloves, could make a boy suspect.

In the type of macho culture outlined above, feminine qualities are not valued and women themselves are seen as inferior. As men's inferiors they should be subordinate and primarily see their role as looking after men and their offspring. Since child rearing is seen as women's work men therefore distance themselves from nurturing or bringing up children.

Another issue is the extent to which historically women were dependent on men. In 1861 37.13 per cent of the workforce in Glasgow was female but by 1901 this had fallen to 31.06 per cent. Most of these were single women as 'women of marriage age were forced out of the labour force'.[33] According to the 1911 census only one in 20 working women was married – this was a much lower rate than England's. Men were seen as the breadwinners and men themselves, trade unions and employers conspired to keep married women out of work. Formal and informal marriage bars operated in Scotland until after World War II. Although it was not considered 'respectable' for married women to work, out of sheer necessity many did work part-time and their jobs were often a bone of contention and resentment within the household. These women's jobs were often in the informal economy – 'helping out' in shops or families and being employed in a range of exceedingly low-paid part-time work. Even when women worked full-time they earned less than men. For example, in the 1900s women workers in Scotland earned about 45 per cent on average of male wages.

Even in teaching they only earned around 80 per cent of what men earned.

In Dundee women became the main labour force in the Jute industry. It is estimated that in the heyday of jute (mid nineteenth century to after World War I), women predominated in the labour force by as much as two to one. The Checklands write that because so many working families had women as the principal wage earners 'there was often a reversal of sex roles: masterful women dominated husbands who 'boiled the kettle'.[34] However, leaving Dundee aside, one historian maintains that before World War II, 'Scotland was distinctly patriarchal. It had fewer women in work than in England, bigger wage differentials between the sexes and sharper divisions in terms of domestic roles.' [35]

A culture of honour

Given Glasgow's problem with violence it is worth enquiring if it can be traced to other aspects of the city's history and if we can learn anything from other cultures which are particularly scarred by violence. If we turn our attention to the USA we see that the country's violence figures are not uniform and vary from region to region. The states which chalk up much higher murder and assault rates are in the south. Black culture is generally more violent than white culture but the southern figures for violence are not simply about higher concentrations of black people as white people in the south are much more violent than white Northerners. What's more, these southern, white offending rates are simply about violence, since crimes of property, for example, are actually lower in the southern states. Another intriguing fact is that this is not so much about violence in cities as small towns. [36]

In the early 1990s psychologists at the University of Michigan began to stage experiments which shed light on what lies behind the violence differentials in the USA.[37] They recruited young, white male students to participate in an experiment and split the group into those from northern or southern states, based on where they had lived for most of their lives. The students thought they were participating in cognitive tests but in one study a man bumped into a student when he was on his own in a corridor and said to him – 'Asshole'. The study showed significant differences in the two groups' reactions – the Northerners tended to laugh off the incident whereas the Southerners were more likely to respond negatively to the person and become affected by what had happened. In one study the southern, but not the northern, students tended to show increased levels of cortisol, a stress hormone, and testosterone after the incident. The students also tended to respond differently to a scenario about a man making a pass at his girlfriend: the southern students were much more likely to suggest an aggressive response. What is fascinating about the Michigan studies is that the differences they report can only be accounted for by whether the students had lived most of their lives in northern or southern states. Variables such as socio-economic background, religion, intelligence, personality, and emotional stability were irrelevant. These findings may help account for why the south is very lenient towards people who have been violent in the face of insults and adultery and why southern states are vehemently opposed to gun control.

The Michigan psychologists explain their findings in the light of what is known as a 'culture of honour'. This term is used by sociologists and anthropologists to describe a culture in which a man will fight to defend his honour against any slight or transgression. Cultures of this type are most likely to emerge in highland areas or marginal areas of limited fertility such as Sicily. The explanation is that, whereas farming leads to co-operation and a sense of security, in these marginal areas, where it is more difficult to make a living, individuals often base their livelihood on herding animals. Animals, unlike plants, can easily be stolen and so herdsman have to be vigilant or they will lose their means of survival. Moreover, in areas which are geographically remote, law and order is less likely to depend on the authorities and more on men looking after their own interests.

One cultural historian, David Hackett Fischer, points out that in such societies honour is not about 'gentility' but 'valour and virility'. In short, it is about a man asserting and policing his masculinity. In these cultures mothers bring up their sons to respond aggressively to any slights. Fischer also maintains that when fear predominates in a society then it 'exalts. . . men above women' and leads to:

> . . .clear-cut ideas of men as fighters and women as workers; exceptionally sharp distinctions between masculine and feminine roles; extreme male domination and female dependence within the family; intense expressions of love and violence between wives and husbands; and sometimes a great aching silent distance that kept them apart. [38]

Living conditions in the old tenements, particularly 'the backlands', were ripe for the development of a culture of honour. People were living on top of one another and co-operation was necessary but, given the insecurity and poverty, everyone had to be vigilant and protective of what little they had. In the nineteenth century Glasgow had a reputation for 'lawlessness', partly as a result of the huge problem with alcohol. However, one Chief of Police believed much of the problem related to the design of tenements themselves: their open nature meant that anyone could gain access thus making it easier to commit crime and almost impossible to police. [39]

In such an environment being prepared to assert yourself and your rights was fundamental to survival and so a 'culture of honour' would have been an essential feature of tenement society. For men this meant being prepared to respond violently to any transgressions; for women it meant being verbally aggressive by giving transgressors a 'shirraking' or 'their character' as well as bringing up their sons to be overly sensitive to insults.

Years ago Sydney Checkland said 'people do not expect gentle things to come out of Glasgow'. [40] From the material presented in this chapter it is much easier for us to see why. As we shall see more fully in the next chapter, this has been a tragedy for many women who have had to adapt to a hard, masculine environment and while they too could be aggressive they were more likely to be the victims of selfish, cold or violent men. It has also had profoundly negative consequences for the nurturing and rearing of children. But it has also been a tragedy for the men themselves. They did not choose much of the path they have trodden. Sadly they were pushed down it originally as the result of a culture of fear and insecurity, dislocation, brutal living and working conditions, pronounced inequality, and an acquired taste for strong drink.

CHAPTER 7

Women and children last

I'VE BEEN continually struck by how traditionally relationships between men and women in Glasgow have been based on conflict and contempt, not love and affection. The internationally acclaimed relationship researcher, Dr. John Gottman, has studied couples' interactions for years and his research shows that the biggest slayer of marriages is contempt.[1] In *The Patter*, a compendium of Glasgow words and phrases, Michael Munro lists 'her/him' as two commonly used words. He explains their meaning:

> The Anonymous Spouse. Many married people tend to speak of their beloved without referring to her or him by name. It is almost as if the marriage partner has attained such a talismanic status that it would be bad luck to utter the name aloud. 'I'll need to be away hame to give Him his tea.' 'I'm taking Her an the weans to the pictures the night.' [2]

My reading of this is different from Munro's – calling people 'him' and 'her' in this way is mildly contemptuous. It depersonalises the partner so that he or she loses any individuality and only occupies a role. We've seen something of the intense conflict between husbands and wives in previous chapters in terms of drink and domestic violence but this is only the pointed, hostile tip of a massive iceberg. Before looking at what lies beneath we need to know a bit more about women's lives.

Poor, clean and exhausted

As William Bolitho's report on slum conditions in 1924 testifies, even when housing was at its worst, tenants – usually women – tried to make something of it. He tells us that in the poorest and smelliest slums there was the bare minimum of 'bed, hearth and chair' yet somewhere on display there was usually ornament of some kind – often wally dogs or pictures but more commonly brass objects, usually miniature women's boots or ships. He writes that while the slum dwellers may feel humiliated at being kept in conditions 'no domestic animal in England knows' nonetheless 'they keep their bits of brass polished'.[3] Indeed many commentators on Glasgow's slums expressed surprise that many of the people still looked personally clean, despite the hovels they lived in. Others said that some of the most appalling buildings still had residents who tried to keep a decent house.

My mother recounts how in the 1920s and 30s it was common for poor folks' houses to be almost bare but everything about the place had a clean, scrubbed look. The desire for cleanliness was facilitated by the provision of clean water, piped into the city from Loch Katrine in 1859. This was the first in a long line of municipal services. Ralph Glasser, who grew up in the Gorbals, gives an interesting account of women's hard labour at the Gorbals Baths:

> One of its departments was a wash-house, aptly known as the Steamie, a long barn-like room kept in perpetual twilight by clouds of steam rising from

washing boiled in rows of coppers, a miasma in
whose crepuscular depths one dimly saw figures in
kerchiefs, long fustian skirts and dark cotton blouses,
sleeves rolled up above the elbows, hauling and
lifting, scrubbing and banging and carrying, moving
with the heavy measure of fatigue, enchained in
punishing ritual. In a clangour of boiler doors, iron
buckets and chains, rumble of slack gears in the
mangles, scrape and clatter of metal-lined scrubbing
boards, and counterpoint of shrill voices calling, they
heaved bundles of clothing and bed linen and
blankets about, banged press irons, turned the drive
wheel of a mangle with rhythmic pulse of straight
arm and shoulder on the handle projecting from the
rim, and then a pull back with the whole upper body,
while the other hand fed layers of wet washing, like
lumpy slabs of glistening clay, between the thick
wooden rollers. [4]

In a city where many people lived in such close proximity
to others, often without sinks, indoor toilets and bathrooms,
these communal facilities were a godsend, at least for those
who could afford to use them.

While there could be something of a pecking order among
the women, there was a huge amount of support as well: camaraderie bred by the experience (past or present) of terrible conditions and constant insecurity. Even the families of skilled workers,
living in the better tenements, knew that an economic downturn, accident or illness, could destabilise them and they would
slide back into appalling slums. In this supportive community,
neighbours were continually borrowing from one another – a
cup of sugar, a needle and thread or a shilling till the end of the
week. It was also common for women to organise a 'menodge'
(derived from the French word 'menage'). This was a way of
everyone in turn getting a lump sum, for a big purchase, by

paying in a small amount each week. Saying someone 'couldnae organise a menodge' is still a term of derision in Glasgow. Other forms of sharing were apparent in the tradition of making extra batches of soup or scones to be shared with neighbours as well as taking turns to keep an eye on each others' weans.

This support ethos was also evident in various formal and informal women's organisations ranging from the successful rent strike during World War I to women's extensive particip- ation in the Co-operative Women's Guild. One of the most moving accounts of women's solidarity I have read is in Meg Henderson's autobiography *Finding Peggy* which describes strong bonds, not only within families but also in the wider communities of the Gorbals and Blackhill.

However, even with this support network the lives of poor Glasgow women were hard and exhausting: a fact admirably summed up in the title of a book about women in tenements – *She was Aye Working*. In an earlier chapter we saw how Glasgow was a low wage but high price economy. Household income was low, and often made lower still by men's drinking habits. It was women who had to try and square this circle. Inevitably many women found it difficult to feed their families properly and it was not uncommon for folk to live on porridge, bread and margarine. Doctors and teachers often recount how, even in the early twentieth century, children were often suffering from malnutrition if not outright starvation. Infant mortality was high.

At the turn of the twentieth century Scotland's rate of infant mortality was the same as the rates for England and Wales but by 1937 the Scottish rate was a third higher. The two factors most influential on whether a baby survived past six months were poverty and overcrowding: these made Glaswegian infants particularly susceptible and the city's figures particularly troublesome. Richard Finlay reports that 'the figures for the mid twenties and early thirties. . . reveal that Glasgow was the only city which failed to improve its rate of infant mortality.' [5]

The health of mothers was also poor – many were exhausted by multiple pregnancies and commonly did not eat much themselves so that they could give more to their children. This inevitably took a toll and many suffered from anaemia. The health of women who had part-time jobs, as well as domestic and mothering responsibilities, was particularly poor. The following reminiscence by a daughter shows the lengths women went to for their families' comforts and to make ends meet:

> In the middle of winter my mother used to get up very early about four a.m., and she would get the old pram out and push it up to the gas station where she would stand for ages so she would be the first to be allowed to buy the dross. She would bring it home, mix it with flour and salt. . . and cook in the oven. This made her own briquettes. God, I loved my mum. She would stand up to her knees in raw sewage to clear blocked toilets on our stairhead so that we didn't have to wade through it. She was a real mother to us. [6]

No wonder many historians and contemporary commentators point out that family life was sustained by women's self-sacrifice.

Suiting himself

The same could not be said of their men. T.C. Smout argues that as working hours were restricted, 'the benefit of increased leisure fell very unequally between the sexes.' Men often used their Saturday afternoons to go to football matches. Coupons, betting and gambling also became popular. These male pursuits, along with drinking, all cost money which could have been spent on the family. Smout points out that married women with families

> . . . gained nothing at all: the children had still to be minded, the shopping done, and the house cleaned, for nothing entered the market to save labour for the working-class housewife until the 1950s and 1960s. The air of pinched desperation and the symptoms of chronic illness that doctors and other social workers so often noticed among mothers in poor families surely had much to do with the fact that for them the house was a perpetual prison. [7]

The novelist William McIlvanney, originally from Kilmarnock, fell in love with much of Glasgow's traditional culture: his novels on the Glasgow detective, Jack Laidlaw, and many of his newspaper columns and articles, read like extended love letters. In a passage in one of his crime novels McIlvanney praises the tenacity and resilience of the Glaswegian male:

> Laidlaw had a happy image of the first man out after the nuclear holocaust being a Glaswegian. He would straighten up and look around. He would dust himself down with that flicking gesture of the hands and, once he had got the strontium off the good suit, he would look up. The palms would be open.

> 'Hey,' he would say. 'Gonny gi'es a wee brek here?

What was that about? Ye fell oot wi us or what?
That was a liberty. Just you behave.'

Then he would walk off with that Glaswegian walk,
in which the shoulders don't move separately but
the whole torso is carried as one, as stiff as a
shield. And he would be muttering to himself,
'Must be a coupla bottles of something intact.' [8]

As usual McIlvanney writes well about the Glasgow character. You can see what he is getting at. However, if this is a 'happy image' of a Glaswegian male no wonder many of them are dying young. Why would your archetypal Glaswegian male not emerge after the nuclear holocaust and ask 'where's my wife and weans'? McIlvanney's astute observations help us to grasp a fundamental truth about Glasgow's macho culture: it is not only the negative effects of alcohol and tendency to aggression which have damaged, and continue to damage, health in the city, but the fact that for many Glasgow men drink, or doing their own thing, became more important to them than their families.

I am not suggesting that *all* Glasgow men were drunks who spent every night propping up a bar, or ignoring their families, but I am suggesting that traditionally there was a strong current in Glasgow which easily swept men up and deposited them in the pub or encouraged them just to suit themselves. Indeed just about every person I've met who grew up in a working class Glasgow household has a story to tell about a father or grandfather who suited himself and acted as if they were the Lone Ranger. This might mean out boozing or gambling, with or without Tonto. But it could also mean just sitting in a chair watching the telly and not interacting with the family or opting out of holidays or other family occasions. Indeed most of the Glasgow-born men I know, from working class backgrounds, who grew up in the 1950s or earlier, recount that their fathers were almost shadowy figures in their childhood. Many men also had huge conflicts with their sons and this further alienated their wives.

The birth of the Lone Ranger

Dr. Annmarie Hughes, a historian who has made a study of gender relations and domestic violence on Clydeside, particularly between the wars, has an interesting perspective on the dynamic between men and women. She argues that throughout the UK in the interwar years there was a new view of the family. As a result of the propaganda round 'homes fit for heroes', the domestic ideal of the new garden city, growing consumerism and the freedom many women enjoyed as a result of war work, family life was reconceptualised. This was the era which seriously began to promote the ideas of 'companionate marriages' and of men pursuing leisure in the home.

However, according to Hughes, this idea had less appeal and relevance for the men of Clydeside. This may have been for reasons related to material presented in the previous chapter about 'the culture of honour' and exaggerated notions of masculinity and gender differences. But there were other reasons. For example the new consumer industries were mainly located in the south and 'heavy industries continued to predominate' in the Glasgow area. [9] This meant that it was very easy for men to continue with traditional ways based on strict gender roles. A second reason was that housing, though beginning to improve, was still poor and overcrowded by English standards. House ownership was also low in comparison to England and many families could hardly afford the rents for a new council house let alone buy a home. Unemployment was also high in Glasgow, leading to widespread poverty. None of this helped to support a strong focus on the home. According to Hughes, these, and other factors outlined below, led to profound conflict between husbands and wives.

Women in Glasgow had been employed during World War I and enjoyed more social and economic freedom. But between the wars, men's economic insecurity, and traditional working patterns and values, meant that they did not want women working and competing in the labour force. Many men had to accept that their wives worked as it was difficult to bring up a family on one wage but generally they resented this development. Their version of masculinity was as providers and authority figures within the family. Instead of the companionate marriage ideal of shared leisure time, west of Scotland men continued with their tradition of separate pursuits.

In previous chapters we've seen how men in Glasgow may have been particularly keen to drink because of problems with dislocation and to escape from overcrowded slums. But Hughes argues that men invested heavily in traditional male pursuits such as drinking, gambling and football in order to shore up their insecure male identity which was threatened by unemployment and job insecurity. This way of expressing their masculinity created huge conflict in the home.

We've already seen what a problem drinking was, but so too was gambling. In the 1930s the Royal Society for the Prevention of Cruelty to Children argued that throughout Scotland it was having a negative effect on women and children:

Every weekend from Friday to Sunday night great

> 'gambling schools' gather at different places and play
> at 'pitch and toss' and it is not an infrequent
> occurrence for men to stand at the 'school' and
> gamble away all the money they have received from
> the Labour Exchange or in a few cases their wages.
> The mother in such cases is usually the complainer,
> but it is remarkable how often one finds she is
> unwilling to take the extreme step of having her
> husband reported to the Procurator Fiscal. [10]

Of course, women would not make formal complaints about such incidents but it is not difficult to see how drink and betting created a running sore in many homes.

One strand of conflict in the gender war was simply about money. Male pastimes consumed much needed household income – effectively taking the food out of the mouths of women and children. Oral history testimonies confirm that many arguments between husbands and wives were about money. Household management, including managing the money, was women's domain. Women wanted their standard of living to rise but this wasn't possible if men continually blew it on their own pleasures.

However, what was perhaps worse than men spending precious money on themselves, was that they did not spend much time at home, thus neglecting their relationships with their wives. In the words of Professor Smout: 'Drink plus bad housing equalled male self-indulgence and female isolation.'[11] Richard Finlay agrees that up to World War I at least, 'men tended to spend most of their time in the work and at the pub in the company of other men' adding that the home was 'reserved for sleep and dinner'. [12] Many women became bitter and resentful. Who could blame them for picking at this scab and resorting to the only weapon available to a powerless woman – nagging. This then worsened the relationship between the couple, no doubt making it even more likely that the man would resort to violence or escape to the cheery ambience of the pub, or the gambling den, and the numbing embrace of a few halfs.

The two-step resulting from this scenario – man goes to pub, woman feels alienated and resentful – is admirably demonstrated in *The Shipbuilders*. Blake's novel starts with a launch day and Danny goes to the pub after work with some mates. He then makes his way home and decides, spontaneously, to 'nip' into another pub to have a drink, put on the coupon and talk about football, before going back to his wife and family. When he finally gets home his wife is alone with their baby, cooking kippers. Here's how we are introduced to the relationship between man and wife:

> 'On the booze again, I suppose,' she said.
> 'Shut your face! ' he retorted, but without passion. 'Is ma tea ready?'
> 'Aye, when I'm ready. I take my own time for them that take theirs.'
> Danny was not put out. He had never expected exchanges of any other kind as between spouses of eighteen years' standing. [13]

This contemptuous exchange between Agnes and Danny is nothing compared to what often passed between man and wife. We've seen something of domestic violence in the last chapter – violence made worse by drink. Sometimes this violence was verbal rather than physical aggression. Eric Bogle is one of Scotland's finest exports: a folk singer, now living in Australia, he is the composer of 'And the band played Waltzing Matilda' and 'No Man's Land' often hailed as the finest anti-war songs. Unusually for a Scot, Bogle displays a real tenderness for women and his 'Glasgow Lullaby' recounts the predicament of countless thousands of Glasgow women:

Glasgow Lullaby

Hush wee babby, for yer daddy's comin' in
Stumblin' up the stair and missin' every yin
Rotten wi' beer and stinkin' o' gin
He's drunk again – as usual

Chorus:
Oh my God, it's a weary, weary life
Who wid be a drinkin' man's wife
Who wid thole a' this trouble and this strife
Who but a silly woman

Hush wee babby, he's comin' in the door
Drunken big feet are skitin' over the floor
He's had a bucket, but he's thirstin' for more
He disnae ken when he's beaten

Hush wee babby, listen tae him sittin' there
Wi his bloodshot eyes and his tangled hair
Mooth fu' o' big talk and eyes fu' o' despair
And blaming me – as usual

Hush wee babby, yer daddy's gone tae bed
The morn he'll no' remember a' the things he said
But his tongue wis sharp and a' the wounds they bled
But then I'm used tae bleedin'

Hush wee babby and close yer weary eyes
Cuddle intae mammy and stop yer tired wee cries
And in the mornin' when ye decide tae arise
Yer mammy will be here waitin'

'The Gorbals Doctor' recounts how drink was a 'shameful' feature of Gorbals life and how when visiting local tenements he could not help but hear 'the never-ending squabbling between husbands and wives'. [14] He even linked the number of late night medical calls to the drink culture and arguments between men and women:

> The proportion of late night calls was always high, not because the baby or child had turned ill late at night, but because it was then that the parent became worried or developed a bad conscience over previous neglect during the day. In many cases a husband would arrive home about 11 p.m. after an evening's hard drinking. His wife would immediately set about upbraiding him for wasting his time and neglecting the children. In order to hammer home her feelings she would point to the baby, who, due to the surrounding row, would almost certainly be awake and crying through fright and the pain of teething troubles. This provided a cue for the husband that he would 'bloody soon get her a doctor' and off he would stumble to the nearest telephone. [15]

No matriarchal society

With men frequenting the pub regularly, home became women's domain. So too did childcare. Even when I was a teenager I remember people saying that they were going home to their 'mother's' at the weekend even though both parents were still alive. It is common for people to suggest that Glasgow was 'a matriarchal society' as women 'made the decisions'. [16] But this is misleading. Of course, some women undoubtedly held the reins at home – not just henpecking their men but generally ruling the roost – but they were the minority. Generally speaking, women made the decisions in the home not because they had real power but because men weren't interested and had abdicated responsibility. What's more, until women started to work in reasonable numbers, most of them were still financially dependent on men. In short, it was men who held the whip hand and whose 'word was law'. This is the picture which emerges from oral history interviews and it is a far cry from a matriarchal society.

Inside the home, as outside, there was a rigid division of labour between men and women in Scotland. Household chores and the care of children were not men's work. Until a few decades ago, no self-respecting man would be seen dead pushing a pram, going for the messages or hanging out washing. So while men's lives improved their wives were still oppressed by too much housework and too little money and time for themselves. It must be said, however, that traditionally many women defended this division of labour, thinking it unmanly for men to carry out household chores. Many mothers ensured that their daughters helped out at home but not their sons thus reinforcing the idea that cooking and cleaning was women's work and that men should be looked after by women.

We will look in more depth in Chapter 12 at child rearing in Glasgow but it is important here to point out that the typical Glasgow working man's penchant for drink, and/or unwillingness to get involved at home, had huge implications for their children and was another source of friction with their wives. The tragedy for many young people brought up in Glasgow is that, as we could see above, they often lived in a household with nagging, fights and a contemptuous relationship between their parents. Certainly some women bore their treatment by a selfish man stoically, thinking that it was a man's right to suit himself since he worked hard. While this may have led to more peace at home it merely perpetuated the problem as these mothers' sons and daughters were then brought up to think that it is right for men to suit themselves and for women to serve them. A recurrent theme in Glasgow literature is young people lying in bed at night desperately hoping that their drunken, violent fathers will disappear, thus giving the families peace. [17] Another is women encouraging their daughters not to get married or take up with men. Cathy McCormack's mother told her: 'A man will give you the moon to get you, once the ring is on your finger, he'll gie ye arsenic.' [18]

However, it would be wrong to insinuate that women were always angels. Glasgow mothers were often good organisers and house keepers but they could be brusque with their weans and neither physically nor verbally affectionate. No doubt there were also cases of good men lumbered with terrible wives who drank and were self-centred.

What every woman wants

Annmarie Hughes's interviews with Clydeside women reveal that what many wanted was a 'caring sharing man'. In fact what these women wanted from their men was rather limited: a man who didn't physically abuse them, who shared his income fairly with his wife and family and who took them on outings and on holiday. In other words, a man who valued his home life and cared for his wife and family. In essence, many women wanted 'a companionate marriage'. Many also wanted something better for themselves and their families. Remember, women did not mainly work full time or have the pub as a refuge, so they were more confined to a home which was often dark, cramped and difficult to keep clean. We must also remember that Glasgow has a cold, wet climate which means that Glaswegians are destined to spend much more time indoors than poor people in warmer and drier climates. Even when these women weren't having to put up with stinking wynds and pends, the buildings they inhabited were often grey and dreary.

However, it appears that women's desires to improve their living conditions and future prospects became another divisive issue between husbands and wives. If women were annoyed at men for their drinking, misuse of money and selfishness, men became increasingly fed-up with women's desires and aspirations. Indeed the idea of men oppressed by their women's wants is one of the main themes in *The Shipbuilders*. In fact this is the story which unites the two male characters – shipyard owner, Leslie Pagan and riveter, Danny Shields – across the great class divide. Danny's wife Agnes makes 'frequent jibes at his working-man's ways'[19] and is under the 'flashy' influence of her sister who has married a man with money and lives in a posh area. Agnes spends much of her time going to the cinema with them, alienating her husband. She is unfaithful and ultimately they part. Leslie Pagan has married an English woman who doesn't like dirty, smoky Glasgow or the industry that's in his blood. All she wants to do is write 'fat cheques' in chic London shops and spend her time jet-setting in places like Claridges. Ultimately she has her way and the book ends with him catching the Night Scot to start his new life in the south.

From my reading of *The Shipbuilders*, Agnes is simply a lonely woman who longs for some love and tenderness in her life. Throughout the course of the book Agnes is critical, and for good reason, of Danny's relationship with their older son. Agnes's crime is mainly that she has a mind of her own and wants more of a life for herself. She is too strong-willed to become the martyr with the pinched face who never goes out of the house. In short, she has too strong a personality to become the long-suffering 'wee Glasgow wummin' with no needs or desires of her own.

This theme of the materialistic wife, intent on improving her, or the family's life, is a recurrent theme in Glasgow fiction. Indeed Neil McMillan, in an article about women in the celebrated Glasgow novelist James Kelman's work, asserts that the author is within a tradition of male Glasgow fiction which 'persistently identifies womanliness with negative bourgeois aspirations'.[20] There's little doubt that women are routinely portrayed in an unflattering light in William McIlvanney's work. These novelists were born in the 1930s or 40s and their female characters often have aspirations for a better house or more money, and they are generally depicted as the carriers of alien middle-class, and essentially English values.

In one of his novels McIlvanney mounts a vicious attack on 'genus surbanus'. 'After mating,' he writes, 'two offspring are produced at intervals mathematically calculated by the female, whereupon the female swallows the male whole and re-emits him in the form of a bank-balance.'[21] In her study of McIlvanney's fiction, Beth Dickson writes that, with the exception of Jenny Docherty (the saintly mother figure in *Docherty*):

> . . .wives are poisonous, brittle, materialistic, empty
> creatures who want to consume their husbands and
> whose main aim is upward social mobility. They are
> almost without redeeming features: it's a great
> mystery why McIlvanney's heroes married the women
> they did. . . Except in lust and acrimony, it seems
> almost impossible for men and women to
> communicate as partners in McIlvanney's work. [22]

The constant tension between men and women over his drinking and desire to spend time with his mates and her material wants and other ideas on life inevitably led to many rows within Glasgow families.

I am no fan of the fashion-driven consumer culture in which we now live. I deplore the cult of celebrity, the labels culture and the wanton waste of our throwaway society. But I find myself an ally with these women who wanted something better for themselves and their families. Many Glaswegian families lived in poor, cramped conditions until well into the 1960s. Many of these women had hard, cheerless lives. Who can blame them for wanting improved living conditions? – bigger, brighter houses that were easier to clean, better furnishings, ornaments and pictures as well as the type of labour-saving devices that we now take for granted such as washing machines, hoovers and fridges. What's more, the data support their case. Even in 1931 an expatriate Scot, living in the USA, wrote 'From the standard of living point of view Scotland is a backward country, and the Scot abroad is increasingly aware of it and ashamed that others must also see it.' [23] Given the housing conditions in the city, and the amount of money spent on drink, this low standard of living was a particular problem in Glasgow. No wonder the Glasgow woman nagged on about improving her lot.

The great escape

Glasgow men used the pub to escape poor living conditions and a nagging wife and it appears that Glasgow women used the cinema as a refuge from the dreariness of their lives. In short, cinema was the Glasgow woman's 'great escape'. By 1917 there were a hundred cinemas in Glasgow – the highest per head of population in the UK. In the 1930s this had risen to 127. Tom Devine confirms that in Scotland as a whole working class women with children 'made up significant parts of the audiences'.[24] In the 1930s and 40s my mother went twice a week with her granny to the pictures. A friend of mine who grew up in Shotts in the 1950s reports going to the pictures with her mother three times a week throughout her childhood. A 1937 survey of children in West Lothian found that only 6 per cent of children never went to the cinema. Even in 1951 investigators found that 'the Scots went to the pictures far more often than the population as a whole – 38 visits per person per year as against an average of 29 for Britain as a whole.' [25] In Glasgow it was 51 visits – almost twice the English figure. [26] Unsurprisingly, Glasgow housed the largest cinema in Europe – Green's Playhouse. The Glasgow Film Society was also the first of its type in the world.

Glasgow was also famous for its dance halls and in the 1950s it was claimed that 'there is a higher proportion of dance halls to the population than anywhere else in the British Isles.' [27] Of course, both sexes frequented dance halls but young women often went four or five times a week. The radio was the first modern consumer item to 'come into general use' in 1930s Scotland.[28] Television broadcasts started in Scotland in 1952 and proved so popular that within a decade the number of cinemas had halved.

Over the years various people have pointed out that Glasgow
is a city which has been heavily influenced by America. This is
not only to be seen in the grid system in the city's central area
– a street layout more redolent of Chicago than Edinburgh or
Birmingham. But it is also evident in the city's taste for entertainment, such as Glaswegians' love affair with country and western
music. *The Third Statistical Account of Scotland*, published in
1958, claims that 'American films are much more popular than
British films in Glasgow.' It also states:

> Almost every American music-hall, radio and/or
> television star who visits Britain makes an appearance
> at the Empire and is greeted with undisguised
> idolatry. . . American film stars are also greeted
> ecstatically when they visit Glasgow. The time of their
> arrival is carefully announced, and crush barriers are
> erected in the Central Station. The crowd on an
> occasion of this sort may number up to nine or ten
> thousand, and it is customary for a large number of
> them to gather outside the Central Hotel and shout
> for their favourite until he makes an appearance on a
> balcony at the hotel. Most American stars say that the
> welcome they receive in Glasgow is the greatest they
> have ever had. [29]

This love of films, particularly Hollywood films, and going
to the dancing may help to account for another aspect of
Glasgow life – the fact that Glasgow women have always been
much more interested in clothes and fashion than their sisters
in other cities. Even the clippies (bus conductresses) in the old
days were often immaculately made up and glamorous. The
writer Janice Galloway is from Saltcoats but you could hardly
get a stiletto heel between what she describes and what was
common in Glasgow during the same period. She says that

people got 'really dolled up, even just to go to the pictures.' She also recounts how many of the folk she knew 'styled themselves on American movies and picked up the language.'[30]

Going to see, mainly American, films may have been better for women than sitting brooding in a slum, waiting for their men to come back from the pub. However, it did not help to solve the underlying problem: men doing their own thing with their mates and ignoring their wives and weans. Indeed women's escape route may even have made the problem worse. From the 1940s on America was also keen on the idea of the companionate marriage and this was the relationship ideal women consumed at the cinema along with their poke of sweets. Contemporary research shows that exposure to glamorous media images can make people feel more critical of their real partners; such viewing also fuels materialistic desires – already a bone of contention between men and women.

Defining the problem

All of this suggests that many homes in Glasgow resembled war zones where there were daily skirmishes between two people intent on completely different styles of life. The men had the power to do what they liked and all a wife could do was nag or defy her husband. No wonder there was lots of domestic violence and contemptuous exchanges between husbands and wives. Until more recent times, this was not reflected in divorce statistics since divorce, even separation, was often out of the question for poor people.

This is not to say that *every* married couple in Glasgow had a bad relationship. Of course, some men managed to live up to the companionate ideal and were good providers. Also, over the generations there have been lots of Glasgow men who have seen the damage the drink or gambling culture could wreak on families and felt scunnered by it. With effort they could swim against the tide. My own dad consciously turned his back on drink and literally got on his bike, taking up cycling as a hobby when he was young. Some men went out of their way to become involved with their own, or other children, through the Sunday School, football clubs, the BB or scouts. Nonetheless, even when men often hankered after something better for themselves and their families they often just didn't know how to connect with their wives or father their children well. Parenting is not instinctual: it has to be learned and we primarily learn it from the way we were parented. It is also difficult for men to conceptualise better ways of relating to women if they have few positive role models to emulate.

I am also not suggesting that this picture was unique to Glasgow. What I've described here could be found in slum communities not just in the UK but internationally. My argument is that this gender hostility was a fundamental part of Glasgow's culture and may well have enveloped a greater percentage of the population than elsewhere. This then means that in this city there was simply too much aggression, quarrels and anger and not enough love and gentleness. It was a culture too driven by the behaviour and values of hard-drinking macho males which failed to value a more home-centred life or provide space for, softness, nurturing and femininity. Men's definition of a good wife was not someone who was affectionate and loving but simply someone who had your tea on the table and the house clean. There's little doubt that many women suffered terribly at the hands of selfish, uncaring and often violent men. These are the circumstances which can lead women to feel ill and depressed. Men suffered too. Women can have a positive effect on men if they are open to women's influence and love. As we shall see in a later chapter, this can even be beneficial for men's physical and mental health.

Men in Glasgow were once open to women's spiritual influence. In earlier chapters we learned how Glasgow was originally a spiritual settlement based on the cult of Mungo or St. Kentigern. However, Mungo's mother was also a religious figure in her own right – St. Thenew. She was a saint of some significance and worthy of a cult centred on a chapel on the west side of the town some of whose ruins survived into the beginning of the eighteenth century. There was also a well linked to St. Thenew which was reputed to have healing properties. Sadly St. Thenew lives on in Glasgow only in the corruption of her name to St. Enoch, famous for its station and shopping centre.

Men in the medieval period often had a feeling of profound reverence and respect for women. For example the Scottish poet, William Dunbar, (c 1460 – c 1520) wrote the following lines in his poem, 'In Prais of Wemen':

> Now of wemen I say this for me,
> Of erthly thingis nane may bettir be.
> Thay suld haif wirschep and grit honoring
> Of men aboif all uthir erthly thing.
> Rycht grit dishonour upoun himself he takkis (takes)
> In word or deid quha evir wemen lakkis, (deed
> whoever women disparages)
> Sen that of wemen cumin all ar we; (born)
> Wemen ar wemen and sa will end and de. (die) [31]

As William Dunbar also pointed out all those centuries ago to his fellow men (and translated here for convenience): women are 'the comfort that we all have here. . . our very nest of nourishing' – those who foul the nest, pay dear. Sentiments to bear in mind when we remember the violence figures and men's poor health in Glasgow.

CHAPTER 8
Let Glasgow languish?

'L ET GLASGOW flourish through the teaching of the word,' said St. Mungo in one of his sermons. It was shortened in Victorian times to 'Let Glasgow Flourish' and now serves as the city's motto. Flourish is a term originally used to describe the process of flowering. For a plant to flourish its fundamental biological needs must be met – it needs light, air, water and food all delivered in the right way for that particular species.

So what do human beings need, not simply to survive, but flourish? Some of our requirements are similar to plants – temperature matters, so does oxygen, light and the right type of food. But this is where the analogy with plants ends. Human beings have a brain and, unlike many animals, a brain capable of complex intellectual and emotional processing. For humans to flourish their physiological and complex psychological needs must be met. Psychologists often use the world 'languish' as the opposite of flourish. This refers to a state of being where survival is not immediately threatened but where growth is stunted and well-being compromised.

One of the most persuasive ways to think about basic human psychological needs is Self-Determination Theory (SDT). These ideas, first outlined by Richard Ryan and Edward Deci, draw on extensive empirical research undertaken internationally on what human beings require for psychological well-being. [1] These psychologists present evidence to show that there are three fundamental psychological needs or 'nutriments' – the need for *competence, autonomy* and *relatedness*. In this chapter we look at these concepts in the Glasgow context so that we can judge whether the city's culture and circumstances have truly 'let Glasgow flourish'.

The need for autonomy

Self-Determination Theory defines needs as 'innate psychological nutriments that are essential for ongoing psychological growth, integrity and well-being.' Deci and Ryan argue that human beings are naturally inclined to fulfil their needs for competence, relatedness and autonomy and when they are they confer 'considerable adaptive advantage' both for the individual and the group.' Self-Determination theorists also argue that people are programmed to 'seek out novelty and challenges, to extend and exercise (their) capacities, to explore, and to learn. However, the prevailing environment can undermine individuals' natural motivation to grow and develop. Indeed research repeatedly shows that external rewards, threats, pressures and directives, can undermine individuals' natural motivation. Passivity, alienation and apathy can also result when basic needs for autonomy, competence and relatedness are thwarted.

In SDT autonomy does not mean independence from others, individualism, selfishness or detachment. Rather it means having a sense of volition or control. These theorists argue that it makes sense for human beings, operating inevitably in changing circumstances and contexts, to do best when they can self-organise and self-regulate. They write:

> . . . through autonomy individuals better regulate
> their own actions in accordance with their full array
> of felt needs and available capacities, thus
> coordinating and prioritising processes toward more
> effective self-maintenance.[2]

We can see the importance of autonomy in a variety of studies. For example, some medical research projects show that the more patients or clients are given responsibility (for example, in insulin control for diabetics) the more likely they are to adhere to the programme. Research projects with young people and in the workplace also show how external rewards and punishments can undermine intrinsic motivation and decrease performance. A much quoted research project which illustrates the link between autonomy and well-being, this time physical health, is the 'Whitehall study' undertaken by Professor Michael Marmot.[3]

Marmot and colleagues researched the effect of status on civil servants – hence the 'Whitehall' study. These studies show that the higher grade civil servants had fewer problems with their heart, and better health, than lower grade workers. As public servants on the second highest grade had disease rates twice as high as those who were in the top grades, this was not simply about the negative effects of being near the bottom of the status hierarchy. Interestingly, known risk factors for ill-health such as smoking, poor diet or alcohol consumption, only accounted for a third of illness. Marmot *et al.* argue that their research shows that it is not simply status (the psychological effects of being at the bottom of the hierarchy) that matters but the stress generated from lack of control. In short, the more senior you are the more control you have over your job. It is commonplace to see stress as the by-product of a job's heavy demands and responsibility. According to this view, the long working hours culture of senior managers makes them more likely to suffer the negative effects of stress than more junior workers. But the Whitehall study contradicts this, showing that it is not the demands made of employees which is the main problem, it is the *control,* or lack of it, which matters most for health. So lack of control leads individuals to experience low grade chronic stress and it is this which weakens the cardio-vascular and immune systems, thus undermining health.

No one could dispute that in past generations poverty led countless millions of people to feel powerless and greatly stressed. One of the best examples we have of the damaging effects of poverty, and complete lack of autonomy, is the life of Robert Burns. Indeed the most poignant aspect of Burns's writing is that we cannot ignore the desperate cries of an intelligent and savvy man, acutely conscious of his powerlessness and its negative effects on his human spirit. In his poems there is the recurrent theme of human helplessness against God ('Omnipotence Divine'); 'fickle' or 'luckless fortune'; and the powerlessness of the labouring classes. Burns lived through a period of restructuring in which people were at the mercy of factors and landlords, patronage was rife and they could achieve little without the backing of those in authority. The church also wielded power over people's lives, regulating behaviour through kirk sessions and various humiliating punishments and fines. Burns's famous poem where he empathises with the mouse inadvertently turned out of his nest in winter by a stroke of bad luck, no doubt echoes his own experience. However, he also believed that human consciousness makes matters worse:

But Mousie, thou are no thy lane,
In proving foresight may be vain:
The best-laid schemes o' mice an' men
Gang aft agley,
An' lea'e us nought but grief an' pain,
For promis'd joy!

Still thou are blest, compar'd wi me!
The present only toucheth thee:
But och! I backward cast me e'e,
On prospects drear!
An' forward, tho; I canna see,
I guess an' fear!

In 'Man was made to mourn – a dirge' Burns develops the notion of human helplessness and bridles against the unfairness of life and its inherent contradictions. In it he ponders how the desire for autonomy is, for poor people at least, undermined by reality:

If I'm design'd yon lordling's slave –
By Nature's law design'd –
Why was an independent wish
E'er planted in my mind?

Burns is the man of 'independent mind' acutely conscious of his own slavery and dependence. However, it is in Burns's letters that we get the full sense of his personal feelings of powerlessness and how this added to the tragedy of his life. Indeed some of his letters are desperate because he is not master of his own fate and powerless to help his children. In 1793, three years before he died, he wrote to a well-to-do confidante, Mrs. Dunlop:

> . . . these four months, a sweet little girl, my youngest child, has been so ill, that every day, a week or less threatened to terminate her existence. . . I cannot describe to you, the anxious, sleepless hours these ties frequently give me. I see a train of helpless little folks; me, & my exertions, all their stay; & on what a brittle thread does the life of man hang! If I am nipt off, at the command of Fate; even in all the vigour of manhood as I am, such things happen every day – Gracious God! what would become of my little flock! 'Tis here that I envy your people of fortune. A Father on his death-bed, taking an everlasting leave of his children, is indeed woe enough; but the man of competent fortune leaves his sons & daughters, independency & friends; while I – but my God, I shall run distracted if I think any longer on the Subject! [4]

On his deathbed Burns was still worrying about how he would pay his debts.

Burns is recognised internationally as the voice of the poor, the underprivileged, and the underdog. His popularity is not only about his belief in human dignity but also because he understood what it feels like to be powerless – prey to famine, bad weather, misfortune, greedy factors and landlords. In other words, he knows what it feels like for the basic human need for autonomy to be overridden by oppressive circumstances. Burns's work has always proved exceptionally popular in Glasgow. Understandably so, since there is so much in the Bard's work for poor Glaswegians to relate to their own lives.

In the nineteenth century, work for the industrial labouring classes, not just in Glasgow or Scotland, but elsewhere, was dire. Workers were required to labour for long hours, often in the most atrocious circumstances. No one would willingly choose to work like this – workers had to accept these conditions as they had no other option. In such a world there was no room for self-regulation, volition or any other facet of autonomy.

Feelings of powerlessness were particularly acute for workers in Glasgow. Firstly, Glasgow industrial workers were mainly employed in industries providing goods for the international market. This meant that their jobs were particularly vulnerable to slumps or other vagaries of the trade cycle. This chronic insecurity may well have added an additional feeling of powerlessness over and above that experienced by industrial workers in more secure industries. Secondly, trade unions have traditionally been the way that workers have organised to gain some power for themselves and to better their conditions. However, until the twentieth century Glasgow unions were weak in comparison with those in England. This meant that industrial workers had less opportunity to feel they could influence their working conditions. Thirdly, workers were mainly employed in large, and exceedingly hierarchical, organisations run by 'autocrats'. As we saw in a previous chapter many Glaswegian bosses believed that workers were there just to obey orders – 'to be tell't'. Fourthly, the clear divisions created by sectarianism or demarcation were very difficult for individuals to bridge. Being a Catholic, for example, sometimes meant that whole areas of working life, and routes to improvement, were closed to you. Foremen, commonly prejudiced against certain groups, often had the power to hire and fire. Until the 1940s favouritism was rife. Unskilled workers could not scale the skill barriers and get into better types of work. For these reasons alone many workers felt powerless. In today's world of employment and anti-discrimination law, which protects us against this type of unfairness, we may find it difficult to understand how demoralising it is to cope with discriminatory processes at work.

Paraphrasing George Orwell we could say 'all industrial workers in the past felt powerless, but some felt more powerless than others'. From the point of view of autonomy – self-regulation and volition – there was little to commend working in Glasgow's industries in the nineteenth and first half of the twentieth centuries. However, the real challenge to the autonomy of the Glasgow working class was not the workplace but the hearth: while the average English worker of the nineteenth and early twentieth century lived in a four room terraced house with its own toilet in the backyard, the average Glasgow worker lived in a one or two room tenement flat. Overcrowding was much more prevalent in Glasgow than anywhere else in Britain. Overcrowding meant not being able to get away from other family members or lodgers. It meant sleeping in the same room as lots of other people, often six in the same bed, with no space for dressing, ablutions, reading or the pursuit of hobbies. It meant little opportunity for 'self-regulation'. You could not do anything that suited you – the overriding requirement was to 'fit in' with others' needs. Worse still your overcrowded family dwelling was not separate from other families. It did not have its own front and back door, as in England, but in a close often with dozens of other families with whom you might have to share cooking and toilet facilities. As we saw earlier, women often bonded together to provide social support but there were still huge strains – strains often routinely glossed over in rosy pictures of the solidarity of tenement life.

It is this freedom of being able to choose for yourself that Gorbals boy Ralph Glasser found so different when he got to Oxford:

> I had never, for instance, had a room of my own,
> where I could shut the door and read or write or
> dream, or have guests. . . I could burn the light in
> my room at night as long as I liked with no fear of
> having to search for pennies for the meter. For the
> first few weeks this feeling of possessing sovereign
> territory was unnerving. [5]

Sean Damer is an acute commentator on the tenement problem of living on top of one another:

> If you had for a neighbour a roaring drunk, a
> violent man, an exuberant party holder, a shebeen-
> or a brothel-keeper, a bagpiper, a sectarian bigot or
> a filthy dirty demented old person, you had had it:
> you couldn't escape. . . Theoretically, of course,
> you could escape – but where to? Most working-
> class families did not have the money for the rent
> in the new, bigger, airier tenements. The older
> tenements, with their small houses, clustered
> round the big shipyards, docks, locomotive works
> and engineering shops, were effectively prisons for
> their inhabitants. [6]

The Mail published an exposé of living conditions in Glasgow in the 1870s which highlighted the problem of strong social controls. The Parliamentary Select Committee which it spawned recounted cases of 'baby farming' where babies were routinely neglected and mistreated. Infanticide was also a problem. *The Mail* argued that neighbours were often aware of the terrible treatment meted out to many babies and children but their self-interest meant that they could not challenge anyone living nearby. 'We have been told again and again,' they write 'that the dread of making disturbance amongst neighbours in close association causes such cruelties as those we are narrating to be winked at and passed over in silence.' [7]

It is hardly surprising that in this environment the aspirations of Glaswegians was for their 'own front and back door' – an arrangement which affords people more control. Indeed although philanthropic societies were appalled at cellar living, and these were removed early in the city's drive for improvement, living in cellars was popular with slum dwellers because it gave them a 'private' entrance and some degree of autonomy. Of course, semi-detached houses with their own entrances were included in the mix of houses provided by Glasgow Corporation as part of its mission to rid Glasgow of slums. However, a favoured approach from the 1960s on was 'high flats' – a far cry from the independence afforded by your own front and back door.

So, various aspects of life for working class people in Glasgow conspired to mean that they had little sense of autonomy in their lives – far from making decisions voluntarily for themselves they felt compelled and directed, either by those in authority or by the proximity and social obligations foisted upon them as an inevitable result of having to live in overcrowded and inadequate conditions. The one exception to this conclusion about the lack of autonomy was the city's children – they had incredible freedom. When children were not at school, mothers often forced them outdoors to play so that they had peace to cook and clean. In cold, wet weather the youngsters may have been reluctant but generally they went willingly. Most Glaswegians' fond memories of being brought up in the city involve youngsters' street culture and the fact that they were able to run wild – playing in back courts, middens and closes, dreeping over dykes and walking miles to visit parks, canals or bluebell woods miles outside the city.

The need for competence

Much of Glasgow's engineering industry called for craftsmen whose pride and personality were built around their skills and their products, who found a fulfilment in their tasks. A launching on Clydeside was often almost a family affair, the workmen looking on with satisfaction as the ship they had helped to create took to the water.

If the psychological need for autonomy was not met what about competence? In Self-Determination Theory competence refers to the need to experience oneself as capable of controlling the environment and bringing about desired outcomes. In short, to feel effective. As babies we are equipped with a natural tendency for 'motor play, manipulation of objects, and exploration of surroundings'.[8] This primes us for growth and also means that we are naturally equipped to find satisfaction in learning for its own sake. The desire for discovery and exploration has evolutionary value leading, for example, to the discovery of new food supplies and more complex ways for group interaction. The fact that the desire to learn is open, rather than directed to specific activities, leads human beings to be 'curious and assimiliative'. The need to feel competent and effective, together with this broad interest in learning, allows for individual development and specialisation.

It is worth pointing out that Scotland is a country which since medieval times has valued learning and was one of the first countries in the world to establish a national network of schools. The Scottish Enlightenment itself can be characterised as a period when Scottish thinkers used rational thought to help change 'man's relationship to his environment. No longer was nature accepted as given and preordained; instead, it could be altered for the better or "improved" by systematic and planned intervention.' [9] In essence, the ideas prevalent in the Scottish Enlightenment enabled ways for human beings to act out their desire for competence through the development of skills, intellectual approaches and new scientific methods for controlling nature.

Indeed the modern history of Glasgow, and its surrounding area, is about increasing competence and environmental control: even the River Clyde itself was engineered and brought under man's dominion. If we compile a list of all the great scientific and technological firsts for Glasgow and the west of Scotland essentially we are celebrating the competence of her engineers, technocrats and scientists. Leaving aside production of various kinds, Glaswegians were pioneers in trade, navigation, banking and commercial methods. Much of what Glasgow and its environs produced would have been impossible without a highly trained and skilled workforce.

The sense of competence workers could derive from their labour is most evident in shipbuilding – the best known and most dominant of Clydeside industries. Working in shipyards was tough and demanding but it demanded skill and allowed for a sense of satisfaction. One expert on the Clyde estimates that 30,000 ships were produced on the river in under 200 years. He also writes that all the yards and 'the tens of thousands of men employed in them have given cause for the description "Clyde-built" to be one indicating the highest praise.'[10] In his novels George Blake refers to the shipbuilders as 'mighty craftsmen before the Lord' and claims that 'almost every man among them was an artist in one of the arts that go to the building of a ship'. He also equates the tradition of shipbuilding with 'skill', 'glory' and 'passion'. The Labour MP David Kirkwood described them as 'the most expert craftsmen in the world' adding that their 'joy as well as their livelihood lay in converting the vast masses of Nature's gift into works of art, accurate to a two-thousandth part of an inch.' A shipyard joiner commented pithily: 'A job well done. That was us.' In the 1940s V.S. Pritchett described what was involved in the process of riveting:

> The riveter is a member of the 'black squad' – a gang of four who turn up to the job with the misleading nonchalance of a family of jugglers. They are the riveter, the holder-up, the heater, and a boy. . . The 'black squad' can set up shop anywhere and begin performing their hot chestnut act. You see one swung over the ship's side. He stands on his plank waiting with the pneumatic instrument in his gloved hands. On the other side of the plate, inside the ship is the heater with his smoking brazier – a blue coke is always rising over a ship: he plucks a rivet out of the fire with his tongs, a 'boy' (nowadays it is often a girl in dungarees) catches the rivet in another pair of tongs and steps quickly with it to the holder-up, who puts it through the proper holes at the junction with the plates. As the pink nub of the rivet comes through, the pneumatic striker comes down on it, roaring out blows at the rate of about 7000 hits a minute, and squeezes it flat. [11]

Before World War I the most elaborate liner built on the Clyde was the *Aquitania*, built at John Brown's in Clydebank and weighing in at 49,000 tons. She was able to carry over 4,000 passengers in three classes of accommodation and almost one hundred crew. The first-class accommodation included a Louis XVI style saloon; a smoking room based on the Painted Hall at Greenwich; and an Adam-style dining room with panelled mahogany; and a garden lounge. Producing a vessel of this size and fitting it out to this quality required a huge number of workers with different skills. Even the launch of a ship was a considerable feat. It took real skill to get some of these huge ships to glide slowly backward into the river. There was only one major catastrophe: the *Daphne* which overturned during its launch in Govan in 1883 killing over a hundred men.

The *Queen Mary*, also built in Clydebank, was a massive 80,774 tons. John Masefield, the Poet Laureate, was moved to write for the launch of this stately vessel:

> . . . rampart of a ship
> Long as a street and lofty as a tower,
> Ready to glide in thunder from the slip
> And shear the sea with majesty of power. [12]

Public interest in Scotland in the liner was immense. On the 24th March 1936 when the *Queen Mary* left Clydebank for the first time for trials, thousands of people lined the banks of the Clyde to catch sight of her. It is estimated that a quarter of a million people watched the liner from Greenock alone. Accounts of the event in Greenock talk about 'awestruck' sight-seers and 'an audible intaking of breath' when the liner came into view and people were astonished 'when they realised the huge size of the Cunarder.' [13]

The public were more interested in the luxury liners but the Clyde built a huge number of different types of vessels: masted sailing ships; fishing skiffs; steam ships; smacks; puffers; shallow draft vessels; paddle ferries; barges; merchant ships; dredgers; tugs; battle ships; destroyers; submarines; nuclear submarines.

Writers tend to talk about the workers as if they were all men. The majority certainly were but women worked in the yards as tracers, French polishers and riggers. During the war women were trained to undertake skilled work previously done by men and they too experienced considerable job satisfaction. A female jute worker from Dundee who learned welding recalled:

> This was heaven – what a difference from the monotonous clickety-clack of the weaving shed. Here was this ship being built, a thing of beauty. There was a pride in the job they didn't have in the jute trade. I dearly loved that job. [14]

There were three main reasons why shipbuilding as an activity had a particularly positive effect on its workforce. First is what one expert called 'the clear sense of purpose in constructing products of such obvious utility.'[15] In a similar vein another argued:

> There are some kinds of manual work in which men do not easily take pride – work for which there is nothing to show, or only some trivial or rubbishy thing. It is not so with the building of ships. When the riveter's heater-boy said, 'Whaer wid the *Loocitania* hae been if it hadna been for me heatin' the rivets?' he expressed a feeling that runs through the whole of a shipbuilding yard from the Manager down. . . Each man or boy employed in building a liner or battleship feels himself to be part-author of something organic, mighty, august, with a kind of personal life of its own and a career of high service, romance and adventure before it.[16]

This then leads to the second reason why shipbuilding should particularly elicit pride and positive feelings. Getting feedback on performance is an important part of feeling competent – it confirms your effectiveness and mastery. As we've already seen it was not only the workers themselves who thought they were creating beautiful majestic objects; the admiring reactions of the general public became part of a positive feedback loop.

The third reason for the obvious pride of the workforce was 'the overawing scale of both the ships and the shipyard environment. Ships were punched, bent and forced into existence out of a reluctant material.' [17] Undoubtedly the sheer scale of the ships built on the Clyde was part of the industry's romance and admiration for the skill of the workforce. The BBC's reporter Fergal Keane recounts feeling 'Lilliputian' when he worked in an equivalent yard in Belfast. [18] Tom McKendrick, a shipbuilder turned artist, reminds us that these yards, often at the end of ordinary looking streets, built the 'biggest man-made moving objects on the planet' – objects bigger than the pyramids. [19]

Shipbuilding was not the only heavy engineering industry to elicit a sense of awe and pride. Glasgow novelist, Margaret Thomson Davies, describes how the locomotive engineering community in Springburn viewed the product of their labours: 'The big gates of Hyde Park swung open at last,' she writes, 'and there were appreciative grasps from the crowd as the gigantic work of art fashioned in shining steel, a thing of beauty and power moved forward.' [20]

This is not simply the idle speculation of a novelist. Look at the pictures of the locomotives produced in Glasgow and you cannot fail to be impressed by their majestic elegance and stirred by the fact that a community like Springburn produced engines to cross continents and foreign lands.

It also appears that other Clydeside workers, even if not directly employed in industries producing ships or locomotive engines, still felt pride in the accomplishments of their fellow workers. Miners, steelyard workers, instrument makers, carpet weavers and countless more occupational groups produced the energy, raw materials or equipment needed to produce the ships and locomotives. They too had an emotional investment in the city's achievements.

There's a story told of a young visitor to Glasgow asking a policeman, 'Can I get from here to Kelvingrove?' and the policeman answering with pride: 'Laddie from here you can get to anywhere in the world.' [21] Reading history books on Glasgow you cannot help but be affected by the Clyde's staggering achievements.

Glasgow workers may have achieved considerable feelings of competence but unfortunately this mastery came from jobs which were insecure and subject to the vicissitudes of international markets which meant that whole yards could shut as a result of orders drying up. In places like Govan, Clydebank, Greenock and Dalmuir this could mean thousands of men – whole communities – queuing up outside the labour exchange.

We can get a good sense of what happened to men as a result of these lay-offs from George Blake's *The Shipbuilders*. The book is set during the Depression. It opens as Leslie Pagan launches the last boat from his yard. This has a negative effect on the shipowner but at least he has other options (the book ends with his move to a small estate in the south of England). The effect on the workers is much more devastating. Blake suggests that the loss of money is nothing to the loss of skill and purpose. The riveter Danny Shields is even drawn to stand looking into cobblers' shops so that he could see 'the deft, rapid hands of the cobbler working'. [22] Danny knocks over something and his wife shouts at him calling him a 'clumsy big lout'. When he says it was an accident, explaining he was only helping to clear away, she retorts, 'Aye, and ye're not even fit for that' – a criticism which elicits such anger in him that he 'swings his fist back to hit her'. [23]

Another issue worth pursuing briefly is that the working conditions in the yard were atrocious. Many visitors compared them with Dante's Inferno. Workers laboured on average 55 hours a week often in atrocious weather and exposed to extreme cold. Few would have done this willingly. They had to do it for a living. Of course, as we have seen, it had its recompense but their need for autonomy was never met no matter how competent they might have felt as workers. Moreover, not all Glasgow workers were skilled. Professor Smout estimates that 'over 70 per cent of the employment in the Glasgow region at the start of the twentieth century could be classified as more or less skilled.' [24] An unskilled job simply meant that anyone, at least with the requisite amount of strength and stamina, was capable of walking off the street and filling the position. A skilled job would require some amount of training, usually in an apprenticeship. There's little doubt from the various historical accounts of Glasgow that the biggest social problems involved the thirty per cent of workers who were unskilled. Some of their problems came from their lack of money and the fact that they were most likely to be housed in the worst slums. But we can also see that, unlike Glasgow's skilled workers, they were less likely to get their psychological need for competence met through their work.

The need to relate and connect to others

In Self-Determination Theory relatedness refers to the need to feel a sense of belonging and connectedness with others. Since children have a long dependency period on adults, our species would not have survived if we were not programmed for attachment, and caring. Indeed Deci and Ryan argue that it became adaptive for human beings to extend feelings of attachment and altruism to 'non-kin group members'. This shift allowed for larger and more cohesive groups which afforded greater protection to their members.

An influential theory advanced by Robin Dunbar maintains that human beings have large brains so that they can process the huge amounts of information needed to relate to others and live successfully in a large group.[25] So relatedness involves sexual partnerships and families as well as feeling appreciated and valued and able to participate in social groups. As we have already discussed the relationship between men and women and their families, here we concentrate on other types of social bonding.

The old tenement communities in Glasgow involved a great deal of social interaction – remember people often shared cooking and toilet facilities. This encouraged people to be familiar and open with one another thus creating the friendliness for which Glasgow is still famed. At the height of the squalor there was a real sense of being in it together. This is succinctly shown in an 1858 report on terrible slum conditions, when the journalist asks one of the elderly women tenants how she manages to live in such dirty and overcrowded conditions and she answers, 'Deed, sir, we're nae waur than our neighbours, an' we dinna think onything aboot it.' [26] For women in particular there was real cohesion and a sense of community. For all that they might have differences, they would pull together to support one another in the face of common problems or a common enemy – factors, bailiffs, beasties, middens or drunken men. It is also important to point out that not only did neighbours generally support one another but there was also a very strong extended family – grandparents, aunts and uncles often lived in the same street, giving a real sense of security for children.

Despite the huge housing and social problems, Glaswegians had an enormous sense of belonging. There was also a great deal of what psychologists now call 'pro social values'. One of the most commonly reported aspects of life during these times was trust: few people locked their door or worried about lending to neighbours. The fear of crime in general was minimal.

Academics refer to social cohesion and interaction as 'social capital'. Robert Putnam, author of *Bowling Alone* and the main thinker behind these ideas, defines social capital as 'the collective value of all "social networks" and the inclinations that arise from these networks to do things for each other.' [27] Other thinkers define it as a collective mental disposition towards community life. Putnam argues that participation in local groups is both an expression, and a builder, of trust and co-operation and is fundamentally important to the running of good societies and the creation of 'civic mindedness'. Where social capital is high people trust one another and interact in various social ways, and are also more like to read newspapers and vote in elections. Putnam makes a distinction between two different types of social capital – bonding and bridging. *Bonding* social capital refers to the social networks valued and created by members of socially homogeneous groups. Gangs or sectarian groups such as the Orange Order are high in bonding social capital. *Bridging* social capital refers to social networks which 'bridge' socially heterogeneous groups. Glasgow's Orpheus Choir, for example, demonstrated bridging social capital as did the Independent Labour Party as both drew members from across the city. Putnam's research shows that both bridging and bonding social capital are advantageous for individuals as group membership confers health benefits. However, it is only bridging social capital that really benefits society. If we turn to men's alliances we shall see how Glasgow has often excelled at bonding, but not bridging, social capital.

In the past few centuries, as now, men's friendship and alliances with other men were often played out in public houses and in passionate support for football teams, such as Rangers and Celtic. Celtic Football Club was formally founded by Brother Walfrid, an Irish Marist brother, in 1887. The purpose stated in the official club records was 'to alleviate poverty in Glasgow's East End parishes'. The following year Celtic played their first official match against Rangers in what was described as a 'friendly encounter'. Rangers later came to be identified with the Scottish Protestant community and until very recent times, Rangers had an 'unwritten policy' of not playing Catholics. Of course, football in Glasgow has always been more than just the Old Firm. The erudite Bob Crampsey illustrated how important football had been in Glasgow's history:

> During the first sixty years of this [twentieth]
> century, Glasgow could make a very plausible claim
> to be regarded as the football capital of the world.
> For almost all of that period, the city could boast six
> First Division clubs, two grounds that would and did
> accommodate more than 100,000 spectators,
> another that would hold upwards of 80,000, and a
> fourth with a capacity of 50,000. These hordes would
> stand on railway sleepers, perilously close to ash
> banks, and they would endure the Scottish climate in
> all its rigorous variety. They provided their own food
> or feasted upon cold mutton pies of doubtful vintage
> and pedigree. (A long-standing joke at the ground of
> Partick Thistle, where for a while the pies were of a
> brand known as V.C., was that you really should have
> won it before eating one.) [28]

In the twentieth century there was a large number of clubs
and societies men and boys could become involved in, such as
socialist Sunday schools, cycling clubs, harriers, improvement
societies and the Boys' Brigade. There's little doubt that the
adverse conditions in Glasgow led to a great deal of social
bonding for men. Social commentators also point out that gangs,
common in Glasgow since the 1930s, are often based on close
relationships within the gang. Indeed members are often
prepared to die to protect one another.

In workplaces too solidarity was common. In 2001 Martin
Bellamy compiled *The Shipbuilders: an anthology of Scottish
shipyard life*. This gives a detailed picture of what life was like
in the shipyards and is drawn from a wide variety of sources.
One of the striking features is how inhumane the working
conditions were – the dirt, the noise and the continual bitter
cold in winter. Many of the jobs were dangerous – deaths and
serious injurious were common. In this environment men were

aware that life and limb depended on their workmates and there are plenty of examples, in this and other industries, of men who were prepared to risk their lives for their workmates. This mutual dependence encouraged camaraderie both in and out of the yard. Indeed it is common for ex-workers and managers to point out that the shipyard was a highly charged, *emotional* environment.[29] There were constant battles with management over tea breaks and conditions of service. By all accounts managers were fairly ruthless, unsympathetic to the hard conditions and prepared to blacklist complainants. By the twentieth century there was a pronounced 'us and them' feeling between workers and management. This provided fertile territory for communist and socialist groups which were always very active in the yards though they never had majority support. There was also lots of underhand dealing in materials and goods belonging to the shipyards and pilfering was common. All this added to the emotionally charged, us and them atmosphere.

Glasgwegians really pride themselves on their humour and workplaces were full of comedy. Much of Glasgow's humour also comes from inflation and exaggeration. 'The most characteristic rhetorical form is hyperbole,' writes Ian Spring, who then treats us to a few standard examples: 'bite an ear (verbally pester); away with the fairies (out of touch with reality), I could eat a scabby dog (I'm hungry), his face trippin him (looking unhappy), hair like straw hingin oot a midden (untidy coiffure). . . [30] Encouraging people to exaggerate for laughs and for effect is a good recipe not just for fun but for the creation of larger than life characters. The humour and characters in Glasgow workplaces, particularly the shipyards is legendary. The artist and former shipyard worker Tom McKendrick argues that the yards were so noisy that it was difficult to communicate and so miming became the order of the day. When they could talk at breaktime:

> . . .it was a grand opportunity, after you had been forcibly quietened for four or five hours, to come out with the boasting and the great tales and all that kind of stuff. Out of that grew a kind of mythology; a kind of bravado, macho tale-telling where you were the hero. . . When anybody ever told a good story it would eventually come down through the generations and be embossed and embellished. [31]

So the yards provided a great environment for the patter merchants and those with the gift of the gab. Given the size of the yards there were bound to be extremely talented men, like Billy Connolly, in their midst. Spontaneous events sometimes happened at lunch time where some of the workers would entertain their mates. Graffiti and cartoons appeared everywhere. Just about everyone had a nickname. The trick here was to latch on to something different about the person and use that for their name. So a man that liked to keep his boots clean was 'Cherry Blossom' and a couple of fat guys would be 'Pinky and Perky'. My favourite is the name, 'Bonus Notches', given to a bloke who wore a baseball cap back to front on his oversized head. . . Practical jokes were also common and could often involve minor injuries – for example, putting lighted cloths in the toilet trenches. The apprentices often bore the brunt of this humour. We've all heard about being sent for 'long stands' and pots of tartan paint. Tom McKendrick says, 'Apprenticeship was a strange sort of business. You're sort of taken into their care and taken the Mickey out of simultaneously.' Some of the men talked to you but generally it was a kind of abusive situation'.[32]

Much of Glasgow's humour in the past and now is funny and creative but, as McKendrick indicates, there can be a negative side to it as well: it often involves finding people's weak spot or exaggerating something different about them. This can be their hobbies or interests but it is often things they can't help, like a speech impediment, their families or where they come from.

There was another dark side to the yards – the support between working men could easily be undercut by tribal allegiances:

> Religious conflict was never far away in shipbuilding
> . . . Sectarian slogans were found everywhere,
> chalked all over bulkheads and on workshop walls,
> and discrimination on religious grounds became
> simply a fact of life. Much of this friction was
> resolved in good-humoured banter, but inevitably,
> when tensions became unbearable, violence would
> break out. [33]

There was also, in the words of Martin Bellamy, 'a rigid caste system that developed among the different categories of workers' and which led to 'conflict'. [34] This was not only bad for the relationships between the men but ultimately for the viability of the yards themselves as it led to demarcation disputes and 'craft jealousy'. As new ways of working evolved each trade was more focussed on its own interests than the long term survival of the industry.

Many commentators on Glasgow, and the west of Scotland, throughout history noted how friendly the people were – how they talk to strangers at bus stops, will go out of their way for people who need help, will share their last crust of bread and generally seem open and supportive. This is often talked about in terms of Glaswegian's basic 'humanity' and feelings of social solidarity.

William McIlvanney has written on this aspect of life in the west of Scotland. He tells us that he loves the people, particularly their scepticism, deflating humour, creativity with words, resilience and generosity of spirit. McIlvanney, however, is aware of the irony of Glasgow – the friendliness and kindness alongside the aggression and violence. 'Kind people who batter unkindness – the rose with the thorns.' [35] Thus he tell stories of men helping out defenceless strangers, or youngsters using violence themselves. He tells us that, as a young man, he had to come to terms with some of the city's contradictions:

> . . . the ferocity of its sectarianism, that weird,
> warped creature that haunts the Scottish psyche,
> sustaining itself on the iron rations of Rangers-
> Celtic games and offering meaningless aggression
> like a Japanese solider lost for years on some
> Pacific island and still fighting a war that is long
> still over; to understand the strong, instinctive
> socialism of the city. . . [36]

Of course, particularly in the twentieth century, Glasgow has seen the rise of strong trade unions and a rich seam of socialist activity has developed, some of it admirable. But we must be careful not to see Glasgow's past through rose-coloured spectacles as this blinds us to essential truths – most notably that Glasgow hasn't a particularly egalitarian culture but does have a rigidly policed pecking order. The hurt inflicted by this pronounced social hierarchy cannot be dismissed as superficial. Historically and contemporarily, Glaswegians can be friendly, supportive and humorous but many bear deep physical and psychological scars. Taking a leaf out of one of McIlvanney's books we could call them 'the walking wounded' and I'm thinking here of the men who are dying at 55 or on incapacity benefit; the boys who are involved in nightly gang fights.

If we bear in mind the poor relationships traditionally between men and women – soured by whisky and selfishness; poor paternal relationships; and the violence and aggression inherent in many Glasgow men's lives, then it is clear that the psychological need for relatedness has not consistently been met for many male Glaswegians. What they often had instead was a general feeling of bonding with the city ('I belong to Glasgow') or its culture; a close association to their workmates or trades union; and the bonds formed though regular drinking and support for football teams – bonds often made tighter through sectarian allegiances. Traditionally women may have fared better on relatedness, usually forming closer relationships with their children than their husbands and often with other women in a similar position. However, relationships with men, particularly when men were so often absent or violent, would have detracted considerably from the basic psychological need to feel supported, valued and appreciated.

So, does Glasgow's history suggest that overall basic psychological needs for autonomy, competence and relatedness were met?' Well, we've just seen the assessment on relatedness. On autonomy, the answer is emphatically no: Glasgow folk have had little control over their lives. It was much more about oppression than volition. On competence, Glasgow men, in skilled work at least, had important opportunities to experience themselves as effective and capable but they were always prey to their job disappearing in an economic downturn.

So all things considered, Glasgow's culture has failed to

provide a fertile soil to fulfil all three psychological needs. The fact that the old traditional industries went into terminal decline in the 1970s and 80s, weakening competence, by far the strongest of the three psychological nutriments for Glasgow's men, was sure to spell disaster for many of them, and ultimately, their communities and families. This simple fact can help us see why so many of Glasgow's men languish, rather than flourish.

CHAPTER 9
Edification, elevation and dependency

A STUDY of the history of Glasgow makes one thing clear: state intervention improved the lives of ordinary Glaswegians. The market – in the form of private landlords – had failed to provide enough decent houses, not just for the poor but for ordinary working class citizens, thus condemning them to life in the most abject slums. Lloyd George's Liberals had promised 'a land fit for heroes' at the end of World War I but did not deliver. It was ultimately a series of Labour governments, and Labour councils, which did most to provide state housing, benefits and free health care. It was the Westminster government which forced employers to operate within a regulatory framework guaranteeing fair treatment for workers. It was state planning too which bailed out the economy making sure that workers on Clydeside and other regions had a job. But, while for the people of Glasgow this state intervention was necessary and saved lives in the short term, it came at a huge cost.

Socialist politics

In the nineteenth century Glasgow was predominantly a Liberal city but with the extension of the franchise came the support for more radical politics. Keir Hardie, the founder of the Labour Party, was from Lanarkshire and by the beginning of the twentieth century the west of Scotland had developed into a socialist hub. Given the rent strikes, anti-war protests, trade union agitation and strong support for socialist candidates during elections, the term Red Clydeside had some justification in fact. In 1922 ten of Glasgow's fifteen parliamentary seats went to Independent Labour Party candidates. Understandably it was the appalling poverty of thousands of Glaswegians which was the major focal point for the city's ILP MPs.

Marxist 'scientific socialism' had some influence on the Clyde – mainly through the activities of the revolutionary socialist figure John Maclean – but it was more common for local socialists to have an ethical and idealistic base to their beliefs, ignoring the more economic arguments for large scale change. Indeed many writers on socialism in Scotland point out how religion played a greater part in the movement's ideology than Marxism. For example, the influences on Keir Hardie were mainly religious. An ILP colleague said of Hardie: 'So far as he was influenced towards socialism by the ideas of others it was. . . by the Bible, the songs of Burns, the writings of Carlyle, Ruskin and Mill, and the democratic traditions in working class homes in Scotland in his early days'.[1] James Maxton always said that socialism was his 'religion'.

One of the most striking features of the socialist movement which developed in Glasgow during this period is that it had a holistic notion of people – this was not only about material improvement but the full development of individuals and communities – and not in some vague future but now. This is why there was a flowering in Glasgow of a whole range of specifically socialist organisations – cycling clubs, rambling associations, Sunday schools, drama groups, youth groups and choirs. Education too was a major motivator and socialist discussion groups, reading groups, lectures and evening classes were common. Many of the movement's leaders had been teachers. Glasgow's ILP was not a centralised organisation but a loose federation of branches as well as women's organisations and other radical groups. Its main means of communication was via its newspaper *Forward*. The movement's vision was often expressed in terms of 'well-being' and 'happiness' and also emphasised the importance of 'spiritual emancipation'.

If we see spirituality as a way of entering into communion with others to celebrate the importance of human beings' higher nature, or willingness to uphold human values, we can see how it was indeed an essential element of Glasgow's socialist movement. For example at a Socialist Sunday school, 'there was a naming ceremony where a big crowd sang socialist songs. . . four little girls put flowers on the baby for purity'.[2] From the 1890s on, cycling became a favourite pastime and resulted in some thriving clubs dedicated to the competitive side of the sport. However, what is more interesting for our purposes is that many of these outdoor, recreational organisations had political leanings. For example, the Clarion Cycling Scouts was a socialist organisation which considered itself part of the labour movement. It used fields near Carbeth to camp out *en masse* in summer months. This was an area which attracted many working people from the city. Ralph Glasser describes the Socialist Camp at Carbeth Muir in his autobiography. Even on the long walk from the tram terminus at Milngavie, on a Friday night after work, there was plenty scope for support and solidarity. It was common to meet folk having a 'drum-up' at a fire and, although you were a stranger they would invite you to join them. Glasser recounts:

> A space was made for you, and someone with
> spare tea in a billy can would pour you some, to
> refresh you while you brewed up your own, to be
> shared in its turn, and you moved into the flow of
> talk as if you had been there all the time. . . Staying
> and tending the fire while you finished your own
> drum-up, you might hear other footfalls approach,
> and you in turn would hail a pack-laden figure or
> little group to join you at the fire. [3]

Indeed it was this constant trek of folk which led people to talk about 'the Everlasting Fire' at Craigallion Loch. In 1919 the local landowner at Carbeth gave some working folk permission to erect huts on his land, though the main development took place in the 1930s. In researching this book on Glasgow, the fire at Craigallion has constantly served as a beacon of hope – proof that there was a point in Glasgow's history where some poor people pursued a life which not only helped them to cope with the stresses and strains of daily existence but also to gain a sense of meaning and fulfilment – a spiritual experience.

The ritual of sharing a campfire and tea with strangers walking the same path is a communion of sort, whose spiritual sense would have been heightened by being out in the natural world. The underlying spiritual values of the movement can also be seen in what Professor Smout calls the 'Messianic scenes' when the Clydeside MPs were sent off from Glasgow in the train following their success in the 1922 election:

> . . . the MPs publicly pledged themselves to 'abjure
> vanity and self-aggrandisement' and to recognise
> 'that their only righteous purpose is to promote
> the welfare of their fellow-citizens and the well-
> being of mankind'. The ringing echoes of a
> tradition as radical as it was socialist were caught

again in the mass singing of two Covenanting
psalms, the 23rd and the 124th. 'Had not the Lord
been on our side.' The crowd sang the Red Flag in
a more modern tone as they made their way to St.
Enoch Station. . . [4]

Of course it is easy to be cynical about this chapter in Glasgow's history. We can point out that the socialism of the Clyde has often been exaggerated. More folk went to the football on a Saturday than accompanied the ILPers to the train. We can snort at the gullibility of Clydeside communists who supported the Russian revolution and became apologists for Stalinism and repression. We can deride the mainstream Labour Party of this period for watering down their commitment to real change and scoff at the fact that several ILP firebrands became establishment figures.

Nonetheless we cannot take away the fact that during the dark years when living conditions were so bad, this socialist movement gave people hope. It is much easier for people to endure if they think that change is possible – if they feel hopeful for the future. Contemporary psychological studies show that hope is important not just for achieving goals in life – without it we are likely to give up – but hope also benefits our well-being. [5]

Moreover, the basic creed to which these socialists cleaved concerned fundamental human equality, respect and human dignity. It contained, therefore, some of the necessary ingredients to heal some of the damage wrought by profound inequality and the indignity of living in such atrocious conditions. By continually emphasising the importance of community and sharing, it also had the capacity to heal some of the fissures evident within the city – between skilled and unskilled labour or between Catholics and Protestants. Yes there was a split to some extent along religious lines with more Catholics drawn to Labour politics and Protestants more to Conservative Unionism but this was not a definite divide. The socialist movement drew in people from all denominations as well as atheists and agnostics.

The ILP was founded in Bradford in 1893 and throughout the UK the party pursued a broad agenda for change and operated in ways which were not overly centralised. However, there's little doubt that it was 'in Glasgow. . . that this crusade reached its height' [6] and Glasgow retained an ILP MP, in the shape of James Maxton, until his death in 1946. In Glasgow's history, Maxton's story is one of the most edifying chapters.

Maxton – man and politician

James Maxton was born in 1885 and raised in Pollokshaws. His parents were both teachers. He went to the University of Glasgow and admitted that his early political sympathies were Conservative. Maxton's conversion to socialism partly came about via the influence of a fellow Marxist student, John Maclean, but was even more the result of his experience of poverty when he became a teacher working in Glasgow schools. He became a member of the Independent Labour Party, as did other members of his family. His personal life was rather tragic: he married and his son was a weak child whose life hung by a thread. Maxton's wife, herself constitutionally weak, put everything into nursing the infant and she herself died when the two-year old was just beginning to thrive. Maxton himself was no picture of health: he was always gaunt, and in most photos he has a cigarette in his hand, testifying to the fact he was a chain smoker. He had a stomach ulcer as a fairly young man and died, aged 61, of stomach cancer.

Maxton was a life-long pacifist and vociferously opposed to World War I. He was imprisoned for a year in 1916, in fairly tough conditions, for his seditious anti-war campaigning. He was sacked from teaching and ended up working as an unskilled labourer in a shipyard not involved in war work. He became a full time organiser for the ILP and in 1922 was returned to Westminster as an ILP MP for Glasgow Bridgeton – a seat he held until his death in 1946. He died a darling of the House of Commons. Churchill described him as 'the greatest parliament-arian of his day' and 'the greatest gentleman of the House of Commons.' [7]

Given these accolades and the fact that fellow ILPers, once great radicals, toned down their politics and became part of the establishment, it is easy to dismiss Maxton as a dilettante and a sell-out. But in his 22 years in the House of Commons Maxton did not depart from his code: he did not take any honour or appointment. He even gracefully turned down the offer of an honorary degree from the University of Edinburgh. He also upheld his decision not to socialise in the houses of the great and the good. He may not have achieved much politically but he was always true to what he believed in and continued to champion the cause of his constituents and the interests of ordinary working class folk round the world who were often trampled on by the rich and powerful. He supported the ILP's disaffiliation from the Labour Party as he would not agree to stop criticising mainstream Labour policies which he saw as a dilution of the party's original aims. It is evident from reading about the man that Maxton was not cut out to be a machine politician. He did not have the politician's instincts to trim beliefs for votes or for political power. Nor did he see himself as a maker of laws or an architect of detailed change. He rightly saw himself as a campaigner and someone who must, no matter what, give voice to what he saw as the truth.

Maxton wanted to see a democratic shift towards a radically different type of society which would meet everyone's material and non-material needs. He did not think this would happen unless the mass of people were convinced of the need to make this change and he would not have wanted a new order imposed against the will of the majority. He hated dictatorship in any form – the idea of the dictatorship of the proletariat, central to Marxist thought, was anathema to him. It was Maxton's belief in the necessity of convincing the majority of the need for change that led him to put so much energy and commitment into his speeches. In other words, talking was his contribution to helping bring about the socialist society he longed for. His official biographer, John McNair, asserts that Maxton 'made more socialists' than any other speaker. It is certainly often said that he gave more speeches than any other politician. A contemp-orary journalist, and former MP, claimed that Maxton was 'the greatest parliamentarian in the House' and 'the finest orator in the land'. [8] No small feat given that he was contending with the likes of Lloyd George and Winston Churchill for this accolade.

Maxton did not make set speeches nor write them in advance. Instead he was a spontaneous speaker, responding to the issues of the day and the concerns and mood of his audience. It was the lack of artifice in his speeches, the naturalness of his communication and the courage of his convictions which meant that people, even those who disagreed with his sentiments and political solutions, appreciated his honesty and integrity. In the words of one South African journalist he had 'a voice that beguiles all who hear it'. [9] One of Maxton's great gifts was his ability to put complex arguments simply and with reason and compassion. In many ways, he stated the obvious and drew people's attention to uncomfortable and inconvenient truths. The following – a speech on poverty in Glasgow in the House of Commons after the ILP had broken off links with the Labour Party – is a brilliant example of Maxton in action:

> . . .The basic cause of the trouble is that the people are poor, and every proposal that is made to make them less poor is rejected with scorn. Whether it is the unemployed man, the sick man or the employed man on low wages, there is a refusal to do anything to alleviate the conditions, and always the reply, which I am accepting, that it cannot be done without bringing the system down in collapse. That is the answer. If you ask for the absorption of the 3,000,000 unemployed by distributing the labour over the whole community by reducing hours, it cannot be done. If you ask for better benefits for the unemployed, we cannot afford it. If you ask the Government to maintain the housing subsidy, and to make a big drive to get everyone in a good house, it cannot be done. I agree. You have proved your case too well. Your capitalistic system cannot relieve the people of poverty. . . You have got to make up your mind consciously to go into the future boldly and with courage. The mass of the people, particularly the upper and middle classes, are afraid to face the future, afraid to go boldly forward facing the world with their hands and their brains. They are afraid that if they have not got their stocks and shares and estates, life will be too difficult for them. The educated people, the aristocracy, the blue-blooded

> people are afraid to face life; the captains of industry,
> the great bankers, are afraid to face life on the same
> conditions as that poor woman in my division who
> faced it with a laugh. [10]

As we have seen, the ILP movement in Glasgow had a broad view of the change they sought: this was not all about material advancement. Maxton too underscored the importance of a broad, humanist agenda. Of course he wanted his constituents to have more money and a better quality of life. But this was not the sum total of his ambition or vision. John McNair sums up Maxton's concerns 'as a complete philosophy of life extending to all spheres of human relationships and with particular emphasis upon the development of the human personality.' [11] Later he adds:

> His vision of the world was of a fruitful and
> beneficent sphere inhabited by reasonable and
> happy men and women. This was his basic political
> philosophy from which he never deviated. It
> dominated his political career. . . [12]

Given that Maxton's vision encompassed how we conduct ourselves in everyday lives he abhorred the idea that the ends could ever justify the means. He believed that nothing good could come from violent power struggles, for example, and always emphasised the importance of democracy. Speaking to a potential biographer Maxton said, 'Write me as one who loved his fellow men.' [13] And it is his personal qualities, and how they were completely congruent with his philosophy of life, that makes him such an estimable character, particularly for a politician where expediency so often has the upper hand.

Some commentators make out that Maxton was neutered

politically; that his opponents could lavish praise on him because he posed no threat and that he allowed his head to be turned. But they are wrong. Maxton believed passionately in basic human decency. He always tried to see the best in people and to appeal to their better instincts. In trying to win people over to the cause of 'truth, justice and prosperity for all' [14] Maxton was more likely to speak of love than hate: more likely to appeal to compassion and tolerance than evoke bitterness or resentment.

This does not mean that Maxton shied away from critical comment and he could be forthright in his condemnation of inhuman conditions. On one occasion he was expelled from the House of Commons for referring to those, who had decided to remove free milk from school children who were already undernourished, as 'murderers'. Some who knew him saw the key to his personality and success as being his fundamental belief in human equality. He could relate to, and was essentially the same with, everyone he met – fellow prisoners in Calton jail or Winston Churchill. This allowed Maxton to be on friendly terms with his political opponents without ever being subservient or compromising his views.

McNair affirms Maxton's character when he writes that his subject: 'was immune from the moral diseases of self-seeking, of material ambition or of the striving after authority or power'. [15]

Inspirational is the obvious term we could use with regards to James Maxton. But nowadays, some psychologists use the world 'elevation' to refer to the feeling often generated by witnessing an act of kindness, for example, or when we feel we are in the presence of someone acting out of 'pro-social values'. [16] Even witnessing someone acting in a positive, humane way can make an individual feel dignified and 'elevated' by it. This feeling is then likely to inspire the person to do something positive. This is why the Maxtons of this world can help create virtuous circles. They bring out the best in people and by helping to create a positive atmosphere make it more likely for people to collaborate and get on.

At one level it is easy to say that Maxton as a politician was spectacularly unsuccessful. Unlike his colleague John Wheatley there is no particular piece of legislation which he could claim his own. He did not even bring forward private member's bills. When he died in 1946 he was the only remaining ILP MP and the party was a completely spent force. However, it would be wrong to say that Maxton was unsuccessful. His aim was never to create or sustain a particular political machine; it was to convert people to the need for a new society. Of course, we do not have the socialist society which he sought but many of the changes he championed have come about. Maxton once recounted that in his class of sixty eleven years olds in Bridgeton over half could not 'bring both knees and heels together because of rickety malformations.' [17] Nothing like this still exists in Glasgow. Most of the great scourges of his constituency – TB, infant deaths, insanitary conditions – disappeared decades ago. Many of the measures he desired have been enacted: state pensions, free health care, social security benefits, subsidised council housing. These came about for complex reasons but one of the most important is that the *Zeitgeist* changed. Stark poverty and its terrible handmaidens became indefensible and insupportable. Maxton was the main person who pricked the nation's conscience and kept an entirely expedient Labour Party on its toes.

The ILPers

So what happened to some of the others ILP MPs who were waved off on the London train and what were their political dilemmas? John Wheatley, originally from Ireland was the founder of the Catholic Socialist Society and the man responsible for encouraging Glasgow Catholics to vote Labour, rather than Liberal. A close ally of Maxton's he was considered the ILP strategist. He was the author of the influential ILP publication *Socialism in Our Time* and became a minister in the Labour minority Government in 1923, under the leadership of Ramsay MacDonald. Wheatley became the architect of the only useful initiative of this government: he devised and piloted through Westminster a Housing Act which provided subsidies for public housing and laid the framework for the development of council housing in the UK. He did not dilute his radical politics, was not offered office in the 1929 Government and died suddenly in 1930, aged 61.

David Kirkwood was a Church elder and former engineer. He represented Dumbarton Burghs, including Clydebank, for the ILP and was particularly interested in the fate of the yards and the high unemployment rate on Clydeside. Kirkwood was instrumental in clinching the deal which saw John Brown's win the contract for the *Queen Mary* in 1933. Kirkwood left the ILP for the mainstream Labour Party. He became a Privy Councillor and also accepted a Peerage, ending his life not simply as Baron Kirkwood, but as an establishment figure. Fellow radical MP Emmanuel (Manny) Shinwell did likewise.

The man who helped these ILPers get on what, for some of them, became a gravy train, was Patrick Dollan, an early pacificist and rent strike organiser. He was later to defect to mainstream

Labour and ran the city's political machine. He became a Glasgow Provost and later accepted a knighthood.

The more complex character on board the train to Westminster was Tom Johnston. He founded and edited the ILP paper, *Forward*. He was a passionate, and steadfast campaigner, for women's suffrage. He also wrote a book still treated reverentially in Scotland – *Our Scots Noble Families*. This was a polemical attack on landlords and aristocrats in Scotland and purported to show that most had acquired their landed estates through theft, pillage or other crimes. Johnston was involved in municipal politics in Kirkintilloch where he successfully cut his political teeth with a number of innovative approaches. Johnston also left the ILP for the mainstream Labour Party. Johnston became Secretary of State for Scotland during the wartime coalition Government and became a great advocate for state planning and control. He never accepted any honours or even fees to chair numerous boards after his retirement from politics.

One of the problems for the radical west of Scotland ILP MPs was the scale of the problem in their midst. Of course, other cities in the UK had slums and some areas where there might be terrible conditions of the same magnitude. But Glasgow's problems were on an altogether different scale in terms of numbers of people affected. A second problem facing these MPs was their nationalism. Wheatley, Johnston and Maxton, for example, were all socialist and nationalist firebrands before they were elected to Westminster. They passionately wanted to see a parliament in Edinburgh which would bring about the socialist policies they longed for. Within a few years of being at Westminster that commitment was overturned – they became convinced that Scotland on its own did not have the resources to solve the huge social and economic problems of the west of Scotland. In short, they believed that that the Union – in the shape of English money – was needed to raise living standards in Glasgow to a tolerable level and improve the economy. Tom Johnston famously said: 'What purpose would there be in our getting a Scots Parliament in Edinburgh if it has to administer an emigration system, a glorified Poor Law, and a graveyard?'[18]

Scotland, socialism and nationalism

Thereafter it was common for some thinkers and cultural figures in Scotland to believe that they were faced with a choice of socialist policies or a commitment to Scottish independence. Writing in 1934, the writer Lewis Grassic Gibbon put the problem thus:

> If it came (as it may come) to some fantastic choice between a free and independent Scotland, a centre of culture. . . and providing the elementary decencies of food and shelter to the submerged proletariat of Glasgow and Scotland, I at least would have no doubt as to which side of the battle I would range myself. For the cleansing of that horror, if cleanse it they could, I would welcome the English in suzerainty over Scotland till the end of time. [19]

It was the failure of the socialists to maintain their interest in Scotland as a nation which led to the establishment of a specifically nationalist party in 1928 and to a massive cleavage in Scottish politics between the SNP (as it became) and Labour. Even though there have been attempts to bridge this divide (such as Jim Sillars' Scottish Labour Party) and the Labour Party reinstated and acted upon its commitment to a Scottish parliament, visceral hostility between the SNP and Labour is still palpable within contemporary Scotland.

As a general rule I think it useful to look at the past to learn from it but not to agonise over it or say 'if only'. However, in Glasgow's case the scale of the social and economic problems were so enormous in the nineteenth and twentieth centuries that it is difficult not to pose the question: would things have been different if Scotland has been an independent nation as opposed to a junior partner in the Union, and governed largely from Westminster? I am certainly not convinced that the values predominant in nineteenth century Scotland were particularly benign or would have led to progressive social policies. Remember there was a strong current in Scottish thought which blamed the poor for their problems and poor relief was niggardly – less generous than in England.

However, if a Scottish Parliament had been solely responsible for dealing with the problems posed by Glasgow they might have taken earlier action to stop the effects of such overcrowding. Having full responsibility for the problem of the Glasgow slums might also have wrought a change of heart. Undoubtedly, Glasgow, indeed Scotland as a whole, suffered from Westminster neglect. There was hardly enough time on the floor of the House of Commons to debate the issue let alone pass the necessary legislation. The people of Glasgow were citizens of the United Kingdom and they were shamefully let down by Westminster politicians.

Even when socialists were elected to Parliament and the pressure for change became unavoidable it was difficult to know what could be done to ameliorate the problems facing the people of Glasgow. By the late 1920s, the economy of the west of Scotland, once dynamic and prosperous (at least for the industrialists), was showing itself to be in a much worse state than the rest of the UK. The economy was too dependent on a few interlocking industries, too vulnerable to the vicissitudes of the international markets and too many employers and workers were inflexible and opposed to change. Large scale unemployment seemed inevitable. Inequality and poverty were the result of the capitalist economic system, and its free market, but no one knew how to manage capitalism better. Given what was going on in Russia, arguing for revolutionary change on socialist grounds was understandably seen as anathema to British values and a vote loser.

Professor Tom Devine argues that in Scotland left-wing politicians, like the Liberals, had 'no intellectual answer to the problems of the inter-war economy.' [20] He also claims that the SNP 'had no coherent alternative strategy of economic reconstruction.' [21] The influential Tom Johnston ultimately changed his basic socialist philosophy. As the editor of *Forward* he had been at the core of a movement which believed in self-help and what we would now call 'empowerment'. The ILP never intended to become a disciplined, centralised party but a loose federation of organisations sharing the same vision of moral, educational and spiritual emancipation of the people through choirs, rambling, evening classes, democratic participation and the like. Of course, better housing and working conditions mattered but they were only the means to better lives, not ends in themselves. However, as T.C. Smout points out, when Johnston, a mainstream Labour MP, took office he basically jettisoned this philosophy in favour of the modern State's belief in the rule of the expert and the consensus of the well-informed. Beveridge and Keynes became his mentors, and committees 'representing all shades of opinion', appointed on his recommendation, his preferred mode of governing Scotland. [22]

This 'democratic deficit' remained until the establishment of the Scottish Parliament in 1999. As Smout also points out, this set-up might well have achieved some practical benefits but it was a far cry from the original political vision of the ILP or Johnston's early political career. The Welsh Labour politician Emrys Hughs said of his visit to Glasgow in the 1950s that 'all the colour and life and vitality seemed to have gone out of politics and apathy prevailed. . . the crusading socialist movement was as good as dead.' [23]

The Labour machine, anglification and dependency

In place of the myriad of socialist groups with their broad humanitarian ideals, there was a well-oiled Labour machine that got its vote out for parliamentary and local elections. The Labour Party easily dominated Glasgow Corporation for decades and in the eyes of many it was not a pretty sight. The historian Chrisopher Harvie describes it as the era of 'the wee hard men'.[24] Sociologist and housing expert Sean Damer refers to the leaders as the 'Murphiosi' – the local term, apparently, for the Catholic mafia at the helm of Glasgow's Labour machine.

Looking at the city's appalling statistics and at the bleak housing estates and housing blocks it is difficult to say that they have managed Glasgow well. In an early chapter we saw how even from the earliest days of housing estates and slum clearance in Glasgow, houses were allocated on a preferential basis to certain types of people thus ensuring the continuation of a strong hierarchy and pecking order. Sean Damer outlines the numerous charges that have been made over the years of corruption within the system in the allocation of houses to tenants and in the awarding of housing contracts. He also claims that 'the Murphiosi' were better on the technicalities of housing than on the 'aesthetic or social side'. Reflecting on developments in the 1930s he writes:

> Such design innovations as did occur were too little too late. The moral inspiration of the ILP and John Wheatley's dream of '£8 cottages for Glasgow Citizens' had been translated into a slick machine particularly adapted to getting the vote in and getting its people jobs in the Corporation – 'in out of the rain', as one uncorrupt retired official put it to me. But it had its successes in the numbers game. Between 1920 and 1939 no less than 50,277 council houses were built in Glasgow, proportionately more than in any other British city: Glasgow had achieved its 1919 target. The irony was this figure was nowhere near high enough. [25]

These figures show the extent of the problem to be solved and how it was almost inevitable that housing in Glasgow was dominated by quantity, not quality, thus leading to massive housing estates and high rise blocks. It also led to Glasgow's status as the city with the highest percentage of council housing outside the old Soviet bloc. Interestingly, Damer recounts taking a Polish film-maker, familiar with Stalinist housing estates, on a tour of Glasgow's council housing and she 'reacted with horror' maintaining that some were the worst she had ever experienced. [26]

Damer puts the blame for the worst problems of council housing at Glasgow Corporation's door. However, the economic and social historian Richard Rodger gives a different perspective. He argues that as soon as subsidies were available for building council houses the Westminster government used them to determine what was built. Indeed he quotes a Glasgow engineer from 1919 who claimed that the new financial subsidy 'gives the Local Government Board (in London) absolute autocratic powers'. [27] The Scottish Office, which Rodger refers to as 'an arm of Westminster-based government' controlled 'the purse strings and sanctioned the design and layout of housing proposals.' [28]

Another of Rodger's arguments is that the underlying design for council housing did not continue in Scotland's urban tradition of tenements, communal facilities or urban density which allowed for local shops and facilities. Instead Scottish housing was forced to adopt English cultural norms:

> The dominant housing ideology was based upon garden-city principles and influenced by English middle-class suburban values. Curved perspective and cul-de-sacs, open spaces and low building densities, broken building lines, rustic aspects, and individual garden plots were the crucial characteristics of garden-suburb design.[29]

Essentially this meant that housing post-1914 in Scotland began to look very different from what had gone before. The compact city was replaced by sprawling housing estates leading to a convergence between Scottish and English cities and towns. It is easy to condemn tenements on the basis of Glasgow's Victorian experience but this would be wrong. As we can see today, tenements can provide attractive dwellings and life-style much sought after by people who have the money to choose different alternatives. If the level of density is controlled properly tenements can provide compact accommodation and support shops and local services. This can sustain a sense of involvement and buzz, absent from many peripheral housing estates. Tenements are popular on the continent and provide good accommodation in urban areas. In many ways it was England, with its emphasis on the pastoral, which was out of step with how to provide houses in urban areas.

What ought to have happened is that when plans were being drawn up for new houses prospective tenants ought to have been consulted on what they wanted. Many might well have said that they were fed up with tenements and wanted their 'own back and front door' – a common desire among working class women with families living in flats. Tenements are attractive to live in but less so for women with families. However, the point is that tenants were not properly consulted. Rodger reports that when officials consulted women they did so once terms of reference on the type of housing had been established and so their input was on details such as the size or location of cupboards, cooking facilities and the like rather then more fundamental design or planning issues. Even if they had said they wanted to live in a garden-suburb Rodger might well be right in claiming that their views on what was desirable had been shaped by cultural 'colonisation'. As bungalows became popular with the Scottish middle classes, and 'bungalow belts' started to ring many Scottish towns and cities, after 1914 Scotland lost its distinctive urban forms and was to all purposes Anglified.

Another of the negative aspects to emerge from Rodger's analysis is that while England dictated the housing styles to be followed and many new houses were built, Scottish overcrowding continued. He quotes figures which show that Scotland continued to build 'undersized' houses. Indeed even as the tenants flitted in, their new house was, by English standards, overcrowded. For example, between 1919 and 1939 the proportion of new Glasgow houses with four or more rooms was 28 per cent whereas in Liverpool it was 89 per cent. That city had 35 per cent of its dwellings with five or more rooms whereas the figure in Glasgow was only 4 per cent. This meant that while more and more houses were built in Glasgow overcrowding, and hence the housing problem, remained right up to the 1960s.

Rodger does not explain why Scottish houses were more cramped but presumably it was due to the sheer number of houses which councils needed to build as well as the available cash. But it may also have been due to the local culture itself. As seen in previous chapters, Glasgow was less of a consumer-oriented culture and men were less involved in family life than many of their English counterparts. This could have affected the attitude of decision-makers who were mainly men. A third of Liverpool's council housing built in the first few decades of the twentieth century had parlours or front rooms, whereas the equivalent for Glasgow was one per cent. No self-respecting Labour man in Scotland would ever have argued for the need for a front room. However, having this extra room can allow families to have hobbies or space for reading, music, doing homework or simply just having some quiet time. Space can help family life: it is not all about bourgeois pretensions.

In *A Century of the Scottish People 1830-1950* T.C. Smout writes the following about Patrick Dollan and the record of Glasgow Labour:

> Dollan manipulated an electorate frightened by the
> immense scale of unemployment and industrial
> collapse, lacking the confidence for new adventure,
> distrustful of Tory and Liberal after the war. . .
> Meanwhile the party kept its pledges to leave the
> Catholic schools with full State support. Labour in
> Scotland became synonymous with the defence of
> council housing, jobs in heavy industry and sectarian
> schools: it had nothing whatever to do with
> participatory democracy, enthusiasm for socialism or
> hope for the future. [30]

Glasgow Labour helped to ensure that people were better housed, clothed and fed, but it did not abolish or reduce real poverty or feelings of powerlessness. The poverty I'm referring to is not just material deprivation, but spiritual deprivation, impoverished relationships and the lack of desire and ambition to make something of yourself and your life. In a previous book I argued that in Scotland the combination of strong collectivist values and the belief in egalitarianism (even though everyone does not start out in life equal) encourages people to know their place. It encourages us all to toe the line and conform. When we add to these attitudes the dependency which welfare policies and corporatism can encourage, it is easy to see why Glasgow should become plagued not just with social but economic problems: low productivity, low business birth rate, and many impoverished communities where people seem to be devoid of motivation and ambition for themselves or their families.

Chapter 10
'The three Bs'

School, even more than home, was a source of
continual tension, a perpetual challenge not only to
your intellect, but to your survival as a free being,
besetting you on all sides with bogey men that sprang
up like dragon's teeth: you seized one by the throat
in desperation and another grinned in its place.
There was little rest. Play was never simply play, nor
learning simply learning. You were always being
tested. Tested in the morning for tables and whack
with the pointer if you were too slow. Tested for the
names of capital cities and dead kings, tested for
writing, up light and down heavy so that your fingers
clawed in cramp from the strain of controlling your
pen, tested for spelling, and spelling and spelling,
tested for the dozen rule, tested for the score rule,
tested every Friday so that your fingers trembled
independently in anticipation when you sat down at
your desk. [1]

SO WRITES Mary Rose Liverani of her 1940s education in
Glasgow. No wonder she sighed with relief as she set sail
for Australia with her family in 1951. But perhaps she was being
short-sighted – after all Scotland in those days boasted that it
had the best education system in the world.

Scotland was one of the first countries in the world to create
a nationwide education system, almost delivering John Knox's

vision of a 'school in every parish'. By international standards Scottish literacy levels were high in the seventeenth and eighteenth centuries. However, the pride the Scots often take in the country's educational achievements go much further than this: for centuries it has been widely believed that Scottish education has particularly democratic and egalitarian antecedents. One of the most influential Scottish books in the twentieth century is *The Democratic Intellect* by George Davie – a term now widely used to convey the democratic and egalitarian traditions in Scottish education.[2] But this is misleading: Davie's book is about the nature of Scottish university education, particularly its generalist and philosophy-based curriculum and how this was expressly designed to counteract the elitism of specialisation. Davie did not himself use the term to embrace topics such as the running of Scottish schools or the type of people able to access university education.[3]

The idea of Scottish education as a particularly egalitarian system is often expressed in the term the 'lad o' pairts' – the idea of a poor country boy who, through access to education, could make something of his life. This is often contrasted with the English education system which is founded on much more elitist ideas and specifically designed to cater for the sons of well-to-do families. But Scotland's apparently radical approach to education was distinctly limited. Of course, there were those who genuinely wanted educational opportunity for all, however many wanted Scottish education to offer a ladder of opportunity for poor but academically gifted children as they saw this as a way to preserve the status quo. In other words, they thought that by allowing the more able of the lower orders to rise through the school system discontent would be controlled thereby constraining the rise of socialism or other radical ideas.[4]

Evaluating Scotland's egalitarian education credentials is not central to our purpose here but nonetheless it is important to point up two reasons for not being too impressed by the egalitarianism suggested by the 'lad o'pairts'. First, the term 'lad' is used for good reason. Girls were educated in parish schools, though not as commonly as boys, but they did not go on to university. For example, women could attend lectures at Scottish universities but not register for a degree until 1892 – fully 15 years behind the University of London. Secondly, there was a distinctly rural bias in Scottish education. Indeed the phrase the 'lad o' pairts' was first coined in 1894 by the man who also introduced the term 'kailyard'. It is an idealisation of parish schools where sons of ploughmen could sit next to children of ministers or even lairds. Indeed prior to the extension of education in the twentieth century, Scotland was one of the few countries where literacy levels were particularly high in rural areas. The usual pattern for neighbouring countries was better educational provision in towns and cities.[5]

The 'lad o' pairts' notion may be overused and the egalitarian nature of Scotland's rural schools exaggerated but it had some substance in fact. However, the story in Scotland's cities was often altogether different. In 1834 the Reverend George Lewis wrote a damning pamphlet, largely focussed on Glasgow, entitled *Scotland: A Half Educated Nation*. At that point there were 200 schools in the city, catering for a population of 200,000 but only eight of them were provided through the original parish framework: the remainder were private, religious or charitable affairs. In Glasgow in 1857 under half of five to ten year olds attended school at all – many of those not in attendance worked in warehouses, shops and factories. Since many of the schools in Glasgow were run by Protestant churches, Catholic children were most at risk of illiteracy. In 1857 only 13 out of 213 Glasgow schools catered for the huge number of children of Catholic immigrants. Despite these various constraining factors Scotland's literacy levels still held up well in comparison with England and internationally.

Attendance at school from the age of five till 13 was made compulsory in 1872 and ensured all children attended primary school but by the late 1890s 90 per cent of Scottish children still did not go to secondary school. Starting from a low particip- ation base, the Glasgow Education Board had a sizeable task in getting all children into primary school. According to an inspector's report in 1897 they did an admirable job:

> One who has visited fine schools in those grim
> streets that fringe the great arteries of traffic, and
> has seen the pale, pinched and joyless faces of the
> children can form some idea of the difficulties of
> the situation. [6]

The school leaving age was raised to 14 in 1883 but there was provision for this to be 'half-time' once the child had reached ten. It was not until 1946 that the age was raised to 15 and then 16 in 1970.

For many gifted pupils from working class backgrounds poverty remained an insuperable barrier to staying on after 14: it wasn't just that parents couldn't afford the uniforms and other school necessities but also that they needed the youngsters bringing in a wage for the family. Despite this, Glasgow University had a higher proportion of students from working-class back- grounds than other places in Scotland and elsewhere. However, most of these came from families of skilled labourers and they usually went to university, not as school leavers, but in their twenties as a result of extensive study at evening classes. Many working men chose to study because, from the early twentieth century on, educational qualifications were essential for access into most professions. In 1938 Adam Collier published a study on the social background of university entrants in Glasgow which shows the extent of inequality in access, despite these mature students:

> In the post-war period 1926-35 there was roughly one entrant to every 20 children born in Social Class 1; in Social Class 2 (Artisan) the figure was one in 212; and in the lowest Social Class it was one in 550. . . Whereas in Social Class 1 the number of children born per entrant for law was of the order 200 to one, in the lowest social class this ratio was of the order 20,000 to one. In the case of medicine these ratios were approximately 70 to one and 6,000 to one. [7]

The number of girls from the lowest social classes reaching university was tiny. Even in 1968 when I first attended Strathclyde University as the daughter of an engine driver the number of girls like me from semi-skilled working-class backgrounds was under one per cent.

In urban areas, like Glasgow where there was pronounced geographical segregation by wealth, when local authority schools did appear they tended to cater for specific social classes. Indeed even though the egalitarian aspect of Scottish education was often played up, prior to 1914, there was open acceptance by some Scottish politicians and educational elites that secondary schools were largely middle class institutions as so few children from poor or working class backgrounds were admitted as pupils. Once secondary school education was extended to all pupils a system was devised to divide pupils, or schools, into 'academic' or 'non-academic'. This was the start of the notorious 'qualifying examination' which reigned in Scotland from the early twentieth century until the 1960s and, crudely speaking, was designed to separate the minority intelligent from the 'thick'. Once entrance to higher quality secondary education was based on formal academic selection decision makers interpreted the absence of children from the lower orders as proof of their intellectual inferiority. Thus the Scottish Education Department (SED) in 1921 declared:

> . . . there is no denying the fact that in every country only a relatively small percentage of the population will be endowed by nature with the mental equipment which they must possess if they are to profit by Secondary School or University study. A frank recognition of this truth is essential, if a proper organisation is to be established.[8]

In 1923 the SED issued its notorious 'Circular 44' which stopped common schooling after the age of 12 and laid out the structure for a twin track system – non-academic schools, latterly known as 'junior secondaries', and academic 'senior secondary' schools. This meant that at twelve children should be selected who showed 'promise of profiting' from a full five-years of study for Highers. The bar for success was set very high and those who were unable to make it were effectively deemed failures. The alternative was a more 'open system' which would allow pupils to benefit from this type of study even though they might not want to stay on to 17 or go on to university. Their achievements could have been recognised by Intermediate certificates. These certificates had existed but were abolished under this new system. What's more, the SED wanted the senior secondary schools located in better-off areas. Some local authorities, such as Dunbartonshire County Council, showed their opposition by continuing to send all pupils to the one school, though there they were streamed into academic and non-academic courses on the basis of their performance in the qualifying exam.

The SED's twin track system largely remained in place until the coming of comprehensive education in the 1960s. Devine maintains:

> The critics are correct to point out that these policies branded the majority of pupils as 'failures', intensified social divisions and produced a secondary educational system with glaring inequality. The SED strategy was imposed against the virtually unanimous opposition of Scottish educationalists, including the government's own Advisory Council on Education. . . In 1944 the Scottish Council for Research and Education estimated that at least a third of all pupils had the ability to be admitted to a full senior secondary course. But as late as 1951 only 5 per cent of school leavers had stayed on to complete the five-year course between the ages of 17-19, with nearly 90 per cent leaving at or before their fifteenth birthday. [9]

Indeed up till 1961 and the creation of 'O grades', almost 94 per cent of Scottish pupils left with no certificates whatsoever.

For decades Scottish education was dominated by discussion on how to cater for the differing abilities and needs of different classes of pupils. Some educationalists thought it best to accept that the vast majority of children would benefit most from a practically based education which would equip them for the world they were likely to inhabit. The authorities did not, however, dedicate the time and resources to make this happen. This strong academic bias in Scottish education was supported by teachers. Indeed the teaching profession itself was rigidly hierarchical. Status was given to male secondary teachers, with honours degrees and not to women, primary teachers or those specialising in practical subjects such as domestic science or technical. This does not mean to say that they were opposed to good educational opportunities for all, but they did see this in fairly conventional academic terms.

Circular 44 created an inherently elitist, academic system. Its strong bias towards the educational needs of the tiny minority of academic pupils, who would go on to university, meant that working class pupils were educated on the basis of a largely second-rate, watered-down academic curriculum which would never recognise their achievements. My father recalls that in his working-class Glasgow secondary school in the 1930s he was taught algebra but with no attempt to make it relevant or meaningful to his world, or the world he would ever inhabit as an industrial worker. Richard Finlay also maintains that in the 1930s, and earlier, in schools catering for working class children, class sizes were around fifty and 'the main teaching implements were the "three Bs": the Bible, belt and blackboard.' [10]

As this suggests, rote learning was common as was physical punishment. Indeed almost all Scottish teachers bought a tawse, a leather strap hardened with pig's blood, 'which was considered as vital an educational tool as the computer is today.'[11] Given the copious autobiographical accounts of teacher sadism, every school seemed to have its quota of nasty, neurotic, belt-happy teachers. Indeed in *Our Glasgow*, a series of personal reminiscences, the school recollections are mainly about being belted.

One man recalls being given an envelope in secondary school for art work:

> . . . I must have had a mental aberration. . . I drew
> a pair of lips on this envelope of mine. Big red lips,
> and I was taken out into the corridor and I was
> given six of these (*sic*) from the art teacher. This
> was a thrashing. I mean this guy wanted to kill me
> . . . psychopathic. There was a deathly silence
> when I went back in the room. Now they would be
> jailed for doing that. . . [12]

One of the best accounts of the unfairness of corporal punishment in Scottish schools, even in the 1960s, is cited by the novelist Janice Galloway. There had been some commotion when the teacher was out of the P6 class and so the head teacher belted everyone for 'disruptive behaviour'. She says that the worst case was of a 'scared little boy' who was so frightened he kept pulling his hands away. Once he was finally belted 'he dropped on his knees' but still was given another for good measure.[13] On the subject of unfairness, another man in *Our Glasgow* recalls that his teacher never marked his composition yet gave him fifteen of the belt – one for each word he spelled incorrectly. [14]

As the last story shows the belt was not reserved for behavioural misdemeanours, but handed out to any child not keeping up with the academic work such as making mistakes in spelling, reading or arithmetic. This meant that slow learners or those with learning difficulties were particularly vulnerable. Even 'nice' teachers used the belt – partly because it was the done thing and also because they feared losing the respect of pupils and colleagues if they were seen as being soft. The aggression didn't always involve the belt: my father recounts being late for primary school one day and the teacher (a future member of a Labour cabinet) taking him, and another latecomer, by the ear and running them along the corridor banging their heads together. Often the aggression was verbal as well as physical. One Scottish writer from the 1930s recalls how, even twenty years after leaving school, he could 'still wake up afraid, dreaming that I am in the infant room and that my teacher is enjoying a half-hour's sarcasm enforced with the tawse on a class of an average age of nine.' [15]

Scottish education also had a strongly competitive ethos – not just 'the qualy', determining the secondary school you attended or the subjects you were intellectually capable of handling – but also how your test marks determined your ranking in the classroom: even in the early 1960s where a pupil sat in a Scottish primary school was decided on the basis of their performance in tests. Those who did not excel academically were constantly exposed to the fact that they weren't 'brainy' or 'clever'. Those who fell behind for any reason – learning difficulties, repeated absences from school through ill-health (their own or parents'), or an unsupportive 'home learning environment' – continually came up against the idea that they didn't just lack brains but that they were thick, stupid and hence worthless. As I know from my extensive training experience in Scotland where I often discussed the topic, negative labelling of children by teachers was extremely common. Youngsters were often repeatedly denounced as 'sleekit', 'useless', 'a dunce', 'dross', 'as thick as mince', 'a big stiffy', 'a waste of space'. One man recalled in one of my sessions that one of his teachers continually called him 'a wee flyman'.

I have little doubt that within Scottish schools there were

also many good, inspiring and gifted teachers dedicated to their pupils and their development. One such teacher was John Boyd Orr who later became one of the most distinguished scientists of his generation and whose name lives on as an ugly Glasgow University tower block. He became a teacher in 1902 in a Glasgow slum school but resigned after a short time as he did not think he could do anything as a teacher to help alleviate the misery of the children in his classroom. He found working in his father's business preferable to 'trying to forcibly feed education down the throats of children who did not want it and received little or no benefit from it.' [16] But he returned to teaching poor 12-14 year olds in Saltcoats and managed to get six of them bursaries as a result of extra teaching. He also spent considerable time in class getting them to sing Scottish songs which the youngsters loved though it wasn't entirely to the liking of the inspectorate. Boyd Orr could see that helping some of his boys excel academically did wonders for their 'self-respect'. But I think it is fair to say that unless a pupil was particularly gifted academically, or had a teacher like Boyd Orr, Scottish education was not traditionally designed to encourage either a love of learning or feelings of self-worth.

On top of this there was the constant problem of language. Scottish schools, even in Gaelic areas until more recent times, used standard English in the classroom. Children growing up in homes where parents spoke Scots, or various types of dialect, ran into particular problems. Thus they could be belted or ridiculed for using language which was natural for them but deemed unacceptable by the teacher or education authorities.

William McIlvanney, a former teacher, gives us a brilliant example in his novel *Docherty* of how dangerous it could be to speak in your native tongue. His character, Conn Docherty, is accused of fighting in his primary school and is brought before Mr. Pirrie:

> 'What's wrong with your face, Docherty?'
> 'Skint ma nose, sur.'
> 'How?'
> 'Ah fell an bumped ma heid in the sheuch, sur.'
> 'I beg your pardon?'. . .
> In the pause Conn understands the nature of the choice, tremblingly, compulsively, makes it.
> 'Ah fell an bumped ma heid in the sheuch, sur.'
> The blow is instant. His ear seems to enlarge, is muffled in numbness. . .
> 'That, Docherty, is impertinence. You will translate, please, into your mother tongue.'

Once Conn has dutifully obliged and said he fell and bumped his head in 'the gutter' Mr. Pirrie replies: 'Not an inappropriate setting for you, if I may say so.' [17] Research conducted by linguists in 1970s Glasgow shows that many teachers disliked the local accent.

The 1944 research quoted above suggested that at least a third of pupils leaving school at 14 were capable of more. In terms of potential this would have been far higher. Experts now realise the importance of what is called 'the home learning environment' for how youngsters do at school. This includes the vocabulary used at home, the availability of books, parents reading stories, their attitude towards learning, and help and encouragement with homework assignments and so forth. Indeed it is these factors which matter more than the actual quality of school provision. It is this educationally rich home environment which not only encourages positive attitudes to learning but also helps to develop the brain and children's actual cognitive abilities.

Recent research suggests that children from disadvantaged backgrounds in the UK are, by the age of three, a whole year educationally behind those from more privileged backgrounds.[19] From this point of view the children of the poorest Glaswegians hardly stood a chance. Many were so undernourished that their height, let alone their brain development, was undermined. Of course, there were exceptions: some had parents who particularly valued learning and who were able to provide a home environment which was sufficiently stimulating and supportive of education. But more commonly youngsters who would have performed very differently educationally if they had been adopted by middle class parents were routinely seen as stupid and incapable of learning. Glasgow's particular problems with overcrowding contributed enormously to this problem. Where was the space to read or concentrate on homework?

But this is not the whole issue. Big differences in educational performance are also, according to Richard Wilkinson and Kate Pickett's data, part of the negative effects of pronounced income inequality. Countries, like the USA and the UK, which now have large income differentials have much more variance within their educational performance than more equal societies like Japan, Canada or Sweden. Wilkinson and Pickett argue this is not about poverty as such but the 'psychosocial' effects of being at the bottom of an extremely hierarchical society where you feel that you are not as good as others. Various psychological experiments have now shown how stereotypes can have a negative effect on people's performance. These stereotypes can be about gender (girls can't do maths), race (black people have a low IQ), or social class (these children aren't likely to perform well).[20] The important point is that countless experiments show that 'stereotype threat' affects how well people perform tasks. For example, an experiment in India earlier this decade showed that high and low caste boys (unaware of each others' identities) were able to do puzzles equally well as one another (indeed the low-caste boys did slightly better). But after they were asked to announce publicly their families' origins and their caste, the performance of the low-caste boys dropped significantly. [21] Given the undermining impact of stereotyping it is not difficult to see how, if you were a poor Glaswegian and you felt that teachers looked down on you, your language and your community, it would affect your educational performance.

The educational legacy

Given that there was some mobility through education in Scotland, and Glasgow, (just not quite as much as some of the myths suggest) it is clear that there were a number of working-class parents who wanted their offspring to get on and who knew that education was the key. Often these were parents who scrimped and saved for bus fares, uniforms, and equipment so that their children could go to state-aided independent schools such as Allan Glen's School in Glasgow. I knew a boy at university who came from Pollok and whose father worked in Fairfield's shipyard. He went to Allan Glen's in the city centre and in so doing completely cut himself off from his neighbourhood – a common pattern.

But while some parents wanted their offspring to get on, many saw school as a waste of time. For years critics have realised that for the mass of the working population, their experience of Scottish schools turned them off education. One manifestation of this is that those who got on educationally were often ostracised. Ralph Glasser, for example, recounts being hated for excelling at maths in his Gorbals school. No wonder it was so common for youngsters to want to leave school as soon as possible. This is still seen in Scotland today. The percentage of young people who leave school to do nothing (not in education, employment or training) is the highest in the thirty OECD countries. Within Scotland, Glasgow has the highest figure which means that the city has the highest percentage of 16-19 year olds in the OECD who have not left school for a 'positive destination'. Many are in this position with the approval of parents and relatives who also think schools a waste of time.[22]

If schools had been different they might have helped to break down the limited, inward-looking aspect of Glasgow's working-class culture which we shall analyse in the next chapter: they would have helped broaden youngsters' horizons, opening their eyes to possibility and all that the world had to offer but in general they didn't. Those who wanted more, or something different from the world they inhabited, were more likely to emigrate than risk staying and being different.

Glasgow's housing problems also presented a serious barrier to the participation in many complex, stimulating, engaging learning activities. Remember Glasgow was not only intensely urban but also many people suffered from serious overcrowding. Quite simply there wasn't the space to get involved in various pursuits. The historian Christopher Harvie makes this point generally in relation to Scotland in the period 1922-64 but it was a particular problem in Glasgow:

Scotland was weak in family activities: gardening, for instance, increased, but not to the same extent as in England with her lower-density housing. Coarse fishing never became, as in the south, the most important participatory sport. Those who lived in the country, or could afford it, caught trout; the rivers and canals in the industrial areas were too polluted for roach or bream to survive. Hobbies requiring house-room, like model engineering, wood-working, motor car maintenance, and 'do-it-yourself' projects were virtually ruled out. Educational reports commented on the inadequacy of Scottish girls as cooks and dressmakers, citing the same reasons. The growth of domestic science classes in the schools was a response. In the long run such factors probably had some part in the decline of skill within the Scottish working-class. [23]

So Glasgow's terrible overcrowding and poor conditions were not just bad for health and relationships, opportunities for amusement, stimulation and learning were also removed. This does not mean that Glasgow's traditional working class were confined to a cultural desert. Music was always big in Glasgow and lots of people played, and continue to play, musical instruments. For many dancing too was an engrossing hobby. Whatever we might think of betting, once a major male pastime in Glasgow, it is also a complex and stimulating activity. Glasgow also had high newspaper and magazine readership. As we saw earlier there was lots of opportunity for involvement in social activities and the communal nature of the housing cemented women's relationships with one another and the wider community and provided a fair level of stimulation particularly given the humour and the sheer number of folk around. But, as we are about to see, for some of Glasgow's working class its culture was stultifying and literally had them on their knees.

CHAPTER 11
Glasgow limited

A T THE END of the Glasgow novel, *The Dear Green Place*, Mat Craig, the hero, is suffering such an existential crisis that his body and mind are wracked by nausea. At the height of the crisis Mat realises that he is 'divided against himself': his thoughts filled with the contemptuous outbursts of an inner 'Glasgow keelie voice' provoking within him a 'deep spiritual boke'.[1] Mat had been walking aimlessly through Glasgow's streets for days and once onboard a Clyde ferry the rising tide of nausea overwhelms him.

The problems of industrial Glasgow were hardly recorded by Scottish authors in earlier decades but with the publication of Hind's novel in 1966 all that changed – Archie Hind did not just spit out the problem he gave his readers something much more dramatic to analyse. No wonder, in her extensive survey of Glasgow fiction, Moira Burgess writes: 'It is hardly possible to exaggerate the importance of *The Dear Green Place* to Glasgow fiction.'[2] The world Hind describes is late 1950s Glasgow and for working class folk it is a considerably more civilised city than the one we've encountered in previous chapters. Overcrowding was still common and many lived in housing poor by English standards but nonetheless the abject squalor and stench of the Glasgow wynds had disappeared. Hind's Glasgow is also the era of the new welfare state with its access to benefits and free health care. Unemployment is low and the standard of living increasing. Hind reflects these improvements in his novel: 'All his life up to then Mat had thought of domestic life, family life, as a life of sordidness and squalor. Then all of a sudden it had become decent,' he writes.[3] But, as we shall see, these improvements were simply not enough.

The Shipbuilders was hailed as the first great Glasgow industrial novel but in a sense it was an outsider's view: Blake was a journalist and from Greenock. Archie Hind's background mirrors so much of what we have encountered so far in this book. He was raised in Carntyne in Glasgow's east end in the 1930s. His father was an ugly drunk who severely beat his wife and children. Indeed Hind's mother left the marital home for years only returning when her grown sons were able to protect her from her husband. Hind did fairly well at school and could have gone on to higher education but his father insisted he left to earn a wage. Hind then did a variety of menial jobs before being conscripted to fight in World War II. On his return he managed to secure a place at Newbattle Abbey, a college specifically designed to educate mature working class students.[4] The principal was the poet Edwin Muir and it was Muir, not his family or community background, nor the schools he attended, who nurtured and encouraged Hind's talent.

In some ways *The Dear Green Place* tells a familiar tale about writing: the hero longs to express himself, to be a novelist, and he has to struggle hard to find his voice, his theme and his confidence. But, as the title suggests, this is quintessentially a Glasgow novel and its drama revolves round the culture's hostility towards this type of literary expression – a hostility Mat experiences existentially and viscerally.

Mat wants to write and his mother, Jetta, is appalled. For all that Jetta plays a pivotal role in the book, in her attempt to clip her son's wings, Hind portrays her sympathetically. She is a limited and somewhat inadequate woman who was humiliated in her early married life by sisters-in-law who looked down on her and taunted her for not 'being respectable'. She is hostile to Mat's literary pretensions for a variety of reasons. First, she doesn't much like ambition. She thinks Mat should be content to live a life similar to his parents and relatives. In short, to join the ranks of the industrial working class. Second, she is particularly hostile to Mat's ambitions because writing books is not 'practical'. Finally, if he is to get on he should do something 'respectable' which means doing a job wearing 'a collar and tie'. For Jetta, becoming a writer is beyond the pale – 'fancy', 'high-falutin' ideas which are 'no for the likes of us'.[5] What's more he has a responsibility to his wife, and latterly, his son. Mat's father, Doug, is less hostile than Jetta but still not supportive. He has read extensively himself, and is politically radical, and can only understand Mat's desire to write in terms of 'getting on', 'ideals' or to show that he's 'cultured'. His advice to Mat is to get a job and write as a hobby. Mat's brother Jake is also unsympathetic: 'I slaughter beef. Ye can eat it. Ye get money for daein' it. Ye cannae eat stories. Ye get nae money for writin' them.'[6]

Mat is a serious intellectual, at home discussing complicated literary ideas with his new bourgeois friends but his confidence in himself is continually shaken by his own thoughts. He is embarrassed, to the extent of blushing when he thinks about his 'presumption'. He often uses his brother's term 'guff' when referring to his own writing. The tragedy for Mat is that he has internalised the 'aggressive philistinism' of his culture, yet still feels he has no choice but to express 'his primal, creative passion'. His existential crisis at the end of the novel takes the form of his inner 'Glesca keelie voice' berating him and his realisation that he is 'divided against himself': 'Ye're nut on, laddie. Ye're on tae nothin'. . . Ye're nut quoted. A gutless wonder like you that hasn't the gumption of a louse,' [7] the inner voice tells Mat.

Mat's saviour is his wife Helen: beautiful, loving, generous and from a middle-class background. In one of the most dramatic passages of the book, she turns on Mat's family for not supporting his ambition to become a writer:

> 'You people. . . seem to be in a perpetual state of
> apology for your very existence. Well I'm not in
> that frame of mind and – ' Helen suddenly broke
> into broad Glasgow speech – 'if ma man wants to
> acquire any fancy notions he needn't look to me to
> reprove him for them. You're a' entitled to a bit
> mair than a mess o' pottage.' [8]

It is Helen who encourages Mat to believe in himself. When Mat rips up his manuscript in anger at his family Helen picks it up and holds it to her bosom as if she were nurturing their child. Helen is a shadowy, undeveloped character in the book but there's little doubt that without her Mat would never have the confidence, or opportunity, to write. Hind's wife Eleanor, from a middle-class Jewish background, performed a similar role in his own life.

As a child of this city Mat feels affection and a sense of belonging and he does not want to cut himself off from his culture. Yet he is acutely aware that his problems stem not just from Glasgow but from his native land. Thus he decides 'to attempt the difficult, almost impossible task of making art out of his Scottishness. . .' [9]

So what are these problems? Hind acknowledges that within Glasgow's socialist tradition there is an intellectual strain but generally Glasgow (and Scotland by extension) is portrayed as intellectually and spiritually deficient. For Hind, like his mentor Edwin Muir, Glasgow, despite the number of Irish Catholics, is essentially a 'Calvinist, Protestant city', 'A city whose talents were all outward and acquisitive.'

> A dirty filthy city. But with a kind of ample vitality
> which has created fame for her slums and her
> industry and given her moral and spiritual existence a
> tight ingrown wealth, like a human character, limited,
> but with a direct brutish strength, almost warm.
> Glasgow! [10]

It is this limited, if warm, humanity which Mat continually bumps up against in his own family – limitations which make writing, or other forms of expression, or being different, well-nigh impossible.

Archie Hind's character Mat is not the only one to experience such feelings. In his short book *The Dear Green Place: the novel in the West of Scotland* (1985) Professor Douglas Gifford argues that a long list of contemporary novelists, poets and playwrights from the region echo one another by presenting. . .

> . . . a sensitive protagonist struggling to articulate
> his reactions to his environment; in ways, firstly, in
> which he has been encouraged at university, at art
> school, or even within the book he's read and the
> company he's kept. Gradually he will realise that
> he cannot accept these ways – or it will be borne in

> violently upon him. A failure of language, of
> communication will take place. He will turn in
> upon himself in increasing solipsism, rejecting his
> art, his friends, and tormenting himself with the
> destruction of anything he has achieved in art and
> in relationships. Alienation or nervous breakdown,
> mocked by a sense of total loss of 'green places of
> the mind', will often be the end; or a sense of
> bewilderment about future evolution.[11]

Gifford, like other experts, attributes the problem to language: for these writers there is indeed a sizeable gap between their local dialect and the formal English of educated pursuits. Another relevant factor is that in advanced capitalist societies mobility is individual – someone from a low social status manages to get on as a result of his or her individual achievements but is thereafter cut off from the everyday reality of family, friends and neighbours. Of course, there is merit in these explanations but is there something about the culture of the region which makes the 'alienation' and 'bewilderment' of those who feel different, or who want something more, even more likely?

The origins of an insular culture

A few reasons for the limiting aspects of Glasgow culture have already been mentioned in earlier chapters – for example, how social cohesion made being different from others difficult and how lack of opportunities for social advancement pushed the most optimistic and aspirational to emigrate rather than stay and change the culture. But there are other reasons. T.C. Smout, an outsider, argues that the problem is Scotland-wide and inherent within our system of education:

Perhaps. . . it is in the history of the school more
than in any other aspect of recent social history that
the key lies to some of the more depressing aspects
of modern Scotland. If there are in this country too
many people who fear what is new, believe the
difficult is impossible, draw back from responsibility,
and afford established authority an exaggerated
respect, we can reasonably look for an explanation
in the institutions that moulded them. [12]

I agree with most of Smout's characterisation of typical
Scottish attitudes but, as is clear in my previous book *The Scots'
Crisis of Confidence*, I would not lay them all at the door of
schools and think that our education system was a reflection of
wider values and practices. Nonetheless, I see what he is talking
about clearly in my own family. My parents attended a conference I was organising a few years ago. We had decided when
people arrived to ask them to write on a card their hope for
Scotland and pin it on a board. My parents were paralysed –
flummoxed not just by the newness of the experience but the
fear of participating. It was as if they were frightened that their
cards would go on the wall and someone would appear to
shirrack them for a wrong answer: 'who wrote that? What
rubbish, Mary Craig come to the front of the class.' It was only
when they were assured that not only were the responses
anonymous but also there were no right answers and no people
to monitor the quality of responses, that they happily wrote
their contributions.

However, in the case of Glasgow manual workers, for all
that they might hang back in unfamiliar situations, their experience did not breed a respect for education and authority in
the way that Smout suggests. Contempt for teachers and schools
was strong, partly because of the inherent unfairness and

arbitrary punishments. Glasgow industries were often run by authoritarian bosses and there was a strong 'us and them' mentality which bred contempt for those in authority. Glasgow's macho culture also encouraged men to look down on males who did white collar jobs. In today's parlance they were seen as wimps.

Richard Finlay thinks this attitude was widespread throughout the country. 'Working-class male culture in Scotland,' he writes, 'held that any man who did not work with his hands was a poof, a skiver, a snob, an upstart or any combination of the four.'[13] For reasons advanced in earlier chapters, this working class machismo was certainly at its peak in Glasgow and these attitudes permeate Hind's novel. Even Mat, the aspiring writer, is contemptuous of white-collar workers – a 'hen-pecked nyaff that couldn't punch his way oot o' a wet poke'.[14]

Mat ultimately escapes, as Hind himself did, from the stifling grip of this limited, deprecating world as a result both of his own tenacity and the love and tenderness he experiences in his relationship with Helen – a woman who does not come from this culture. The story has a hopeful end with Mat discovering his theme and readers realising that the book he is going to write is the book on Glasgow they have just read.

But many Glaswegians are held fast in a set of self-limiting beliefs. If we want to understand why working-class Scottish, but particularly, Glasgow culture is limited and inward-looking, we must cast our net wide and bring in other things for inspection. For example, Glasgow's industrial make-up encouraged the sense of being stuck in a time warp – lives repeating themselves from one generation to the next. Traditional heavy engineering industries dominated and the city had fewer new technology and consumer-oriented industries than other UK industrial centres. All this shored up traditional job patterns, skills and work culture leading to the sense of Glasgow, and Glaswegians, being insular and unwilling to change.

In the ILP and other left-wing political circles education and cultural pursuits were often valued – seen as a tool in the service of political agitation and change. But for huge sections of Glasgow's working-class, particularly those who were unskilled or semi-skilled, airy fairy book learning, the arts or anything that smacked of social climbing or pretension was detested and ridiculed. In other words, what they particularly valued was their own skills, culture and experience. Essentially this meant that as working hours reduced, and leisure time increased, a variety of pursuits and interests (and different career paths), which could have provided stimulation, novelty and satisfaction were closed off.

This notion of working-class Glaswegians living in a very small world is a major strand in the work of Willie Gall, a cartoonist for the *Evening Times*. Years ago I did a rough analysis of the story content of *The Broons* – the famous comic strip from the *Sunday Post*. One of the most recurring themes is a family member trying something new, such as water skiing, relatives then 'taking the mick' and the water skier falling flat on their face before returning to the security of the family. But trying new things isn't part of Gall's satire of Glaswegian life. What he commonly portrays are Glaswegians, ostensibly know-ledgeable about social trends or big national or international events, in sport, politics, entertainment, yet trapped within the prism of their very limited experience. In short, everything is turned back into the world they know and they are pictured as confidently ignorant and naive. 'If Wullie wis Ian MacGregor he widnae close any pits, sure ye widnae, Wullie?'; 'If ah jined the Sloane Rangers wid ma man huv tae gie up his season ticket at Parkhead?'; 'If it wisnae fur the bingo an' the bettin' shop this place wid be a cultural desert.' [15]

It is fairly common for local writers to praise Glasgow's working-class, or even underclass, for being positive and defending their values against the middle classes. But often this means praising a very narrow view of the world. For example, one writer recounts positively the story of a drunk staggering accidentally into Rogano's – an upmarket restaurant and bar in the city centre. He is asked to leave and as he goes he tells the staff and customers that the atmosphere is duff; that they need music and dancing to liven it up. Of course, music and dancing can enhance pubs greatly but that doesn't mean there is no place for restaurants dedicated to good food and conversation. In the UK as a whole eating out in really good restaurants has a class dimension but elsewhere in Europe ordinary people appreciate fine dining and treat themselves to the experience when they can. In Glasgow it is much more likely to be mocked and disparaged by anyone who doesn't see themselves as middle class – even left-leaning middle classes and academics often collude in these values The same is true of opera and other high culture.

The difficulty with this is that these values (it's no for the likes of us and it's crap anyway) keep people in a restricted world and encourages time and money to be spent on drinking, watching telly, bingo, gambling, football or consumer goods. In short, limiting them to what workers or the poor have tradit-ionally done. Of course, there were, and still are, individuals who break free from these cultural constraints but what I'm describing here is what often passes as traditional Glasgow working-class culture.

Glasgow's version of confidence is often summed up in the word 'gallus'. Originally used negatively to refer to someone who was destined for the gallows it was then redeemed and used, generally in a positive way, about someone who is cheeky, dresses stylishly or acts with bravado. But examples of gallus behaviour often illustrate limitations as much as confidence. Janice Galloway's autobiography gives a fascinating account of working-class women's lives in the 1950s and 60s and it is relevant here on two counts. First, her big sister is depicted as gallus personified – outspoken, ultra-stylish and outwardly confident in her dealings with the opposite sex. But her confidence is often little more than breathtaking prejudice and myopia. So, for example, she pronounces that she'd never read a novel written by a woman as 'women canny write' and she disparages the young Janice for buying herself a book on wild flowers.[16] Also, Galloway is clear that all that obsession with appearance which was common in the world she grew up in masked a general negativity about the self. In an interview, reflecting her family's penchant for getting dressed up for photographs, she muses:

> We came from a period where, like the photographs, you wished to be portrayed quite different to how you actually were. Because how you actually were was either a source of shame or embarrassment – you weren't good enough. . . It's about looking better than you actually feel, because how you actually are is poor. I've never felt that was healthy. Some of the excesses of misery into which members

of my family were led came from the feeling of not being good enough. . . I got my mother a phone, and she only ever spoke on the phone in a Yorkshire accent. Because a Scottish accent was plain. [17]

When people report self-criticism and self-hatred in the west of Scotland it is often played out in relation to language. Community activist Cathy McCormack reports that when she was interviewed on television she was repeatedly told by locals that the way she spoke 'shamed' them and that she should 'learn to speak English' before she went on television. [18]

None of the culture described in this chapter has been good for the city's economy or politics. It was a world of low expectations and limited horizons; a world where it was all too easy for political representatives to think that ordinary people did not expect, or deserve, too much. It also led to an uncreative, unenterprising culture, which was stuck in the past – undermined by outmoded work practices and demarcation disputes and increasingly dependent on the state.

What's more, this environment undermined Scotland as a whole. Between 1821 and 1945 over two million Scots migrated. Over half these migrants went to the USA, Canada, Australia and New Zealand and were intent on finding a better life. In the 1960s, when Archie Hind wrote his novel, as many as 40,000 Scots a year left their homeland. Many were from Glasgow and the west of Scotland. [19]

CHAPTER 12
Love actually

In the second city of the Empire
Mother Glasgow nurses all her weans
Working hard to feed her little starlings
Unconsciously she clips their little wings
(Verse from 'Mother Glasgow' by Michael Marra)

GEORGE ALBEE, a distinguished American psychologist, of international renown, died in 2006; he was in his 80s. A mere six months before his death he visited Scotland to give lectures on mental health. Albee was principally interested in the prevention of mental illness not the treatment and, given the level of problem in the west of Scotland, we should take particular note of his ideas. Albee's research convinced him that the principal causes of mental illness is not brain disease or disorder but poverty, exploitation and lack of love. He often said that the best, single way to improve mental health was to make sure that all children were wanted. He firmly believed that 'if children sense in their bones that they are wanted, loved and appreciated, they develop a great internal self-confidence that resists all kind of stress.'[1]

Albee is right to emphasise the importance of feeling loved. Those specialising in child development tend to talk about this in terms of 'attachment' – the psychological connectedness human beings need which begins in the early bonding between mother and child.[2] The psychiatrist John Bowlby, who came up with the concept of attachment, speculated that it was necessary for human survival. Children who find it difficult to become securely attached often have problems later in life with relationships and behavioural problems. Attachment difficulties often result from neglect, abuse and severe stress.

Research now confirms what many psychologists and those working with children have always suspected: stress and trauma in childhood is hugely important affecting not just childhood development but later mental and physical health. So why are children so vulnerable and childhood stress so damaging? One reason is that babies' brains are not fixed at birth but ready to be primed for the type of society and relationships they are born into. Thus it is through interaction with the mother that babies learn, or do not learn, the basic skills of empathetic communication, for example – a skill at the heart of all good relationships.[3] It is only in recent years that researchers have discovered that childhood trauma can actually alter a person's DNA and shape the way their genes work. One Canadian study found that the brains of people who had been abused in childhood had 'different epigenetic markings in the brains of the abused group. These markings influence the hypothalamic-pituitary-adrenal (HPA) function, a stress-response which increases the risk of suicide.'[4] This study confirmed in humans earlier findings in rats, that the quality of maternal care significantly influences the genes that control their offspring's stress response.[5]

There are now countless studies which illustrate various

ways in which babies' experiences and care have a huge impact on their later development and life chances.[6] One of these studies, on macaque monkeys, has had a major impact on Dr. Harry Burns, Scotland's Chief Medical Officer. Researchers varied the ease or difficulty for mothers in retrieving food.[7] When it was difficult mothers were away from their babies for much longer periods. What the research showed was that baby macaques whose mothers found it easy, or difficult, to find food were much less stressed and had better brain development than those baby monkeys whose mothers sometimes found food easy to acquire and sometimes difficult. This unpredictability led them to exhibit symptoms similar to depression. This echoes other research which shows that mothers from poor backgrounds are more likely to be stressed, hence pre-occupied with things other than their babies, and that this stress can easily lead to a mothering style which is unpredictable, cold or neglectful.

Childhood experience and stress is not just damaging for mental health: physical health too is affected. One of the studies which could shed some light on why Glasgow has such a poor health record is a major American research project on Adverse Childhood Experiences, known as the ACE Study.[8] This large-scale collaborative research project studied 17,000 adults' responses to questions about childhood abuse and household dysfunction. They were mainly middle-class, employed Americans living in California. The average age was 57. The questionnaire also asked respondents to outline their current mental and physical health. Individuals scored one point for each adverse experience they recalled. This gave a score between 0 (no adverse experiences) and 8. Its findings were startling:

The ACE Study reveals a powerful relationship between our emotional experiences as children and our physical and mental health as adults, as well as the major cause of adult mortality in the United States. It documents the conversion of traumatic emotional experiences in childhood into organic disease later in life. How does this happen, this reverse alchemy, turning the gold of a newborn infant into the lead of a depressed, diseased adult? The study makes it clear that time does not heal some of the adverse experiences we found so common in the childhoods of a large population of middle-aged, middle-class Americans. One does not 'just get over' some things, not even fifty years later.[9]

Table I shows the prevalance of ACE scores:

Table I: Prevalence of 'Adverse Childhood Experiences'

Number of Adverse Childhood Experiences (ACE Score)	Women %	Men %	Total %
0	34.5	38.0	36.1
1	24.5	27.9	26.0
2	15.5	16.4	15.9
3	10.3	8.6	9.5
4 or more	15.2	9.2	12.5

The Study showed a strong relationship between the number of adverse experiences and self-reports of cigarette smoking, obesity, physical inactivity, alcoholism, drug abuse, depression, attempted suicide, sexual promiscuity and sexually transmitted diseases in later life. Researchers speculated that smoking, drug taking, alcohol and so forth were coping devices to help alleviate stress. More importantly, the more adverse childhood experiences people reported, the more likely they were to have heart disease, bronchitis, cancer, stroke, diabetes, skeletal fractures, liver disease and poor health as an adult.

The relationship between the ACE score and medical problems is striking. For example a person who scores 4 is 260 per cent more likely to have a chronic obstructive pulmonary disease (such as bronchitis) than someone with an ACE score of 0. A male who gains 6 on the ACE questionnaire has a 4,600 per cent increase in the likelihood of using heroin intravenously than another who scored 0. An individual who scores 4 or more is 460 per cent more likely to be suffering from depression than an individual who scores 0. Those with high ACE scores are at much higher risk (3,000 to 5,100 per cent) of committing suicide. Researchers point out that there is a 'strong graded relationship' in the data between what happened in childhood and later health. [10]

Table II shows how the figures for the Study broke down into categories. Remember that the average age is 57 which means that most of the respondents would have been brought up in the 1940s, 50s and 60s. [11]

Looking at this list, my speculation is that people growing up in Glasgow during the same period probably had similar levels of sexual abuse (given current estimates), even more alcohol consumption (given that Americans consume less on average than the Scots); more domestic violence given its prevalence in historical accounts of Glasgow, its link with alcohol, and the Scottish Government's current estimates that 20 per cent of women suffer domestic abuse as opposed to the 13 per cent reported in the ACE Study. I also suspect that more than 28 per cent of people of this age group brought up in Glasgow would report being physically abused (at least being

Table II:
Prevalence of Specific 'Adverse Childhood Experiences'

ACE Category Data collected 1995-97 (but relating to childhood of respondents with a mean age of 57)	Women (n 9,367) %	Men (n 7,970) %	Total (n 17,337) %
Abuse			
Emotional abuse	13.1	7.6	10.6
Physical abuse (smacked or hit)	27.0	29.9	28.3
Sexual abuse (by anyone 5 years older)	24.7	16.0	20.7
Neglect			
Emotional neglect	16.7	12.4	14.8
Physical neglect	9.2	10.7	9.9
Household Dysfunction			
Mother treated violently	13.7	11.5	12.7
Household subst. abuse (alcohol or drugs)	29.5	23.8	26.9
Household mental illness (depression, attempted suicide)	23.3	14.8	19.4
Parents separate/ divorce	24.5	21.8	23.3
Incarcerated household member	5.2	4.1	4.7

spanked or hit). I also think that Glaswegians, particularly those from poor backgrounds, would report much higher levels of what the ACE researchers call 'emotional abuse' and 'emotional neglect'. So what's my evidence for this?

See you?: Emotional abuse Glasgow style

In the ACE questionnaire a respondent is asked to rate 'emotional abuse' on the basis of whether, in the first 18 years of life, 'a parent or other adults in the household often, or very often, swore at you or insulted, put you down or humiliated you or acted in a way that made you afraid that you might be physically hurt'.[12] I believe that the vast majority of Scots, let alone Glaswegians, would respond positively at least to the first part of this question. Scotland has traditionally been a put-down culture. We're good at criticism and cutting people down to size – in fact, we think it is good for them. And this is particularly true in Glasgow where folk hate others 'bummin their load'.

Look at *The Patter: the guide to common Glasgow usage*, originally published in the mid 1980s, and you'll see how so much of the language is critical.[13] Many of the terms listed are insulting ways to label people – *nyaff, flyman, bauchle, heidbanger, sweetie-wife, tumshie, tube, daftie, hairy, keelie, breenger, balloon, eejit, haddy, no-user, queerie* and countless more. This is a culture that really goes in for name calling. There are also lots of negative adjectives such as *haunless, torn-faced, shilpit, glaikit, away with the fairies* and *hackit*. There are also numerous ways to describe dirty things – *mockit, honkin, bowfin, hoachin, mingin, clarty, boggin*. . . and these can also be applied to people. In contrast there is only one term of endearment – *hen*. I could only find, or remember myself, two common positive nouns to describe people – *stoater* (often sexual) and *soul*. *Stoater* is also used to refer to anything good.

If Glaswegians want to be positive about something they don't usually use traditional Scottish adjectives such as *bonny* or *braw* and, with few positive terms of their own, would be more likely to use English/American words such as brilliant, fantastic, smashing or fabulous. The only positive adjectives for a person I found listed are *gallus* and *hoachie*, meaning lucky. Words to praise or encourage people are almost non-existent in Glaswegian – *gaun yersel* is one, another is *come away. . . Aw the nice* may be used but it is often deprecating.

No self-respecting Glaswegian male, let alone female, is likely to use English words like dear, dearest, darling, beloved or sweetheart. Men would be more likely to use American terms such as honey or doll. As in the rest of Scotland Glaswegians are often likely to use the diminutive if they want to be positive about something: 'Would you like a wee cup of tea?'; 'I just bought this wee skirt in Marks' – a language style which suggest you have to make something trivial before you can be positive about it.

By contrast there are lots of terms for giving folk a row (e.g. *shirrack* and *slag*) and also for hitting or being violent – *scud, laldy, tank, burst, molocate, melt, blooter, skite*. *Malky* means to cut with a razor, *chib* means to stab and *mark* means to give someone a scar. There are also lots of words for being drunk but this is common in other places as well.

Literary commentators consider Michael Munro, author of *The Patter*, the leading expert on Glasgow language and describe his book as 'excellent'.[14] In the introduction he writes that the book is a 'true reflection' of Glasgow and its people 'with all their unattractive features, such as deprivation, bigotry and pugnacity, but with all their virtues too, such as robust and irreverent humour, resilience, and abhorrence of pretension.' [15] There's little doubt that Munro has done a good job of crystallising Glaswegian – essentially the language of the old tenements. Given what we saw in previous chapters it is hardly surprising that the folk who lived in some of the world's most terrible, overcrowded slums created many of their own words for dirt, drink, physical aggression and maintaining your position by being prepared to argue for your rights. The words are grittily onomatopoeic and if you grew up with them, as I did, there is a familiarity about them that is almost comforting. But look again at what Munro sees as the 'virtues' of the language and you'll also see that even here, one way or another, it is about putting folk down. This is not a language which encourages or expresses respect and I'm talking here about basic human dignity rather than observing status. Nor is it the language of support, emotional expression and tenderness. In short, Glaswegian is particularly good for emotional abuse. This is not to say that people weren't kind to one another and that there was no love in families just that the local language didn't support or encourage this.

Visitors to Glasgow, or anyone who has considered the issue, are bound to have noticed in the street cases of gross emotional, and often physical, abuse. I'm thinking here about a parent hitting a small child, or giving them a mouthful of foul language, for a trivial misdemeanour. What I'm concerned about here is the endemic, *low-level* abuse in west of Scotland culture. When carrying out my research I came across one passage which epitomised to me the way that many Glaswegians would, at least in the past, routinely talk to their children. This autobiography does not suggest gross abuse of any kind but even this type of constant, low-level aggression would at least score one point on the ACE Study. The time is 1940s Glasgow, the setting a tenement in Plantation near the docks and the 'he' is her father:

> He suddenly noticed me sitting beside the table.
>
> 'Christ, it's no show withoot Nosey. What are ye doin', sitting there wi' your lugs flapping?' He turned angrily to my mother. 'There's nae blasted privacy in this place. That big yin listens to everything. It's got its lugs glued tae the door from the time it gets up tae the minute it goes tae bed, an' it wouldnae surprise me if it works a night shift as well.' [16]

Notice the disparaging labeling and the use of the word 'it' in this sentence. This is something which seemed to be pretty widespread in Glasgow but referring to a child as 'it' is humiliating and contemptuous. Mary Rose replies 'indignantly' that she doesn't have to listen as everyone 'shouts a' the time' but still her father 'sarcastically' makes another remark about her ears.

Others had a much harder time. Robert Douglas grew up in Maryhill in the 1940s and 50s. His father was a drinker who violently beat his wife and son. The author is great at depicting the day-to-day aggression and criticism (emotional abuse) meted out by his father. In the following passage his father has just belted him on the ear in front of his mates for being late:

> As we headed for our close I knew that I'd spend the rest of the evening wondering what to do to avoid him getting onto me. If I sat quietly, it would

be, 'Whit's yer face trippin' ye for? Dae ye think ye
shouldnae be telt aff for being late?'

If I sat in a corner and read: 'That's aw you ever
dae, sit wi' yer face buried in a fuckin' book.' The
book would then be snatched out of my hand. He
liked that.

If I got on with some homework: 'Get that put
away! You should have been in early if ye knew ye
had homework. Ye can go tae school the morra
without it done. If ye get the belt you've naebody
tae blame but yourself.''

At last bedtime would come and I'd climb onto the
bed-chair. I'd start to read a comic, and he'd maybe
let me have five minutes. As usual I'd quickly
become absorbed in a story. . . Snatch!

'Never mind lying therr reading. Turn your face tae
the wall and get tae sleep.' [17]

What about 'emotional neglect'? In essence, this is about
whether there is love and warmth not just shown to the child
but evident in the wider family unit. This love could be physical
(affectionate hugs and cuddles) or verbal. This is not just about
being told you are loved but other types of verbal affection such
as words of encouragement, appreciation and praise and
someone showing empathy and support. Again Mary Rose
Liverani (née Lavery) tells us: 'In our house, the only four letter
word never voiced aloud was love.' [18]

The most poignant reminiscence I have heard personally
came from a man in his fifties whose mother used to take him
with her on a Friday to his father's work when she was trying to
get his paypacket. 'It didn't feel great to know that your ma
couldn't trust your da to make sure that his kids had food in
their bellies the following week.' And he then added, 'what did

it say about him that he would rather get pissed in the pub than look after his family?' That's emotional neglect.

Many others report of their 1940s or 50s upbringing that physical affection – hugs, kisses, and cuddles were non-existent. There is no specific Glaswegian term for this type of affection as the word *winchin* refers to a sexual embrace. I have found it common for people brought up in Scotland right up to the 1960s to report that families were not physically affectionate. It wasn't just that open displays of affection were frowned on – affection itself was uncommon. The problem was partly about the size of families and being too busy with chores. But it was also about a lack of gentleness in the culture – a gentleness absent through-out Scotland but particularly in macho Glasgow. Perhaps mothers were right to withhold this type of affection: sadly, young people had to be prepared for a tough, aggressive environment. If they had been emotionally open or needy, or simply used to gentle treatment, they could have been mercilessly picked on in a culture where people had to know how to hold their own.

Gordon Williams in his late 1960s novel *From Scenes Like These,* set in the west of Scotland, has the young Dunky Logan reflect that his experience was different from what he saw in the cinema: 'Funny how in the pictures you often saw kids give their mothers a kiss or a hug. He could no more have done that than shagged a horse.' [19]

Glaswegians are also very dismissive of animals or children who are affectionate: 'He's nothing but a big sook,' they'll say. Variations on this theme are calling someone who likes physical contact, a 'plaster' or a 'poultice'. Folk that show their emotions may be dismissed as a 'big wean' and when children cry they can be called 'bubbly' and given a row. Cliff Hanley gives a good example in one of his novels. A grannie has burnt herself in front of her grandson: '. . . the poor wee wean frightened out his wee wits. There, son don't greet, your poor old Gran's aw right. Aw shut your girnin' face, you snivellin' wee get,' she added, as the pain gives a jump. . .' [20]

Openly discussing and supporting each other's emotional needs also appears to have been in short supply in many families. Children commonly listened to parents arguing all the time or were aware of a lack of conversation and emotional connection. In the words of the community activist and author Cathy McCormack, 'I didn't like the way my da treated my ma. I didn't feel there was a relationship – they never sat down and had a blether.'[21] For many others it wasn't just the absence of conversation that was a problem, but persistent fights and arguing. Indeed if we fast forward to 2005 we can note that research conducted with young people living in a Glasgow scheme highlighted 'family conflict' as a major issue which needed to be addressed. A study in 2005 amongst S1 to S4 pupils in Glasgow Schools showed almost one third were worried about 'family rows'.[22]

Children were also routinely brought up to be 'seen and not heard' and could have a hard time if they stated their own emotional needs. A tragic example of emotional neglect is given by the journalist and writer Meg Henderson in her autobiography. Her father was a heavy drinker who, she claims, constantly put his own desires and wants before his family's and was a poor provider for them. What is most shocking, however, is the story she tells about being sexually molested by an older family friend when at a party with her father. When they got outside she told her father (Skip) what happened:

> Skip's response was a mixture of anger and annoyance, as though I had broken some unwritten social code by mentioning it. It wasn't that he didn't believe me, it was that he didn't want to know. It was as though these things happened, but they shouldn't be mentioned and he was ashamed of me for not adhering to that social nicety. His ten-year-old daughter had been sexually assaulted by someone she should have been safe with, but it would upset his life to acknowledge it or do anything about it.
>
> I felt ashamed, dirty, unclean. . . [23]

Meg Henderson rightly goes on to say that her father's attitude to her lowered her self-esteem and made her feel worthless. This is indeed what research says: sexual abuse, severe physical punishment, emotional abuse and neglect all have an extremely negative effect on a child's self-esteem.[24]

Given the name-calling, put-down basis of much of Glasgow's verbal expression, I think it fair to assume that just growing up in the city meant that many children would automatically score one point for adverse experiences. But the problem is wider than this. The ACE researchers point out that adverse childhood experiences tend to be cumulative.[25] Of course, people can score one point but it is common for children to be brought up in families where the adverse experiences reinforce one another: if a father drinks (one point), he is more likely to hit his wife (one point) and the prevailing stress may well make hitting the child more likely (one point) as well as emotional neglect (one point). These conditions may well lead one of the parents to feel depressed (one point). For people who are already quite poor then money being spent on drink will mean less money to feed and clothe children (one point). That's us at seven points already if we count in one for routine emotional abuse. If we then note that for women there's a one in four chance of sexual abuse (either in the family or, commonly, the dirty old man in the close) then that's another possible point. If there was real relationship breakdown then the parents may well separate and that's another point. As crime was fairly high in poor areas of Glasgow, and because Scotland imprisons a high rate of offenders then it wouldn't be that difficult for an unfortunate Glaswegian child to collect the full ten points thus making it almost certain that he or she would go on to drink and smoke heavily, use heroin, and have chronic ill-health. . .

Given the culture and history I outlined in previous chapters it seems reasonable to speculate that Glasgow, and the west of Scotland as a whole, may have produced a higher number of people encountering multiple adverse childhood experiences. If this is the case, it may go some way in helping us explain why the city has a higher percentage of people with alcohol and drug problems and various types of ill-health. It may also help us understand the violence figures for, as we saw in Chapter 6, a propensity for violence often results from childhood neglect and abuse and problems with 'attachment'.

But what of resilience? Over the years an impressive liter-ature has accumulated on this subject. It is now well-understood that some children can experience terrible abuse and yet still grow up to be well-adjusted and live good lives.[26] Researchers have identified some of the factors which foster resilience and one of the most important is for a young person to have at least one adult in life who can give him or her some amount of emotional support. This could be an auntie, a neighbour or a teacher. But what is important about the ACE Study is that it suggests that while people may, on the surface, survive abusive childhoods reasonably well, their physical health is likely to suffer at a later point in life.

In a paper on the ACE Study, Dr. Felitti, one of the researchers, argues that adverse childhood experiences 'are the most important determinant of health and well-being of our nation' [the USA]. [27] Another argues that the prevalence of these experiences in the population is a 'modern drain' reducing economic performance by increasing sickness and absence rates and undermining employees' productivity. [28] This is an argument we should pay particular attention to in Scotland given that Scottish productivity is lower than our competitors [29] and Glasgow has exceptionally high numbers of people claiming incapacity benefit.

However, while there may be strong social and economic reasons for trying to reduce these adverse experiences in childhood they are often ignored. 'Unfortunately, these problems are painful to recognise and difficult to deal with,' writes Felitti. 'Most physicians would far rather deal with traditional organic disease.'[30]

This is likely to be as true in Scotland, and the UK as a whole, as in the USA. But I think there is an additional factor which should be considered here and it is this: Scottish literature, particularly from Glasgow and the industrial west of the country, heaves with examples of physical and emotional abuse and neglect and household dysfunction. Yet, as we are about to see, this *crie de coeur* is frequently interpreted as the result of a largely unrelated matter – constitutional politics.

Chapter 13
Lanark on the couch

S COTLAND'S culture and history is unusual: a once independent country, not colonised as such by England, yet in some respects taken over by its culture, language and values. However, this take-over needs to be put in perspective. In 1707 Scotland was a reluctant party to an incorporating parliamentary union with England but the country won the right to maintain its own traditions and institutions in religion, education and the law. In short, Scotland maintained much of its autonomy on matters critical to the continuation of its separate identity.

Given this history, it seems right for the poet Edwin Morgan to maintain: 'The fact that Scotland has nationhood without statehood must leave its cultural life with a sense of the unfinished, the provisional, the potential, a situation that. . . every writer inherits willy nilly.' [1] In other words, it is not difficult to see why this tension between being Scottish and British would influence writers and affect our literary tradition. However, Scottish literary analysts believe that this history has had a huge impact on the country's culture. In their cultural critiques it is easy to discern four inter-related themes – all related to the country's political history.

The first is the idea that there is something inherently divided, schizophrenic almost, about Scottish identity. Thus it is claimed that the country's literature is riddled with divided selves and doppelgangers. Some would even have us believe that only a Scot could have created Jekyll and Hyde. It is an argument which I find utterly unpersuasive but there's no doubt that the notion of division dominates the thinking of Scotland's literary analysts.[2]

A second related idea is that the Scots have weak, even 'damaged identities' and that individuals, communities and the country as a whole are constantly threatened by 'disintegration'. A third theme concerns problems with language and 'narrative voice'.[3] The language problem can take various forms. For example, Edwin Muir's version is that unlike the Scots of pre-Reformation Scotland who were able to think and talk with one mind, contemporary Scots 'feel in one language' (Scots) and 'think in another' (the English of the classroom).[4] In short, Scots suffer from 'dissociation'. Muir saw the origin of the division not in the Union with England but in the advent of 'strict' Calvinism which was opposed to 'poetic drama' and so disrupted Scotland's 'homogenous literary language'.[5] Other literary problems with voice stem from the difficulty Scottish writers have in resolving the dialect spoken by characters and English as the accepted medium for narration.

Douglas Gifford, reflecting on literature from the west of Scotland, argues that there is a particular concern with 'the debasement of character and language' and the failure to find a voice which will connect with the aspirant's dreams and confused sense of self. He later adds: 'The gap between local (and perhaps debased) dialect and formal English is a part of the problem. But the failure to find a self-confident register of expression, style, *voice* matters so much more.'[6]

This leads into a fourth theme in Scottish literature identified by Cairns Craig: 'In Scotland our cultural analysis has been obsessed with images of our self-hate'. [7]

At one level these are interesting ideas which have some-thing to contribute to our understanding of Scottish literature and culture. But there is also something bizarre about the fact that everything Scottish writers say – even when it is about a failure in their personal relationships, or a mental breakdown – is seen through the limiting filter of Scotland's difficulties with identity and voice or some specific aspect of the country's political history.

We must remember that there is a strong psychological basis to the standard political analysis: schizophrenia, the divided self, confused identity, problems with self-expression and self-hate are intrinsic to psychoanalysis. This means that when the characters in Scottish novels have psychological problems these can be most easily interpreted in line with the country's dominant psycho-political themes and, as a result, what is happ-ening at the individual level can be completely played down or ignored.

The effects of a frozen childhood

This tendency to overpoliticise personal themes can be seen very clearly in the treatment of Alasdair Gray's *Lanark* – an important milestone in Glasgow's cultural history. Gray was born in 1934 and came from a working-class background. However, his experience is a far cry from some of the problems we saw in earlier chapters. Gray mainly grew up in Riddrie which, he claims, was the 'best planned housing scheme' to come out of the Wheatley housing reforms.[8] His parents came from respectable working class homes – not slums – and met since they both liked wholesome outdoor pursuits. His father worked in a factory but was highly educated and Gray grew up in a home which appreciated culture. His mother worked in a shop but also sang and was in the Orpheus Choir. According to Gray both home and school were very supportive of his intellectual and artistic development, though his parents were keen for him to be educated in a way which would allow him to enter a well-paid professional job.

The naturalistic account of Duncan Thaw's childhood in *Lanark* is, according to Gray, essentially autobiographical. From this we can see that Gray managed to escape many of the horrors of Glasgow children, not just because he lived in much nicer circumstances but also his father was no drinker or wife beater and even handed over his unopened pay-packet. Yet in a recent biography Gray confirms that his nice, interested and supportive father beat him and his sister with a belt.[9]

The details Gray outlines in *Lanark* are even more disturbing. The five year old Duncan Thaw is disgusted when his mother gives him food such as tripe and sheep's hearts. He refuses to eat them and his mother forces him to sit at the table and eat the offending food. He then vomits and is confined to his room until his father gets home. Then his father appears and 'thrashes' him.[10] This makes Duncan hysterical and he starts to beat himself. When this happens again, his father undresses him and plunges the child in a cold bath. This isn't an isolated incident but is repeated. Later, when Duncan does something which he considers to be a much 'horrider crime than not eating dinner' he is not only confused when he escapes punishment for it but also believes that he 'deserved to be hurt'.[11]

In the section in *Lanark* where Gray outlines his plagiarisms – books and ideas which he has drawn on in his own story – he writes the following under Brown, George Douglas: 'Books 1 and 2 owe much to the novel *The House with the Green Shutters* in which heavy paternalism forces a weak-minded youth into dread of existence, hallucinations, and crime.' [12] Gray's father ultimately regretted the beatings but as Gray says himself 'it was the done thing in those days.' [13] Gray presents the cold bath incidents as having a major emotional impact on Thaw telling us that he was dried and put to bed and then, 'Before sleep came he lay stunned and emotionless while his mother tucked him in.' [14] A verse of one of Gray's later poems reads:

MOTHER, LOST MOTHER/WHERE HAVE YOU
TAKEN ALL MY HEAT/LEAVING ME ALONE/
AS COLD AS WATER, AS COLD AS STONE? [15]

Gray's mother died of liver cancer when he was only nineteen – a tragic incident which he hardly experienced emotionally. Indeed on the morning of her death he ate breakfast and then put on the radio to listen to a comedy show. His father had to ask him to turn it off as he thought the neighbours would be offended. Until recently Gray has been uncharacteristically silent about his mother and he hardly mentioned her in written accounts of his life. However, in a recent biography, compiled by his secretary, he recalls that she was 'physically, slightly cold' and didn't cuddle them much and was a 'lonely' woman who didn't have much fun. He also recounts that it was years later before he could release 'an emotional iceberg of tears' about his mother's death. [16]

From interviews, and the account in *Lanark,* it is difficult not to conclude that Alasdair Gray's emotional life was frozen as a child and that this chill blighted his life and his relationships. Indeed words related to cold, such as frozen and ice, permeate Gray's work and he depicts himself as a man who lacks heat, warmth and passion. From childhood, Gray suffered hugely from asthma and eczema so severely that it was often disfiguring. Doctors told him that both conditions were partly psychosomatic. In *Lanark*, the young Thaw is a gifted painter and confident in his skills but he is always aware that this can never compensate for the fact that he is 'an inadequate man'. He longs to find love but, lacking 'sex appeal', and unable to relate well to people, is destined to be rejected by women and his simple, human longings unfulfilled. Plagued by self-loathing, his body is wracked by asthma and, following a psychological breakdown, he commits suicide. Thaw is then reincarnated in the character Lanark.

Colin Manlove, an expert on Scottish fantasy literature, points out that *Lanark* is similar to most Scottish fantasy novels (and unlike English ones) in that the hero, both as Thaw and Lanark is a 'social misfit'.[17] They are continually depicted on the edge – not part of the world they inhabit and unable to bridge their isolation and loneliness. Lanark, like Thaw, finds it difficult to connect with women. Indeed towards the end of the book, when contemplating an attractive woman, he 'looked inside himself and found only a hungry, ungenerous cold, a pained emptiness which could neither give nor take. . . a dead man.'[18] In the main part of the story the object of Lanark's desire is Rima but emotional connection, even good sex between them, is problematic. They are both covered in 'dragonhide' – a mysterious disease redolent of Gray's eczema but also used by him to suggest Reichian emotional 'armouring'. Lanark's dedication to Rima saves her life yet it isn't enough to bind her to him. She leaves for another man, telling him 'you are the most selfish man I know'. [19] Lanark has the insight to realise that he is no hapless victim; that he was faithful to her 'not because I loved her but because I wanted love' [20] and that she was right to reject him.

In *Lanark*, time and time again, relations between men and women are like a dance where neither partner knows the steps. If they do manage to hook up and waltz off they are soon tripping each other up, leaving not just bruises but a sense of frustration and resentment. Nonetheless as Janice Galloway points out:

> Thaw/Lanark's wish for female companionship rises chokingly from between the pages, as heady as aftershave. Whatever bitterness he falls into, a masculine need to cling, to seek protection and communion, recurs with near-pathetic regularity. Gray's hero expects the wrong things from his women, confesses his stupidities, does it all over again. And how he yearns. The drenching sadness of his blighted need to bond more fully with the unknowable sex is powerful, poignant. . .[21]

Confronted by death at the end of the book the chamberlain asks Lanark if he has a complaint. He answers, 'I ought to have more love before I die. I've not had enough' to which the chamberlain replies, 'That is everyone's complaint.' [22]

Of course, in the modern world with its materialistic obsessions, it is easy to see why disenchantment with the quantity of love in one's life may well be universal. Nonetheless, people will experience this feeling to varying degrees. Feeling that we want more love can simply be the sense that something is missing, like being peckish between meals, or it can involve a hunger so profound that our very being is threatened. And it is this latter sense of lacking love that pervades *Lanark* – leading the young Thaw ultimately to suicide and creating Lanark's and Rima's hideous, life-threatening dragonhide.

The individual, starved of love and affection, can be found in any society but could it be the case that this theme is particularly apposite in a city with an emotionally abusive culture as this is likely to create psychological problems and strain relationships to breaking point?

Gray was 27 before he managed to have a relationship with a woman – a Scandinavian called Inge who was 18 years old. He married her within a couple of weeks. The marriage produced one son but was emotionally disastrous for both partners and finally ended in separation. The simple yearning for love, and the despair engendered by feelings of disconn-ection, are at the heart of *Lanark* but its meaning is easily obscured, muffled by the political and philosophical complex-ities of this multi-layered novel.

It is in Gray's poems that his heart-felt sorrow at the emot-ional disconnection in his life finds uncluttered expression. Indeed the volume, dedicated to his mother, is called *Old Negatives.* The cover tells us that the verses are 'negative because they describe love mainly by its absences and reverses.' The image accompanying the poems about Inge are of a woman, half-dragon, piercing a man through the heart.

The final verse of a poem called 'Woundscape' reads:

> To enjoy the wife who is his, lovingly legally
> Is to be silent. How can he be silent and be?
> He imprisons his heart and will not allow a door.
> By fearing the gift of love he loves fear more.
> It is not fulfilment he wants, but to be wounded regally.[23]

Are these lines not eerily reminiscent of what the historian David Hackett Fischer argues happened in cultures which reinforced differences between the genders? – 'a great aching silent distance that kept them apart'.

Lanark is about the 'quest' to find more 'love and sunlight' where sunlight means quite simply a better life.[24] At the heart of the novel is Gray's simple mantra: 'Let Glasgow Flourish by Telling the Truth.' But what are the truths Gray wants us to hear? When interviewed about his work Gray claims very little about *Lanark's* meaning and what people should take out of it. Indeed he says that if his work has deep meaning then it simply echoes what Chekhov claimed for his plays: 'My friends you should not live like this.' [25]

But what does 'this' refer to? Partly this is about socialism although Gray makes it clear he is not setting out a political manifesto of any kind. But what I find dispiriting is the way that the basic human story of the quest for love and the damage wrought by childhood experiences is ignored by so many commentators. Instead we are more likely to be told that *Lanark* is essentially a variation on the Scottish divided self and a commentary on the stasis of modern Scotland. What this approach ignores is the writer's own motivation for creative endeavour. There is even a line in *Lanark* where Sludden says: 'An artist doesn't tell people things, he expresses himself.' [26]

We know that Gray wrote out of despair and his own personal experiences. He was a sensitive, imaginative child and the abusiveness inherent in his culture had a crippling effect on his emotional development and no doubt his physical health. Gray has suffered from depression, had periods when he consumed too much alcohol, and has numerous health problems. His work also gives repeated insight into feelings of self-hate. [27] Given this, how helpful it is to see his first novel – twenty four years in the writing – mainly as the result of Scotland's relationship with England or with capitalist exploitation?

Feminists used to say 'the personal is political' in that our personal relationships have a political and economic dimension. In this book I have also shown how economic and social forces, affecting jobs and living conditions, forced men out of the home and into pubs and how this simple fact had a profound effect on relationships with their wives and children. As we have seen, some of the desire to drink may also have been attributable to the severe dislocation people experienced as a result of the rapid destruction of old ways of life. In this respect it is impossible to separate the political and the personal. Nonetheless we must be aware that when examining individuals' lives these factors can either be in the foreground or the background. I believe that the constant attempt to link the personal problems that surface in novels with Scotland's constitutional and cultural position leads to a distortion. It encourages us to miss the obvious: authors who write dark, gloomy novels about the quest for love and sunlight are doing so because they didn't have enough of it when they were growing up or are missing it in their personal lives.

Exactly the same instinct to overpoliticise the meaning of a novel can be seen with Janice Galloway's *The Trick is to Keep Breathing*.[28] This charts the mental breakdown of Joy Stone. This novel too has been interpreted in conventional Scottish political terms. Thus the problems it outlines are about 'damaged identity' and the author's problems with 'voice', albeit from a woman's perspective.[29] But Janice Galloway has now published the first part of her autobiography and it recounts a story which would make the ACE researchers weep and should force analysts to look at her first novel in an entirely different light. Galloway's mother was over forty when she was born and repeatedly told Janice that she 'thought she was the menopause' and 'things would have been different' if she had known – the implication here being that she would have ended the pregnancy. (Remember George Albee's claim that the most important factor in a child's life is to feel loved and wanted.) Janice's father was a drunk who was emotionally abusive and threatening (though not necessarily physically violent) to her mother. Understandably the father had a negative effect on young Janice:

> You knew he was in because of the way the air sat in
> the house, the displacement of dust. It was some-
> thing animal that gave him away, something animal
> that picked him up, sent the message for the chest to
> tighten, the ears to prick. In the right mood, I could
> feel him through walls. It was the sensation of being
> in an open field, losing the hand you thought you
> were holding, the ground sinking underfoot. [30]

After a particularly ugly incident the mother leaves home, taking Janice with her. They live in tiny accommodation and are very hard up. The father eventually dies and they return to the matrimonial home. Janice's mother clearly suffers from depression and at one point tries to commit suicide. By my reckoning the child Janice has encountered at least five 'adverse childhood experiences'. But there is more to come. She has a much older sister who, in the book, she calls Cora. Aged twenty-one she leaves her husband and baby and returns to live with Janice and her mother. Janice talks about her as 'sprung like a steel trap'. [31] As described by Galloway in the book, Cora has some type of personality disorder. She completely lacks empathy and regularly subjects her much younger sister to extreme verbal and physical abuse. For example, she locks Janice in a cupboard, sets her hair on fire and often punches her. On other occasions she could be generous and do interesting things. So being with Cora Janice felt she 'had to be braced':

> Want something nice? she'd say and hold out her
> hand. It could be chocolate, a wrestling match, a
> feather, a belt to the side of the head, no clues which.
> I didn't even have to choose a hand. That's what want
> got, she'd say, whether the surprise was nasty or nice.
> That's what you get just because. What she was trying
> to teach me I have no idea: what I learned was a
> lifelong suspicion of treats, promises, the expectation
> of pleasure. [32]

A highly intelligent and sensitive woman, and one of Scotland's most gifted writers, no wonder Janice Galloway went on to write a novel about a woman's mental breakdown. Interestingly, in an interview Galloway says that 'there is no such thing as a dysfunctional family – we're all dysfunctional in some way. This is normal.' [33]

Galloway's and Gray's stories set in Scotland portray a negative and unnurturing world. They are not lone voices. Gavin Wallace in his survey of the Scottish novel since the 1970s describes a 'spectacular tradition of despair'. [34] One survey of Scottish literature claims that there is a 'persistent dark strand in twentieth century Scottish writing. [35] This darkness deepens if we examine the literature of the west of Scotland from the 1960s on as so much of it is about couples arguing, kids growing up without love and affection, women getting beaten up, fathers totally estranged from their children, women popping painkillers to get through the day and mad, belt-happy teachers. For all that we often hear about great social cohesion, many Glasgow novels report a great deal of alienation from the community and arguments amongst neighbours. As well as these dysfunctional relationships life is described as lacking in spiritual meaning or personal fulfilment. This negative view of day-to-day life can be seen clearly in the novels of Robin Jenkins, Alexander Trocchi, George Friel, Agnes Owens, Gordon Williams, Alan Sharp, Archie Hind and Alasdair Gray. No wonder so many of their characters long for escape.

It is also unsurprising that in a large-scale survey of Scottish literature the terms 'shadow-land', 'wastelands', 'blighted cities' and 'dystopian visions' are applied when discussing work emanating from the west of Scotland.[36] What's interesting is that these negative perspectives pre-date Thatcherism: the problem is not simply about deindustrialisation, mass unemployment or the disorienting effect of moving from an inner city slum to a peripheral housing estate. It's something deeper than that. A Scottish literature expert from Germany, Peter Zenzinger, argues in an article on modern Scottish fiction:

> . . . contemporary life as depicted by Scottish writers has very few alluring traits. . . all the zest has gone out of life, all prospect of a better future has withered. This complaint is familiar enough in all industrialised countries, and yet the extreme bitterness with which it is uttered in Scottish writing is remarkable. [37]

Zenzinger also maintains that contemporary literature shows that 'the primary curse of Scottish life' is 'the inability to love' which he thinks 'aggravates the sense of loneliness and isolation felt by the modern urbanised Scot to the point of neurosis.' [38] Another foreign commentator gives an insightful synopsis of Gordon Williams' *From Scenes Like These*:

> . . . a father/son relationship based on hatred, a rejection of all that parents stand for, and a resolve to avoid their mistakes; the absence of any goal within reach and worth striving for, and finally, the hero's capitulation and escape towards the life-style of a 'real moronic working man' just to get away from the constrictions of respectability, and the demand for an education that seems to be of no practical value. Primarily, Dunky Logan runs away from a domineering mother and the task of being a grown-up, for a male Never-Neverland of drink, football and sexual fantasy.[39]

Are these novelists using such story lines as metaphors for Scotland? I think not. It is not Scotland's political experience, and history of divisions, which have mainly been responsible for these negative stories but reflections of their real lived experience – their own or that of the people round them. Living in a country where people often see their culture as second-rate only adds another layer of negativity but this is not the major reason for the 'dark strand' or the literature of 'despair'. We should look to the home, our personal relationships or the school, more than to the constitution or our political position.

This does not mean to say that there are no good arguments in favour of independence or more political powers for Scotland. I am a passionate supporter of devolution and would like to see the country have more political and economic power but I also want to see constitutional and identity politics kept in their place. It is gentleness, compassion, encouragement, unqualified love, hugs and affection that writers and others growing up in the west of Scotland particularly missed in their lives.

CHAPTER 14

Dislocation, dislocation, dislocation

G LASGOW has mounting problems with drink, drugs, violence and poor people's health. In some areas of the city these are of such magnitude that we must accept an unpalatable fact: to find populations with equivalent problems as poor male Glaswegians we need to look at the experience of aboriginal people in the New World. In short, it is the Maori in New Zealand, the native people of Canada and the US or Australia's aboriginal population where we find similar levels of addiction to drink and drugs, violence, suicide and health-defeating behaviours.[1] In short, the closest parallels are native peoples whose culture and hopes have been destroyed. In Chapter 5 we saw how earlier in Scotland's history rapid urbanisation may have caused 'dislocation' and fostered the conditions for addiction (in that instance alcohol) to arise. But serious dislocation also befell poor Glaswegians in the past few decades.

Community breakdown

> I remember sitting on the steps at the close,
> unable to accept that I had to stay there, feeling
> totally lost and homesick for Blackhill and Peggy.
> I was on another continent, as far away as the
> people who were emigrating to Australia. . .[2]

So writes Meg Henderson in her autobiographical *Finding Peggy*. The year was 1956 and the young Meg wasn't emigrating to the antipodes: her family had been given a new house in Drumchapel, one of the new peripheral housing estates.

In the late 1950s Glasgow Corporation's assessment of housing stock led them to conclude that they needed to demolish 90,000 houses, in 29 separate areas of the city. Thousands of other houses were also in very poor condition. The Corporation then set up 29 'comprehensive development areas' to help clear the slums and improve these areas. At the same time central government was making plans for two new towns to be built – East Kilbride and Cumbernauld – to help relocate people from old run-down urban areas. Glasgow Council also built huge housing schemes mainly on rural land on the outskirts of the city – Pollok, Easterhouse, Drumchapel and Castlemilk. Easterhouse was so vast that it was reputed to be one of the largest council developments in Europe. These estates were not 'garden suburbs' as they included large numbers of high density, tenement style blocks. As well as these housing projects the Council also embarked on a major new road network – the Inner Ring Road. Effectively this led to vast areas within the old city being demolished or isolated – Cowcaddens, St. George's Cross, Charing Cross, Townhead and others, almost overnight, went from being thriving urban communities to streets overshadowed by motorway fly-overs and poor access for pedestrians. On top of this the Corporation decided to fill some of the gap sites within the city with high rise blocks. This led to multi-storey blocks appearing in Springburn, Maryhill, Ibrox and other places, including the notorious Red Road flats.

Experts estimate that by 1975 the Council had demolished 95,000 houses and large areas had been cleared of shops and industries. Effectively this meant that hundreds of thousands of Glaswegians had to flit and whole communities and areas, such as the Gorbals, were razed. Many tenants probably went willingly and were delighted with their new homes. My own grandfather and aunt were relocated in the early 1960s from a decrepit Maryhill two room and kitchen to a lovely three apartment flat with kitchen and bathroom – a huge luxury for working-class Glaswegians. Others appreciated having a garden or being surrounded, for the first time, by some green space.

Despite these positives, reading various reminiscences, it is easy to see how disoriented people felt. One minute they were living next to neighbours they had known for years, near their extended family and part of a community and the next they were living in a neighbourhood where few people knew one another. Remember in these days most working-class people didn't have telephones so even keeping in touch with family members was difficult. Also transport links were poor. Bus and rail links were limited and so getting into town, or other areas to see relatives, proved time-consuming and extremely expensive. Glasgow once had a public transport system the rival of the world but the Council phased out the trams in 1962 and the city adopted car transportation with such a vengeance that it even remodelled the city centre to make way for the motorway. One problem was that most of the folk, now living on the periphery, were reliant on public transport as they didn't have cars. One early resident of the Castlemilk estate recalls that people were at first happy to go but that the move was often beset with problems:

I often wondered about those folk who moved in,
stayed for a wee while and then disappeared, leaving
the house empty. There was always quite a few
houses empty, brand new as well. . . When people
came to Castlemilk, there was a tremendous change
to their lives. Some people couldn't take the shock.
Others couldn't afford it. We were like early settlers.
We needed an extra wage for bus fares to get to visit
our families, who were all away in another part of
town. [3]

One of the biggest problems with the Council's response
to the housing crisis was their decision to demolish, not
refurbish, most of the old tenements. The planners and
politicians obviously did not grasp that in moving tenants about
in this wholesale fashion they were breaking vital social ties
and family bonds – the very support that people needed to live
meaningful and decent lives. The politicians also decided to
replace many inner city dwellings with multi-storey flats. In the
main this proved disastrous. When we think of high flats it is
easy to envisage American sky-scrapers – often home to some
of the world's richest people. But it is now widely recognised
by social scientists that housing poor families in tower blocks is
a big mistake: they simply don't have the access to facilities,
and green spaces, that makes an apartment lifestyle reasonable.
Also when poor people are confined together in a block of flats,
with its stairwells and dependence on lifts, this environment
can magnify problems with drugs and anti-social behaviour.

Unfortunately, Glasgow built so many high flats that by 1979
there were more than 300 in the city – a higher percentage of
citizens in this type of dwelling than any other equivalent city
in Europe. Two of the tower blocks, known as Hutchestown C,
attracted a huge amount of attention. The city authorities

commissioned the architect Sir Basil Spence to design two high rise blocks for the new, redeveloped Gorbals. Spence based his design on the Marseille apartment building (*Unité d' Habitation*) designed by the famous architect known as 'Le Corbusier'. However, while there were superficial similarities the Gorbals tower blocks had little of the facilities at the core of Le Corbusier's building which boasted a nursery school, hotel, shops, offices and gymnasium. The *Unité d' Habitation* included a sun deck roof-terrace with an unobstructed view of the Mediterranean and was set in landscaped grounds – a far cry from Spence's tower blocks in the old Gorbals which came to be known as 'Hutchie C' or latterly 'Alcatraz'.

In the early 1960s the four hundred families who moved into Spence's new flats were very impressed: they were spacious and bright and a far cry from the one-roomed dark dwellings they had previously inhabited. Indeed they seemed so upmarket some residents likened them to a hotel. The new flats also had large verandas which Spence had designed to jut from each floor, allowing residents the opportunity for space and fresh air as well as somewhere to hang washing. Indeed Spence imagined that the building would look like 'a ship in full sail' when the balconies were filled with sheets billowing in the wind.[4]

Reality was very different. Sitting or hanging your washing out on verandas, high up in the sky, might seem great on paper but, given Glasgow's weather, doing it for real was often miserable. Right from the very start vandalism was a problem. So was building design and maintenance. Spence's design was 'innovative'. In other words, major elements of building design were untried and untested. One of the problems was that rain leaked into the lift shafts causing power failures. Within ten years the building needed to be reclad and windows replaced. By the late 1980s residents were no longer looking for building improvements: they had lost heart and wanted out. The Council demolished Spence's two tower blocks in 1993.

The problems with lifts not working, vandalism and lack of facilities were repeated elsewhere in Glasgow's high rise housing stock and successive Glasgow councils never allocated adequate money for maintenance. But this was a problem with council housing generally in the UK. In 2007 Lynsey Hanley wrote a powerful analysis of council housing in Britain called *Estates: an intimate history*. In it she charts how Nye Bevan's vision for quality council housing to promote the health and dignity of working people, and eradicate inequality, led to the building of huge tacky housing estates and ugly tower blocks. Everything we've encountered so far is all part of the story of housing in Britain, not just Glasgow:

> An unflattering portrait of council-housing policy at the turn of the 1970s would contain the following elements: thoughtlessness; the hard sell of building contractors; poor workmanship; Brutalist concrete designs; lack of maintenance; the well-meant but dippy optimism of local-authority planners and architects; a fetish for quantity over quality; and power-crazed council leadership. [5]

Hanley is great in describing the soulless nature of many estates and how their design often led to wind tunnels and inhumane townscapes but she spends little time documenting the type of problems which beset Glasgow's new housing stock.

Blaming the tenants

As was the case with Spence's flats, many of Glasgow's new houses were poorly designed and built, leading to particular problems with dampness and condensation. Cathy McCormack is one tenant who campaigned extensively on dampness and whose autobiography *The Wee Yellow Butterfly* charts the sorry tale.[6] She moved to the Easthall area of Easterhouse in 1975 into what she describes as a 'concrete bunker'. Within weeks she realised how cold and damp it was – so damp that there were icicles hanging from the windows in winter and various moulds growing on the walls. A house-proud woman, concerned about her children's ill-health, Cathy kept complaining to the Council. Like many other tenants, she was told that the problem was not the houses themselves but her lifestyle: she was boiling too many kettles, not opening enough windows and drying too many clothes. In other words, Cathy and other tenants were to blame for doing the normal things in houses that anyone takes for granted. Some tenants, living in a building with a crack in the gable wall, were even told that they were at fault for slamming doors.

'Blame the tenant' didn't go down well with residents and, given the Council's lack of interest in the problem, some residents, including Cathy, formed an active anti-dampness campaign. What the residents wanted was simple: affordable heating, proper insulation and effective ventilation. The group did a door-to-door survey in the area and found that 60 per cent of tenants reported living in damp houses. The group also brought in independent technical experts to survey the houses:

> . . . we all believed that our houses were made of brick. A lot of them weren't – they were built of

> something called a Wilson Block, which allows rain
> water to come in through the joints, along the
> metal ties and soak the inside walls. Made from
> concrete blocks with no insulation, the houses lost
> heat very quickly. The report showed that a tenant
> in an Easthall council house lost £4 in heat costs
> through a wall of Wilson Blocks for every £1 lost
> through the wall of a Barratt brick house. [7]

These experts also discovered other major problems such as faulty foundations, inadequate damp courses, and lack of maintenance to roofs and windows. As almost a third of tenants lived in hard-to-heat houses, Cathy was one of the first to realise that the large amounts of energy they consumed wasn't just financially ruinous for the families: it also had huge environmental costs. Imaginative tenants' action in Easterhouse led to a grant from the European Union, together with local authority funding, to upgrade a group of houses so that they had better insulation and solar energy. This resulted in decreasing fuel costs from an average of £30 a week to £5.

Cathy wasn't simply joining up thinking between housing and the environment but also housing and health. She and many other residents were convinced that the damp houses were making them ill. For example, one of Cathy's children was plagued with asthma and one of her babies had terrible thrush – a fungal infection. There is now a great deal of evidence that damp housing can have an extremely negative effect on health, particularly for children and the elderly, as well as causing depression and anxiety.[8] But in those days when people claimed that their housing was undermining their health they were ignored. This was the era when it was becoming clear that Glasgow had atrocious health and that the city had the worst figures for heart disease in the world. However, the response of health professionals was to look at other factors. Cathy McCormack recalls:

> . . . the blame was put on our diet and in particular
> our greasy fish suppers and general lifestyle. . .
> One thing I knew for sure was that it was not keep-
> fit exercises that we needed but homes that were
> 'fit' to live in and incomes or benefits that
> prevented us from having to choose between dying
> from hypothermia or malnutrition. [9]

Food was understandably a touchy issue. There were few shops in these huge schemes often selling poor, over-priced food. Some local people undertook research and discovered that the food available in Easterhouse 'was not only more expensive than places like the west end, but the quality of food like fruit and vegetables was sub-standard.' [10] These and other housing and income problems were ignored by council officials and health professionals, McCormack claims, in preference for individualistic solutions which implied that somehow the people themselves were to blame and could solve the problems themselves.

Even in the early days of Easterhouse the scheme attracted notoriety for its problems with gangs. The problem came to national and international attention as a result of the English singer Frankie Vaughan who campaigned for youth clubs in the area and organised knife amnesties. Vaughan was a major UK entertainer and so his interest ensured copious publicity. Some argued that the new tenants had imported the gang problem from old areas and feuds. But Cathy McCormack thinks that the media and politicians continually overlooked 'the political violence that has been inflicted on the hearts, minds and spirits of the people who live here'.[11] In Chapter 1 we saw how inequality can lead to violence as a result of 'the bicycling reaction' – people feeling bad about their low status and so kicking out at others. But there were other reasons why Glasgow's new housing estates were likely to breed violence.

The boredom factor

In undertaking this research on Glasgow one fact in particular has stood out for me. In the early 1960s when Easterhouse was built its population was 58,000 yet it had absolutely no facilities and inadequate public transport. This meant it was bigger than many Scottish towns. For example, Ayr currently has a population of 46,000 and has a cinema, racecourse, sporting facilities, hotels, theatre, library, pubs, shopping centre and countless other facilities. This is what we would expect in a place catering for that level of population. Yet Easterhouse started off with nothing. The city council, mindful of the problem that drink had caused in many working class areas insisted that the new estates were 'dry'. In other words, they had no public houses. As to other facilities they thought it frivolous to spend money or time on such things when the priority was simply to get people out of slums and into better quality housing. Again Glasgow's councillors and officials, like many of their British equivalents, were simply wrong.

The seventeenth century French philosopher Blaise Pascal summed up one of his profound insights in a couple of lines: 'I have discovered that all human evil stems from one fact alone – Man's inability to sit still.' In other words, it is boredom which can easily drive us to destructive or anti-social acts. He would not have been surprised that within a short period of time Easterhouse had a gang problem and violence.

One of the modern thinkers to analyse the importance of stimulation for modern societies is Tibor Scitovsky, a Hungarian-born American economist. He argues that when people are forced to work hard and for long hours boredom rarely presents a problem. In the past it was rich men who often turned to blood-sports, jousting and other various activities to relieve their boredom. Indeed Scitovsky writes:

> Violence seems to be men's instinctive outlet for their pent-up energies; and combining it with danger, especially danger they feel confident of overcoming, makes it all the more exciting and satisfying.' [12]

In his book *The Joyless Economy: the psychology of human satisfaction*, Scitovsky draws on different types of research to help us understand why human beings have such a need for stimulation and complexity. Quoting neurological research he argues that the human brain needs arousal – that too little or too much stimulation can feel painful – and that the organism struggles to maintain an 'optimum' level.

Boredom and lack of stimulation in areas like Easterhouse resulted not just because they lacked facilities; even the housing estates themselves have monotonous layouts with streets and streets of similar houses and design. No wonder the comedian and performer Billy Connolly referred to these estates as 'deserts wi windaes'.

The problem of lack of stimulation was not confined to the peripheral estates as high rise dwellers also often suffered from the lack of facilities. Over the years the city council has built some facilities in these estates, such as community centres and sports centres, and the population numbers have reduced, but there is still not enough to do, particularly for young people. One of the striking messages of a recent Channel 4 documentary on knife-crime in London and Glasgow was that many of the young men in Glasgow particularly cited 'boredom' as one of the main reasons they went about in gangs fighting one another. 'It gies ye somethin to dae,' was a frequent refrain. [13] The tragedy is that gang warfare restricts gang members' movement to a few safe streets, effectively imprisoning them in a small area. This means that it can be harder for them to access facilities which may be there but are outwith their gang territory.

Added to the problem of damp, ill-maintained houses and nothing to do is another important factor – the way that these new areas quickly went to seed. Bored teenagers resorted to vandalism, graffiti appeared and so did litter. This, together with inadequate landscaping and untended green spaces, meant that streets, or entire areas, quickly looked run down. This may seem trivial but social scientists now believe that even small changes in the appearance of a neighbourhood can have a hugely negative effect.

Urban decay

In 1982 James Q. Wilson and George L. Kelling, two experts on crime and public administration, published a now famous paper called 'broken windows'. [14] In it they set out the conditions for 'urban decay'. They argue that if a window is broken and not repaired, another will soon be broken and then another. This can happen in good or poor neighbourhoods. The same can happen when litter piles up, graffiti appears, gardens are ill-maintained or weeds grow through cracks in the pavement. The authors argue that 'vandalism can occur anywhere once communal barriers – the sense of mutual regard and the obligations of civility – are lowered by actions that seem to signal that "no one cares".' In other words, untended property, graffiti, litter all suggest that you can just do what you like; that the area is uncontrolled. This then often triggers the next step in urban decay:

> We suggest that 'untended' behaviour also leads to the breakdown of community controls. A stable neighbourhood of families who care for their homes, mind each other's children, and confidently frown on unwanted intruders can change, in a few years or even a few months, to an inhospitable and frightening jungle. A piece of property is abandoned, weeds grow up, a window is smashed. Adults stop scolding rowdy children; the children emboldened, become more rowdy. Families move out, unattached adults move in. Teenagers gather in front of the corner store. The merchant asks them to move; they refuse. Fights occur. Litter accumulates. People start drinking in front of the grocery; in time, an inebriate slumps to the sidewalk and is allowed to sleep it off. [16]

What then commonly happens is that residents start thinking that the area is dangerous. They don't go out as much at night; they avert their eyes to trouble. This then makes the area attractive for drug dealers and criminals.

This pattern could be seen in many council house areas throughout Glasgow. The new houses were built, tenants moved in and very quickly the area degenerated in exactly the way these authors suggest. Of course, there were exceptions and even within many of the big schemes some parts seemed to degenerate much more quickly than others. Indeed some streets or enclaves have always managed to exude the sense that people do care and have thus managed to ward off the worst anti-social behaviour. Exactly the same pattern of urban decay can be discerned in some of Edinburgh's council estates and those south of the border as well. But for a number of reasons Glasgow's schemes were particularly vulnerable to this type of erosion.

First, the sheer size of the estates encouraged a sense of alienation and estrangement. Second, gangs and violence had bedevilled areas of the city since the 1920s. Third, Glasgow had a tradition of hard drinking. If drunks stoating through the streets was a sign that no-one cared, then right from the start this would have been visible in the new estates. Fourth, Glasgow Council was notoriously bad at maintaining its houses or housing estates. Many estates hadn't been adequately land-scaped in the first place. Finally, a large number of tenants were already suffering from excessive stress in their life as a result of poor family relations (outlined in previous chapters). This meant that many had too much on their minds to bother about litter, rowdy weans or unkempt gardens. In short, in large tracts of Glasgow it was extremely easy for the message to go out – no-body cares – and for decay to set in, creating the conditions for crime and large-scale social problems.

Lynsey Hanley maintains that 'part of the problem with estates was their estate-ness' – the fact that they were built for a specific group, often on the periphery, rather than evolving organically.[17] They were built to cater for a specific social group which meant that others often looked down on the inhabitants. Thus it was all too easy for residents in surrounding areas to 'stigmatise' those who came from estates. Once these areas had a bad name then anyone who could, moved out. The continual creaming off of people who were the most successful was also disastrous. These were the people who could have been role models in the area; 'the Joneses' that neighbours may have tried to emulate. As they leave estates it reinforces the sense of being cut off from normal society and aids the downward spiral. International research shows that as outsiders' opinion of an area becomes more negative then the worse it becomes as only the desperate will agree to go there. [18] This is exactly what happened with black ghettos in the USA. Successful black Americans followed the white middle classes and moved out of the cities effectively leaving them to a black underclass.

One of the most interesting analysts of the problem of black Americans is Harvard sociologist William Julius Wilson.[19] He argues that their plight is partly about the legacy of racism but that the more important factor is their economic marginalisation as a result of 'deindustrialisation'. This marginalisation and weakening of the work ethic happened as a result of large-scale, and effectively race-blind changes in the economy. America increasingly shed well-paid, unionised blue collar jobs and many of the casualties were black people. Similar trends can be seen in Scotland and the rest of the UK.

Deindustrialisation

From the 1960s until the late 1970s economic policy in the UK was dominated by government attempts to shore up ailing industries and to lessen the effect of the decline of traditional industries by offering incentives to foreign-owned, mainly American companies, to invest in areas like Scotland. Thus Linwood, in Renfrewshire, became the site of a car plant in the early 1960s. By the mid 1970s almost 60 per cent of manufacturing workers in Scotland were employed in foreign companies. However, inward investment caused its own problems. Many of these 'branch factory' jobs were low-paid and not particularly skilled and these plants were vulnerable to closure in any economic downswing. What Scotland lacked, and still lacks, is home-grown businesses.

Workers in the west of Scotland did not simply accept these job losses. In 1971 8,500 workers staged a 'work-in' at the yards of Upper Clyde Shipbuilders (UCS) in protest at their impending closure. Their demands for the right to work and their determination to keep the yards open, fulfilling the order book, became international news and financial support poured in from round the world. Part of the appeal was the charismatic leadership of Jimmy Reid and Jimmy Airlie with their pledge that there 'will be no hooliganism, there will be no vandalism, there will be no bevvying. . . '[20] Over 80,000 people took to the streets to support the right to work. Within a year, the Heath Government conceded most of their demands and the yards stayed open.

In 1971 Reid became Rector of Glasgow University. The *New York Times* considered his inaugural speech, on alienation, one of the best since the Gettysburg address and published it in full. The most famous passage is when Reid likens modern society to a rat race:

> To the students I address this appeal. Reject these attitudes. Reject the values and false morality that underlie these attitudes. A rat race is for rats. We're not rats. We're human beings. Reject the insidious pressures in society that would blunt your critical faculties to all that is happening around you, that would caution silence in the face of injustice lest it

> jeopardise your chances of promotion or self-
> advancement. This is how it starts and before you
> know where you are, you're a fully paid-up
> member of the rat-pack. [21]

Some believe that Scotland ultimately paid dearly for the opposition to closures by the extremely punitive inaction of the Thatcher Governments of the 1980s and 1990s when Scottish industries haemorrhaged jobs.[22] Undoubtedly the election of the Thatcher Government in 1979 saw a radical break in economic policy: from one concerned about maximising employment to one focussed on managing the money supply. The effects of this, and other changes happening in the global economy, were huge:

> There was an economic restructuring of a magnitude
> that had probably not been seen since the days of
> the Industrial Revolution. At a stroke, with little
> public expense and within a remarkably short period
> of time, the Scottish economy lost all its traditional
> problems which politicians had endeavoured to
> solve from before the Second World War.
> Unprofitable industries and businesses closed, the
> traditional sector more or less disappeared, services
> took the place of manufacturing. . . [23]

The west of Scotland was particularly affected by this 'de-industrialisation'. By the 1990s there were only a few shipyards left on the Clyde. By 1993, the unthinkable happened – the iconic Ravenscraig steel plant closed. Many of the manufacturing plants fell silent – Singer at Clydebank, Caterpillar in Uddingston and Talbot at Linwood, to name but a few.

Modern historians generally agree that Scotland came through this grim period remarkably well. The new Scottish

301

economy was much more diversified and by 1987 the country's occupational structure was more similar to England's. It is also clear that Scotland generally fared better from this period of economic restructuring than Wales or the North East of England. However, these analysts also agree that this period of economic change exacted a huge price: communities suffered as did the human beings caught up in the turmoil. Scottish unemployment soared, peaking in 1995 at 15.6 per cent. There were huge regional variations. The Scottish figure was generally between a quarter and a third higher than the figure for the UK as whole. Within Scotland the figure for Glasgow was particularly high. It is estimated that around 30 per cent of those in peripheral housing estates were unemployed in the 1990s, with the figure rising to 38.2 per cent in the city centre. Twelve districts in Glasgow had unemployment rates above 20 per cent.

In this period of restructuring and 'downsizing' lots of people lost their jobs – white collar workers and managers as well as workers. But as the economy improved it was manual workers who found it particularly difficult to get work since so many of the new jobs were in services and not the heavy industries where they had served their time.

It is estimated that in 1983 around three quarters of a million Scots were 'dependent on supplementary benefits for a living, and it was reckoned that over a million people were living on or below the officially defined poverty line'.[24] Given that Scotland's population was around five million that is a huge percentage of the population living in poverty. Others estimate that the number of people struggling to make ends meet was nearer to one and a half million. The reason for this was not just unemployment but low wages. Many of the inward investors came to Scotland because labour was cheap and the country had high numbers of employees on low wages. Richard Finlay argues that if overtime is not part of the calculation then one in five male workers was on low pay in the early 1980s. Women workers, many of whom worked part-time, were paid at even lower rates than poorly paid men.

This picture of unemployment and low wages has to be seen in the wider UK context. The Thatcherite revolution ushered in a much more materialistic age. This was the era of 'loadsamoney' and 'greed is good'. It was an era which witnessed the sale of public assets to stimulate the economy and enhance the wealth of individuals: the Government sold off shares in Britain's nationalised industries and gave council house tenants a legal right to buy. Data on inequality in the UK show that from the 1980s on, as a result of the Thatcher Government's economic policies, inequality rose sharply.[25] Thus, while many families in Glasgow and elsewhere struggled to live on benefits or low wages, many professionals and others were beginning to benefit from the property boom and the rise of financial services or other new industries. By the 1990s most of those in work began to see a real improvement in their standard of living. With over 55 per cent of homes now privately owned in Scotland, the majority of people had a place on the property ladder. Cars and foreign holidays also became the norm. Items branded 'luxury' and 'designer' were now marketed to ordinary people and many were living lifestyles that would have left previous generations speechless. Of course, none of this was unique to Glasgow or Scotland as these boom years improved living standards in all western countries.

The New Glasgow

In 1983 those in charge of Glasgow City Council realised that the city's old image of slums, heavy industry, strikes, bigotry and gang warfare was holding the city's modernisation back, deterring potential tourists and investors. Michael Kelly, the Lord Provost, managed to raise money from private and public sources, to launch the 'Glasgow's miles better' campaign, generally seen as one of the most successful attempts to sell a UK city. It was a fairly low budget campaign which used Roger Hargreave's 'Mr Happy' character to project the idea of Glasgow as a friendly, welcoming city which supported a good quality of life. The campaign was aimed at business people, opinion formers and those with money and was hugely successful in improving Glasgow's image as well as increasing feelings of civic pride.

This was not a one-off public relations effort. This was the beginning of Glasgow's very successful marketing campaign to sell the city. As discussed in an earlier chapter, Glasgow has proved itself to be excellent at marketing and culture-led regeneration. It truly has been at the forefront of changing the image of a smoky, slum-ridden city into a post-industrial, designer city based on culture, education, style and shopping. Much of what has happened under the 'culture' banner is not froth – Glasgow is genuinely a city with a great deal of cultural activity and the City of Music title is well-deserved.

Many of the physical changes the marketeers focus on are real and not just based on marketing spin. The old slums and industries have disappeared. Many of Glasgow's old city centre buildings and tenements have been cleaned and areas like the Merchant City refurbished, and are now bristling with upmarket flats, restaurants and bars. Other changes testify to the fact that Glasgow has remodelled itself: service sector jobs increased substantially boosting the percentage of residents in social classes 1 and 2; the city has become popular with tourists, attracted by its shops and culture; and the quality of life in this 'post-industrial' city has received a considerable boost, at least for those with enough education and disposable income.

It is also easy to sympathise with the need to recast Glasgow's image to attract money into the city. Traditional industries were all but gone: the city had to reinvent itself. Jobs and livelihoods depended on it. But I think culture commentator Ian Spring, one of the best critics of the making of the 'new Glasgow', is right to argue that there has been something distasteful about much of this marketing. Spring points out that in much of the material, like the example which follows, 'ultra enthusiasm erupted into excessive hyperbole'.

> Today the latest stage in the renaissance of Glasgow was revealed. Now it stamps the city as culturally the most exciting in Britain. The 'no mean city' image no longer exists. Today Glasgow can claim to rival Europe's top urban jewels such as Paris and Florence. The old Glasgow – perceived for so long as a place of drunks and tenements – has been transformed into a vibrant and confident city with a glittering future. [26]

This was written in 1986 when it was clear that there were considerable problems with the new housing stock, unemployment was soaring and many schemes were still (as now) plagued with gangs. These problems may not have been visible within the city centre but that didn't mean they had gone away. As

Spring points out the 'miles better' campaign never reflected, or even attempted to reflect, the lives or opinions of countless Glaswegians who lived in soulless estates or tower blocks with nothing of the lifestyle, or the 'glittering future', promoted by Glasgow's marketing department. Cathy McCormack maintains that in 1990, the year Glasgow was City of Culture, 29 per cent of its housing stock was affected by some form of dampness, condensation or mould growth: not the type of culture which would have made its way into the city's bid for the title.

The political fall-out of the Thatcher era

Some of the cultural changes in Glasgow, such as the rise of a new generation of artists and writers, would have happened anyway as they were linked to other developments, such as the expansion of higher education and Scotland's changing identity. But undoubtedly the type of changes behind Glasgow's rise as 'Scotland with style' were boosted by the new economy and its emphasis on money and looks. Nonetheless, Thatcher's policies did not prove popular in Scotland or Glasgow. The Conservative vote ebbed, seats were lost at both national and local level and opposition to her style of Government fuelled nationalist, and pro-devolution, sentiment.

Scotland's economy was, as we've seen, much more under-mined by closures and unemployment than England's. The celebration of private industry was more threatening to Scotland than the south of England because of the size of the country's public sector. So it is not difficult to see why the Conservative Government should have been so unpopular. The fact that Scotland was now governed by a party Scots had so emphatically rejected, and continued to reject, was a source of profound alienation and despair. Mrs. Thatcher herself, with her fake accent and Home Counties hair-do, was profoundly disliked my many Scots, though, no doubt, there was an element of misogyny as well. Interestingly William McIlvanney once referred to her as 'a woman who keeps her intelligence in her purse'. [27]

In the 1983 election it was clear that a political rift was emerging within the United Kingdom as Labour retained popularity in Scotland but lost once again in England. Once we add into this difficult political environment, profoundly unpopular policies such as the poll tax it is easy to see why political activists felt they had to fight back against what they saw as an alien and hostile government. All this provided fertile ground for the rise of nationalist and devolutionary sentiments.

During the 1979 referendum campaign much of the pro-devolution argument was based on the idea of a 'democratic deficit'. But within a decade this argument had evolved substantially into the idea of 'civic nationalism'. Scotland, it was claimed by those arguing for devolution, was a more socially-minded country, unlike England, which was individualistic. Richard Finlay admirably summarises the argument and points out the paradox:

> The Scots. . . were more in favour of state
> intervention and the social institutions of the state,
> such as comprehensive education, the National
> Health Service and other organs of the Welfare State.
> Paradoxically, these were all residues of the British
> state which had been created in the forties, but by
> sleight of hand they were increasingly painted up in
> tartan and claimed as part of Scottish political
> culture. The change in ownership was not as
> surprising as at first might appear. The demand for

home rule was driven by organisations seeking to defend institutions all of which had their origins in values and beliefs created in Britain during and after the Second World War. That the rest of the British political nation had rejected these values that the Scots seemed desperate to cling to meant that they had to be increasingly represented as Scottish. In this sense, it was not a perception that the Scots had changed that drove the changes of the eighties and nineties, but rather the fact that Thatcherism had robbed the Scots of an acceptable or credible vision of British identity. Corporatism was transmuted into civic nationalism. [28]

William McIlvanney was one of several cultural figures to espouse hostility to the Thatcher Government, warning of the dangers of acquiescence. Speaking at an SNP conference in 1987 McIlvanney urged Scots

. . . to refuse to go where she is trying to force us to go, with the blunderbuss of her economic policies held to our head. I hope we have the courage to remove ourselves, at least some distance, from the shallowness of her philosophy. I hope we have the wisdom to return to prospecting our own traditions once again.

There is a deeply ingrained tradition in Scotland that we will not finally judge one another by material standards. . . No. We'll use another system – a system long established here; a system developed from the experience and the pain and the long thought and the deep humanity of the Scottish people. And that's not a hard system to apply. Its principles are simple enough. You want a measurement of people? Then, if you wish to remain Scottish, here it is. You will measure them by the extent of their understanding, by the width of their compassion, by the depth of their concern and by the size of their humanity. [29]

McIlvanney bases the idea of Scotland's particularly human-itarian approach not just on the experience of industrialisation but on various aspects of Scotland's history and traditions. In various speeches and articles he makes reference to the 'Scottish tradition' by citing the Declaration of Arbroath, the public riots against the Union of the Parliaments in 1707, the ideas and influence of Robert Burns, the socialist values within his own mining family from Kilmarnock and Glasgow's communal culture.

Yet while I stand full-square behind McIlvanney's rejection of the crude materialistic values of the Thatcher Government his views on these 'Scottish traditions' are no more than myth-making. So far in this book we've seen how ordinary working people in Scotland suffered as a result of Scottish landlords who forced them off the land and into appalling working and living conditions. We've also heard about Burns dying in penury with few coming to his aid; successful Scottish businessmen building huge ostentatious mansions for themselves; greedy factors; autocratic bosses; and guardians of the Poor Law deliberately deciding to pay out money to the destitute which was below subsistence level. These, and other countless examples, suggest that compassion was *not* at the forefront of these Scots' minds.

Of course, we're not alone in finding our history strewn with this type of exploitation: right round the world we can find examples of people paid a pittance for back-breaking labour and living in awful conditions while their masters live in splendour. Inequality is also deeply embedded in many societies. But it is also true that some countries, most notably in Scandin-avia, have managed to create social structures and policies which are genuinely more compassionate and caring than ours. Undoubt-edly good things happened in Scotland, such as neighbourliness and communities supporting one another. We also had our fair share, indeed perhaps even more than our share, of philanthrop-ists and charitably-minded individuals. But it is wrong to make out that somehow 'compassion', 'concern', and 'deep humanity' are stamped in the Scots. Sadly trying to cleave to these notions about ourselves blinds us to the truth of the problems of inequality in Glasgow and elsewhere in Scotland.

'A war without bullets'

Mass unemployment was one of the inevitable outcomes of Thatcherite economic policy. The Government continued to pay benefits, and foot huge social security bills, but took the view that work was available for those who really wanted it. Norman Tebbit, a member of the Conservative Cabinet, famously, but indirectly, told people to follow his unemployed father's example from the 1930s and get on their bikes and go in search of employment. No doubt some did – taking jobs on the oil rigs or London building sites, for example. But it was unreasonable to expect former industrial workers to move *en masse* to the south of England to take up work: their families and all they knew were in Glasgow. This city had made things – big, impress-ive things like ships and locomotive engines. This new economy of services – talking, customer service, processing bits of paper or whatever – did not make sense. Besides they weren't ideal candidates as many lacked the communication skills and attitudes required. Many of the new service sector jobs were ultimately taken by women, often working on a part-time basis. But the women from the schemes often lacked what was wanted. Professor Chris Warhurst's research shows the new service industries put a great deal of emphasis on accents and presentation and poor Glaswegians simply don't have the right image or style. [30]

Given the numbers of people in Glasgow who lost their jobs, and the uncompromising nature of political discourse, it felt like an attack. In her book Cathy McCormack calls it 'the war without bullets' – a war fought with 'briefcases instead of guns'.[31] For Cathy the reason for the war was quite simple: the people in Glasgow who had worked in traditional industries were now 'surplus to market requirements'. They weren't needed any more. They were supposed to be 'free' but in reality could not escape the 'poverty trap'. Cathy became acutely aware that this story was not particular to Glasgow.

As we saw earlier, Harvard sociologist, William Julius Wilson, argues that the problems which beset black communities in the USA are not due to a weak work ethic or poor family values but the fact that many black men lost good, well-paid unionised jobs as a result of deindustrialisation and the practice of 'off-shoring' – manufacturing items more cheaply in third world countries. [32] These practices have taken hold throughout the modern world and have led to a decline in the demand for traditional working class labour: a development with negative consequences for families and communities worldwide.

From 1990 on Cathy McCormack became involved in what was happening internationally. She visited South Africa and Nicaragua; went to international conferences in places like New York where she talked to people from the IMF; and became influenced by thinkers such as Paulo Freire the internationally acclaimed educationalist and theorist on oppression. But Cathy observed an important difference between the oppression she saw in the third world and what she saw on her own doorstep.

In places like Nicaragua poverty was external and obvious with people living in shanty towns and makeshift accommodation. These circumstances led people to understand the source of the problem and have a strong sense of community and shared experience. However, in Glasgow 'the abuse was camouflaged and the pain privatised.' [33] The breakdown of community and the ostensibly better living conditions meant that those struggling to live decent lives behind their front doors were not only isolated from others but somehow personally to blame.

McCormack tells us that when various people came to Easterhouse from third world countries they were shocked by what they found. A social worker on placement from the Congo (then called Zaire) told Cathy: 'I didn't know it was possible to oppress people to the extent that they were oblivious.' [34] A woman from South Africa, who had been active in the African National Council, said after her stay in Easterhouse that it resembled 'a concentration camp'. [35] But if this is the case who are the jailers? Cathy would finger the heartlessness and extreme drive for profit of international financiers and politicians. But interestingly, she also blames the local Labour Party. They were the governing party in Glasgow Council and they dragged their feet on dampness and other housing problems and had to be taken to tribunals to begin to address the issue. She also claims her local councillor disempowered the highly effective local residents group she was involved in and ironically, imposed 'a housing co-operative from the top down'. [36] Ultimately she concluded that decisions were made on the basis of what would be best for the ruling Labour Party – not local people. As we saw in Chapter 9 about the life of the Independent Labour Party, this was not an uncommon conclusion.

Cathy is also critical of health authorities who 'individual-ised' problems making them feel guilty about diet and lifestyle and what she calls the 'poverty industry' – a network of organisations, staffed with professionals on good salaries who she thinks have a vested interest in the continuation of the problems they are supposed to address.

It is very difficult to read Cathy McCormack's book and not feel outraged on her behalf. She has played a part on the international stage, received glowing coverage in media outlets such as *The Guardian* or Radio 4, and yet is hardly quoted in Scotland. She still lives in a cold house in Easterhouse. 'In wars with bullets,' she writes, 'they use mines to blow people up. In wars without bullets, they undermine people.' [37]

In her book Cathy is clear that some of the problems which people in her area face are about money, hard-to-heat houses and the soul-destroying effects of long-term unemployment. But she is also aware that the problems are more psychological and spiritual than material. This is about feeling worthless and excluded – about knowing you are at the bottom of the heap and not part of mainstream society. It is about people not simply refusing to listen to what you have to say but ignoring your existence. This is essentially the argument that Richard Wilkinson and Kate Pickett advance in their book *The Spirit Level*. But Cathy adds another important dimension. She tells us that the problem is also about a lack of hope.

Cathy McCormack's analysis majors on the changes which happened in places like Easterhouse as a result of housing regeneration and the human fall-out from the economic restructuring of the 1980s. But it is also clear from her own narrative that the problems of Glasgow pre-date this. Her description of early family life in the 1950s and 60s is of a self-centred, angry father, parents who hardly talked, no physical affection between family members, child abuse by neighbours and an education system where she routinely felt put-down. Of course, this is not exclusive to Glasgow but it runs so deep it is part of the city's DNA and can never provide the basis for good, flourishing lives. When we put on top of these stresses and strains, housing and employment problems we can see why life imploded for many families, formerly working-class, now labelled 'deprived'. These internal and external fractures created the conditions for widespread dislocation and self-destructive behaviours and ill-health.

Finally, one historian's metaphor is worth citing as it is particularly apt for this conclusion. Christopher Harvie reviews the nature of Scotland's hard, working class culture in the period 1922-1964 and focusses on how men spent time drinking in miserable pubs. He writes:

> If the result was a certain social inadequacy, then it would have been much worse but for the women. They created a home-life and a sort of community-politics, even if only through policing by gossip. They stayed away from drink and crime, saved, organised their families, read. They were a coiled spring. [38]

The spring was sprung, partly by the growing independence of women and the fact that they were less likely to martyr themselves for their families. But the type of profound socio-economic changes documented in this chapter also played their part. None of this was unique to Glasgow but the uncoiling of the spring has had a particularly damaging effect in a city where living a healthy life has always proved difficult.

CHAPTER 15
Straws in the wind

BEFORE the Centre for Confidence and Well-being ran its first big event on 'positive psychology' I explained the content on the phone to a journalist. Hardly able to keep the contempt from his voice, he asked, 'And what has this got to do with the man coughing his guts out in Shettleston?' 'Everything,' was my rapid reply. This event was not about poverty and men from poor areas would not be participating but many policy makers were and, if they are going to come up with policies to help some of Glasgow's problems, they need to hear different ideas and perspectives. In this chapter I look at some of the obvious factors for Glasgow's challenging statistics before considering various pieces of research and different ways to help us understand well-being in the city. Some of these findings are indicative rather than conclusive – straws in the wind which help us discern its direction.

The obvious
At the heart of the journalist's question about the man in Shettleston was his firm conclusion that the problem is simply poverty and unemployment. However, as we saw in Chapter 1, poverty helps us to understand a great deal of Glasgow's problems but it still cannot provide the answer: other places, some in Eastern Europe, have much worse poverty and

deprivation and yet they have less violence, better health and fewer social problems. As Wilkinson, and a growing number of economists point out, the problems with being poor in Western countries is not so much about the money *per se*. Of course some may live in dire conditions such as damp, run-down houses but many do not. What's more, the 'poor' can still have access to goods only available to better-off people in previous times. Indeed those now classed as living in poverty can still have fridges, televisions, cars and foreign holidays.[1] This is one of the reasons why we need to see the problem as more about inequality. This has been a major theme of this book yet even here Glasgow's inequality is not worse than it is in many other places with much better health outcomes.

Another obvious reason for excessive ill-health is having to live in a poor run-down neighbourhood. We looked at some of these issues in the last chapter and certainly they play their part. Nonetheless there is no escaping the fact that Glasgow has spent millions on physical regeneration yet it has not had the expected impact on health or social problems.

What of unemployment and work? Since 2005 a number of important Government reports have been published in the UK which set out the evidence for the benefits of work. [2] These reports argue that work is central to people's individual identity and social status; meets various psychosocial needs; is essential for people to feel full members of society; and is the main way that people can support themselves. In short, work is important for people's mental and physical well-being. On the contrary, those who are unemployed are likely to die earlier and generally have poorer physical and mental health. Getting back to work is therefore a major way to improve individuals' health and life satisfaction. Undoubtedly areas like Shettleston have high levels of worklessness yet we must continually remember that health problems, violence, drugs and alcohol abuse are much worse for the west of Scotland than for many other areas in Europe even though the unemployment rate in this Scottish region is lower than theirs.

Sadly many of those out of work in Scotland lack the skills or attitudes employers are increasingly looking for. Between 2002 and 2006 Futureskills Scotland surveyed 19,000 employers on their recruitment needs and how satisfied they were with their current workforce.[3] Most employers were content, except those in growing companies; those employing school leavers; and those recruiting employees with low skills. What particularly troubled these employers was not so much literacy and numeracy skills but that a growing number of employees were not good at talking, listening, getting on with others in a team, or solving simple problems. Sadly these are the skills we need not simply to survive at work but to navigate life, including family life.

The unexpected costs of family breakdown

In 2006 the Scottish Education Department invited the OECD to undertake an in-depth examination of Scottish schools to ascertain the performance of the country's education system. The review document is extremely positive: investigators considered Scotland's performance in mathematics, reading and science to be 'very high' by international standards and they reported that head teachers and pupils are 'generally very positive about their schools'.[4] They also proclaimed that Scotland 'has one of the most equitable school systems in the

OECD'[5] in that what is on offer in schools across the country is consistently high and that there is a real commitment to the education of all young people 'whoever they may be'.

However, these investigators reported a worrying problem at the heart of Scottish education – there is a considerable 'achievement gap that opens up about Primary 5 and continues to widen throughout the junior secondary years (S1 to S4)'.[6] This then leads to 'inequalities' when it comes to staying-on rates at school and academic achievement, with those from poor backgrounds often leaving with minimal, or no qualifications. Glasgow city, largely as a result of the concentration of poverty and deprivation, has some of the highest under-achievement scores in Scotland (though these figures have improved in recent years).

The OECD investigators thought that Scottish education is consistently good and that variation in performance is largely about *the pupils* not the schools. They referred to this problem as the 'unequal capacity to use good schools well'.[7] The report authors link this underperformance to socio-economic factors but they also point out that poor children in Scotland perform much less well than poor students in many other countries.

So how does this research on Scottish education relate to family breakdown? – the title of this section. Copious research shows that children from single parent families are more likely to have emotional and behaviour problems and fare much less well in life than children brought up in households with their two biological parents.[8] Studies in the UK suggest that those brought up with one parent are 75 per cent more likely to fail at school; are 35 per cent more likely to be unemployed; and are twice as likely to abuse alcohol and drugs.[9]

There are various reasons why children from lone parent families do not do as well – this is partly about poverty since two parent families are generally better off, though even children from wealthier lone parent families are less likely to do well in life. It is often due to the absence of a male role model and the father's lack of involvement in the child's upbringing. Again copious research shows that a child's relationship with his/her father has huge implications for various outcomes in life.[10] Children from single parent families may also suffer from stigma. Mothers who are lone parents are also much more vulnerable to depression than married mothers. These factors taken together may mean that single parents, particularly those having to deal with the stress of poverty, have less energy and resources to provide the type of good 'home learning environment' which longitudinal studies such as 'EPPE', carried out in England, show is more important to youngsters' academic performance than their parents' social class or their mothers' education.[11]

The OECD report on Scottish education repeatedly referred to socio-economic status, poverty and deprivation and did not mention family structure yet this may help to explain why so many children in Scotland, particularly in Glasgow, are not able to benefit from the good education available to them. As we saw in Chapter 1, Scotland has a high percentage of single-parent families and Glasgow's figure (46 per cent of all families with dependent children) is not only one of the highest in the UK but internationally. Why? The political right beat the drum on a return to family values but much of the problem is about opportunities and structures – politics, not morality.

The hidden social costs of unemployment

Detailed research in the USA and on UK census figures suggests that much of the rise of single parent families is due to male unemployment:

> Evidence. . . suggests that being out of work or in unstable employment has powerful effects on the father's position in the family, through such things as his lack of financial contribution, lowered status, and increased interpersonal tensions, and that this tends to undermine stable partnering. It also makes men into less desirable future partners.[12]

This research suggests that what is really going on with family breakdown is that Glasgow's industrial decline and concomitant rise in unemployment has undermined men's position in the family and made lone parent families much more likely, thus opening a Pandora's box of extensive social and educational problems. However, while these researchers argue that their data provide clear evidence of the link between unemployment and the rise of single parent families they accept that it at best explains 50 per cent of the increase in lone parents between 1971 and 2001 with the remaining portion coming from structural issues, such as social security payments, as well as cultural trends. Indeed there is no geographical area in the UK (even the wealthiest) where the proportion of single parent families is less than twenty per cent of all families. [13]

Data on family breakdown and unemployment help us to understand a considerable proportion of Glasgow's problems but again it is by no means the full answer. If we compare the prevalence of families which do not include the two biological parents then the Glasgow figure is very high (52.16 per cent) but only slightly higher than Liverpool's (51.04 per cent) and actually lower than Manchester's (54.74 per cent) [14] yet, as we saw in Chapter 1, Glasgow's health and social problems are considerably larger than both these cities. The figures charting family breakdown and male unemployment come from the USA and the UK but other European countries have not experienced anything like the same rise in single parent families even though they too have areas with exceptionally high unemployment rates. [15] For example, the Greek unemployment rate in 2005 was 10 per cent – more than twice the UK's figure yet Greece had the lowest number of single parent families in industrialised countries and the UK the second highest figure. Data show that in 2004 many German cities such as Dusseldorf, Dortmund and Bremen have much higher unemployment rates yet significantly lower percentages of single parent families.

Table III: Marital Status as reported in the 2001 Census

	England & Wales %	Scotland %	Greater Glasgow %
Single (never married)	30.1	43.9	47.9
Married	43.6	35.8	31.9
Remarried	7.4	4.5	3.0
Separated	2.4	2.9	3.5
Divorced	8.2	5.7	5.8
Widowed	8.4	7.3	7.9

The importance of marriage

If we look at divorce rates in the UK then it appears that Scotland is faring better than England and Wales on relationship breakdown since the rate north of the border is lower. [16] But look closely at the figures in Table III and a completely different picture emerges: many fewer people in Scotland, particularly in Greater Glasgow, are marrying or remarrying. This may have implications for physical and psychological health. Why?

The benefits of marriage to individuals' health and lifespan have been known since the mid-nineteenth century. However, interest in the benefits of marriage has escalated in recent years though this has not been evident in Scotland. Longitudinal research, some of it conducted in the UK, shows that married people tend to live longer, are less depressed and have better physical health. These effects are not small but substantial. It is common to see men's health and longevity linked to employment and income but marriage is a stronger predictor of men's health and life expectancy than these economic factors.[17] Longitudinal research in the UK suggests that marriage may be as important to men's health as whether or not they smoke. Indeed married men live longer than divorced, separated or single men.

One explanation is that married people are better off because they pool their resources. Another is that marriage helps protect against the stress and strains of everyday life. A third explanation is that marriage not only enhances an individual's social network but also provides intimacy and closeness which may be extremely beneficial to health, perhaps by boosting the immune system. Finally, marriage can provide what is called 'the guardian effect' whereby spouses are less likely to indulge in risky health behaviours such as smoking and drinking and are more likely to lead an 'orderly life' with regular meals and sleep patterns. This effect is stronger in men than women.

One of the intriguing findings on marriage is that it confers much greater benefits than cohabiting. In other words, the benefits of marriage are not simply attributable to sharing resources and networks and living in close proximity with someone; there must be something additionally important about marriage and the fact it involves a positive choice and commitment.

It is possible that feeling loved has a hugely beneficial effect on our health. One study showed that when men with cardiovascular disease were asked 'Does your wife show you her love?', those who responded positively had half as many symptoms as those who said no. Another study of 8,500 healthy men found that those who had reported 'My wife doesn't love me' developed three times as many ulcers. Similar findings apply to women. Women who had breast cancer and said they lacked affection in their lives were twice as likely to be dead in five years than those who were similarly afflicted but reported affection. Again it has been found that healthy women who say that their husbands despise them are much more likely to suffer ill-health than those in loving marriages. [18]

Divorce can be particularly damaging to men's health. International research shows that separated and divorced men 'have higher rates of extreme physical and mental health outcomes (including mortality and hospitalisation of all types) compared to separated and divorced women'. [19] Research on 55 year olds in the Clyde area found that divorced and separated men had higher systolic blood pressure than the married men in the study and worse self-rated health and mental health than the men who were married. [20]

Of course it may be the case that by not getting married men spare themselves the pain of divorce. But this must be qualified. Many of those who do not marry cohabit. Research shows that cohabitation is not nearly as stable as marriage. This means than in a city where almost 60 per cent do not marry, there must be a great deal of relationship churn with partners splitting up and moving on. The disintegration of cohabiting relationships can involve considerable stress and pain making it similar to the impact of divorce. What's more, these break-ups are likely to lead to considerable loneliness and, for men, detachment from family life. As we have already seen, around 46 per cent of families with dependent children in Glasgow are lone parent families and around 90 per cent of them are headed by the mother. This means a large number of men in the city are not simply unmarried but are not formally cohabiting with the mother of their children.

Even those men who are married may not reap the physical and psychological benefits. It is possible that in Glasgow – a city where men have had a particular love affair with drink and pubs (rather than wives) and a history of suiting themselves – men do not benefit from 'the guardian effect'. Indeed this was suggested in the Clyde study as it did not find that married men had significantly different smoking or drinking rates from men who were single or no longer married.[21]

We must also remember that it is not any marriage which confers benefits – those who are most committed to the marriage are most likely to reap benefits from the union. Being in a negative marriage is worse for men's and women's health than being divorced or single. Marriage quality is measured not only through the frequency and intensity of disagreements but also by the extent to which people feel they are loved and cared for, listened to and able to share their private feelings and concerns. [22]

Does that sound like the typical Glasgow marriage or relationship as depicted in literature or witnessed in the street? Quite simply, as we have seen in earlier chapters, there is little in Glasgow's history, culture, values and language that encourages this type of positive relationship between men and women. Of course, some attain it but I would argue that they are swimming against, rather than with, the city's emotional tide.

Here's one little vignette I witnessed a few weeks ago in central Glasgow. Three tough guys walking along the street, spitting and jeering, notice an elderly couple and the man is carrying a big bunch of flowers. It is possible he had given them to the woman but it looked to me as if they were on the way to the hospital. But the tough guys point at the old man carrying the bouquet and shout in a menacing fashion 'see you, you're a big f'n sook.'

It is easy to see how men like these are likely to damage their health, and shorten their lives, through gang fights, smoking, drinking, drug taking and worklessness. But I firmly believe that we must also see that they damage their health by not having positive, committed relationships. Surely it is no coincidence that men in Glasgow have exactly the problems which international research shows can result for men from divorce, separation and poor marriages? – high blood pressure, life-threatening health conditions, alcohol and drug misuse, poor self-rated health and mental health problems leading to suicide.

And what of women? Again international research shows that women benefit from marriage though less than their husbands. Some research suggests that for women the physical health impact of marital breakdown is not as dramatic as it is for men (hospitalisation and serious health challenges) but that their health more generally suffers and that they are particularly susceptible to mental health problems such as depression. Again, as with men, research shows that women particularly benefit from a good marriage, and suffer from a bad one, and that the benefits to women's health are particularly strong later in life.[23]

So could poor marriage and relationships in Glasgow be undermining women's health as I believe it is undermining men's? Let me remind readers just how poor women's health is in Glasgow. Women in Glasgow consistently score badly on health measures when compared to their sisters in the rest of the UK. Glasgow women particularly suffer from mental health problems. For example, Scotland's suicide rate is significantly higher than other English-speaking countries yet the rate for women in Glasgow is 53 per cent higher than it is in Scotland as a whole. The equivalent figure for men is 40 per cent. Recent research concluded that the physical health of women in the west of Scotland was the worst out of twenty deindustrialised regions in Western Europe.[24]

The possibility that marriage in Glasgow does not confer positive benefits for women is indeed suggested by the study of women aged 55 in the Clyde area mentioned above. This found that single women had the same health as married women.[25]

And what of happiness? International research suggests that those who are married consistently score themselves happier than those who are single or separated/divorced.[26] If women and men in Glasgow suffer from poor marriages, as I suggest, then surely this would show up in the city's happiness figures? Andrea Nove analysed happiness data collected in the Greater

Glasgow and Clyde NHS area in 2005. Nove's task was not to compare the Glasgow data with other places but to find which 'factors are associated with self-reported happiness.' [27]

Nove found that marriage and cohabitation was not nearly as strong a predictor of happiness as 'satisfaction with adequacy of household income'. In this survey almost 60 per cent of those who were the most satisfied with their household income also scored maximum points for happiness whereas only 13 per cent of those who were married rated themselves happiest and 'never married' people were only slightly behind in the most happy category at 12.1 per cent. Indeed after detailed statistical analysis Nove writes:

> The happiness levels of married people were not significantly different from those of cohabiters, divorcé(e)s, widow(er)s or single people. Only those describing themselves as 'separated' were significantly less likely to be happy than married people. . .' [28]

On the other hand 'the strongest association' in Nove's statistical model was the relationship between happiness and satisfaction with household income: 'the more satisfied a respondent was with his/her income, the happier (s)he tended to be.' [29] When it comes to 'household composition', as opposed to marital relationships, Nove also concluded that any detectable lower levels of happiness for 'lone parents' or single adults was 'related to their having lower levels of satisfaction with their income, rather than being single *per se*.' [30]

The economist Richard Layard identifies what he calls 'the Big Seven' factors associated with happiness.[31] The first is 'family relationships/marital status' and the second 'financial situation'.

In her analysis Nove identifies nine, rather than seven, factors associated with Glaswegians' happiness. Satisfaction with household finance is first and family relationships (first on Layard's list) is eighth (second bottom) on the Glasgow list. The second most important happiness factor in Glasgow is 'personal freedom'. Layard and Nove use similar ways to classify family relationships and marital status; as Layard's work is more in tune with international evidence, then we must ask why Glaswegians' happiness correlates more with satisfactory income, personal freedom and a host of other factors, than to close personal relationships or family life?

Is this indeed hard evidence to support the argument I have advanced at various points in the book that for centuries men and women in this city, and the surrounding region, have not had good personal relationships within the family and that this is undermining well-being? As some longitudinal studies show that marriage quality is the single biggest predictor of well-being, is it surprising that in a city which scores so poorly on health that marriage and family life are not closely associated with happiness?

Let's look more closely at what is most strongly associated with happiness in Glasgow – money.

Money and materialism

For decades economists have equated money (Gross Domestic Product) with national well-being, making the assumption that the best way to improve people's lives is to stimulate economic growth.[32] However, as the economies of western nations have grown substantially in recent years it has become clear that, while poverty is not good for well-being and happiness, continually increasing a country's wealth is not necessarily beneficial. Indeed in the past few decades the UK's GDP has increased substantially while happiness levels have remained stubbornly flat. What's going on is really simple: money is important for happiness and well-being but once basic economic needs are met and people have food on the table, a roof over their heads, and some sense of economic stability then having more money does not inevitably mean more happiness.

The research undertaken by 'positive psychologists' and increasingly by economists shows why people's lives may not be as improved by money as was once thought.[33] Part of the explanation is that human beings have an impressive capacity to 'adapt' to circumstances. This means that when good things happen (such as getting a new car or a wage increase) they can temporarily boost our positive feelings but within a matter of weeks we hardly notice the new thing anymore and our level of happiness returns to its normal level. Pleasurable events too, such as eating wonderful ice cream, are transitory and even when we are half way through the experience our sense of delight diminishes. Robert Burns was alive to this problem when he wrote in 'Tam O' Shanter':

> But pleasures are like poppies spread,
> You seize the flowr, its bloom is shed;
> . . . Or like the Rainbow's lovely form,
> Evanishing amid the storm.

Another problem with trying to find happiness through money and things is that people are 'creatures of comparison':[34] less motivated by money and what it can bring than by the idea of having more than the people around them. So if some people get richer in a society this can breed discontent but if everyone becomes richer then no-one feels better off.

Tim Kasser is a psychologist who has made a particular study of those who pursue a materialistic lifestyle. Kasser defines materialism as 'buying in' to a cluster of goals related to money, fame and image. People's materialistic values can be measured in terms of their motivation towards 'attaining possessions, attractiveness and popularity'. Kasser reports extensive and consistent international research which shows that 'People who are highly focussed on materialistic values have lower personal well-being and psychological health than those who believe that materialistic values are relatively unimportant.' [35] Kasser argues that everyone must place some value on material goods. We need food and shelter to survive. A sense of security and comfort adds enormously to the quality of our lives. From time immemorial people have placed some value on their appearance; wanted to feel some degree of pride in their accomplishments; and have cared to some extent on how they are viewed by others. So Kasser's argument is that:

> . . . materialism is relative. Materialistic values
> become unhealthy when they are highly important in
> comparison with other values for which we might
> strive. The question is one of balance. . . [36]

Kasser's rule of thumb is that materialism is detrimental to our well-being when it compromises the fulfilment of our fundamental psychological needs. For example, those with a materialistic orientation place less value on warm, intimate relationships and take a more instrumental view of others, often caring too much about status, appearances and image. They are also less likely to do things because they are intrinsically interesting or stimulating but because they make the person look good or feel better than others. These behaviours and values are not helpful in creating a truly fulfilling and rewarding life.

The governments of Margaret Thatcher, and those which followed, have particularly promoted materialistic and individualistic values. One of the main purveyors of this philosophy of life is the mass media. Television now beams into people's homes information about the lives of the rich and famous. It provides a daily diet of advertising designed to encourage viewers to want things they do not have. Research shows that the more people are exposed to television images of successful and attractive people the more dissatisfied they are with themselves and their partners. [37]

Since materialism undermines well-being, and as well-being in the west of Scotland is not high, could it be the case that the local culture is particularly disposed to materialistic values? Kasser maintains that feelings of insecurity can lead people to pursue a materialistic lifestyle. Indeed contemporary international research shows that people whose needs for 'security, safety and sustenance' were not met by their childhood upbringing are much more like to develop a materialistic orientation to life. [38] This may well mean that the abject poverty and insecurity of employment in Glasgow may have predisposed its citizens to pay particular attention to materialistic goals. In the story we have encountered so far we have come across other factors which would encourage the west of Scotland to become a particularly materialistic culture: Glasgow's domination for centuries by a money-oriented elite; the city's penchant for American films and celebrity culture – strong purveyors of materialist values; and the importance many women in the west of Scotland (more than other places in Scotland) have attached to appearance. Glasgow's recent rebranding of the city as a shopping Mecca and 'Scotland with style' suggests a materialist citadel.

On balance, however, I would say that up to the 1950s Glasgow may well have been a city with strong materialistic values but that for many individuals these values were still kept in check by the city's emphasis on politics, community and religion. What's more, many Glasgow women could go to the cinema two nights a week and still have hours of time to spend with family, friends and neighbours. But what the city's love affair with America and the cinema may have done is make Glaswegians particularly susceptible to the charms of television – the main conduit for transmitting materialistic values in modern cultures. Historians recount how the advent of television in the 1950s had a dramatic effect on cinema going in Scotland. Within a decade the number of cinemas had halved.

Americans are top of the league when it comes to television viewing. In 2007 the country's average was 4.6 hours per day. The equivalent European figure was 3.5 hours and the UK's figure 3.8. However, Scotland's figure was higher at 4 hours per day. Research conducted in Glasgow in 2003 reported that 35 per cent of people in poor areas watched 5 or more hours a day. Since commercial television is more popular than the BBC that means a great deal of exposure to advertising.[39]

Television viewing can have a negative effect on people, almost irrespective of the adverts and the programme content.

One of the problems with television is that it makes people too passive – even when vewers watch programmes they have selected their mood is slightly below apathetic. Time spent watching television is time lost to other activities which are more likely to lead to a sense of personal fulfilment such as talking to family members, listening to music, reading or pursuing hobbies and sports.[40] High levels of television viewing are also bad for community involvement. Robert Putnam, an expert on social capital, when asked what is the one thing that could build social capital immediately replies, 'turn off the television'. [41] Physical activity is also hugely important for how people feel about themselves and the world and this too is seriously affected by copious television viewing.

Thanks to the media and the internet, young people everywhere are being raised on an unhealthy diet of contemporary American values. In 2009 Jean Twenge and Keith Campbell warned in their book *The Narcissism Epidemic: Living in the Age of Entitlement*, where these values are leading.[42] These psychologists report solid empirical evidence which show that narcissistic personality traits are increasing amongst young people in the USA. In effect this means a rising number of people obsessed with themselves, their achievements and their lifestyles. Child development specialists in America warned that this was likely to happen years ago as they could see that the 'all about me' activities favoured in American classrooms was likely to encourage narcissism. Undoubtedly as Twenge and Campbell point out the media, materialism and individualism have also played their part in this growing obsession with the self.

As Scots we may think our youngsters will be immune to such self-focus. After all are we not a collectivist culture with strong beliefs in society, volunteering and charitable giving? Traditionally yes, but there is undoubtedly a change in attitude. Teachers and youth workers are very aware of a shift in values and report how common it is for young people to simply say 'become famous' when asked what they want to do when they grow up. A 2007 Scottish YouthLink survey gives grounds for concern. Even before the financial crisis the number of young-sters who thought volunteering an important part of good citizenship dropped by 7-8 per cent. Even more worrying is that only 43 per cent of 17-25 year olds think it important to help poor third world countries – a drop of 23 per cent between 2005 and 2007.[43] Yet, as we are about to see, exposure to the third world has so much to offer.

Different types of wealth

In 2006 Ruchazie, part of Glasgow's Easterhouse, teamed up with Baula in northern Malawi in a project which is an inspiration to both communities. The first contact was a group of Malawians coming to Ruchazie to stay with locals. 'What lovely houses you have. Ruchazie is beautiful,' they told astonished residents who were used to the place being called a 'dump'. A small group of folk from Ruchazie went to Malawi. The Ruchazians were treated like royalty: they were the first westerners ever to stay overnight in the village.

The initiative, part of a larger project called 'Together for a Change', was initially funded by the Church of Scotland's Guild (though the work happening in Ruchazie involves both the Church of Scotland and the local Roman Catholic Church). The project aims to twin poor communities in Scotland and the developing world so that they can 'share one another's experiences' and give people in both communities 'a sense of self-worth' not simply by giving hospitality to foreign visitors but also 'through recognising that they have something valuable to contribute to the struggle to end poverty' – a contribution which could influence politicians and policy-makers.

The contact between these two communities has had a hugely transformative effect as I could see for myself when I had the privilege of spending some time with some of the Glaswegians who had been most involved. Their exposure to Malawian culture and way of life helped them to see that the poverty they experience in Scotland is not so much material as spiritual and cultural. Bill Hunter, the local minister, spoke for the views of the group when he wrote:

> Baula is. . . beautiful. Set in the hills of northern Malawi with the most glorious sunrises and sunsets and people who smile from ear to ear and sing like angels when they greet you bringing tears to the hardest Glasgow eyes. And the community is rich – with all the glorious riches we have forgotten about in our 'advanced society'. In Baula everyone volunteers for the benefit of the community and all the services that we expect someone else to provide have to be done by local people whether it is running the baby clinic or mending the roads, running the schools or making sure the water supply keeps running. It inspired us to do more when we came home and to stop moaning. It is rich in its spirituality, people don't hide their faith in Malawi – it shines in their broad smiles and the prayers before everything. It bounces along in the songs they sing and the conviction that God will help them. It is rich in the care that people give one another when children are orphaned by malaria or AIDS or some other tragedy and become part of a relative's

> extended family even though feeding another set of
> mouths is never easy. The elderly are respected and
> their wisdom guides village life. People are in touch
> with their traditions and culture and proud of who
> they are.[44]

The Malawians may lack what we consider basic resources yet they have, as Bill Hunter testifies, strong families and communities. The Ruchazians so admired the Malawians' energy and enthusiasm for song and dance that one of the lasting legacies of contact with Malawi is an appetite for 'African nights' at the local church. Another important gift the Malawian exchange has given the Scots is a strong sense of meaning and purpose. The community, including local youth who are often seen by society as a problem rather than an asset, have been fundraising for Baula. And what did the Malawians get out of their experience of Scotland? – an understanding that Western culture is not what they thought. They could see that not only did Scotland have people who also feel downtrodden and 'poor' but also that communities and family life here are weak and many people, if not depressed, do not enjoy life to the full. Within a week of being in Scotland they advised the locals not to spend so much time watching television because they could see its negative effect. The two communities benefited from the exchange as they felt isolated and marginalised and they enjoyed both the sense of being listened to and the idea that people, thousands of miles away, cared about their well-being.

I know of other projects, linking people in Scotland with poor third world communities, that have had a similar effect on volunteers.[45] For example, Brett (a lad whose troublesome life led him to a secure school) was one of a group of youngsters who went to undertake voluntary work in Ecuador. The young folk had fund-raised for months for their tickets and other expenses and when they were there they worked physically hard for weeks creating a nursery school and running a soup kitchen. Brett proved popular with the group and locals alike and his voluntary work completely changed his perception of himself. For the first time he saw himself as someone with something to give rather than the recipient of other people's time and generosity. He liked the sense of meaning this new role gave him. When he returned to Scotland he felt much more appreciative of his schooling and resolved to turn his life round so that he could make a contribution to society. When he spoke at one of the Centre's events on young people he told the audience that he now wanted to get a job where he could help people. It was moving to hear him talk knowing that probably for the first time in years Brett was energised, not just by his new found purpose, but also a feeling of hope.

Feeling grateful and positive about everyday aspects of life can boost well-being and happiness in adults and gratitude exercises are now promoted by positive psychologists.[46] Dr. Elaine Duncan, a psychologist in Glasgow has even tried these out with people (largely women) in Wellhouse, in Easterhouse.[47] Before reporting its positive findings it is important to know that the initial measurements on those who took part show worrying levels of depression, and exceedingly low levels of self-esteem, optimism, life-satisfaction and happiness. The importance of self-esteem is, as we shall see later, generally over-rated but low levels are linked to suicide and depression and the other measures, particularly optimism, are important for mental and physical health.

The study, run in conjunction with the local housing association, asked participants, on a daily basis, to think and write about positive aspects of their life with a particular focus on gratitude. (During this month long intervention the project's researcher phoned the participants on average seven times and this may have affected the outcomes.) The results of the intervention are very strong showing a significant reduction in feelings of depression and improvements in all the well-being measures (happiness, optimism, self-esteem and life-satisfaction). Many participants kept up the activity once the original project was over and kept thinking and/or writing about gratitude. Some participants reported that the intervention had an effect on their goals and what they did in life in terms of employment, promotion and so forth. In other words by focussing on appreciation and gratitude people went on to make real life changes. What is particularly important and impressive about the findings is that the effects did not just continue, but strengthened, as time went by. The measures taken four months after the intervention were significantly higher than they were after one month.

This is an exercise which has to be handled with extreme sensitivity and caution. Unequal societies breed ill-health and a raft of social problems. Potentially this exercise could tell people to forget inequality and feel grateful for what they have. On the other hand, I have suspected for a long time that part of the problem for the less well-off in the UK is that their 'deprivation' is repeatedly drummed into them by the media and well-meaning professionals. No doubt this is one of the reasons why 'poor people' often spend huge amounts of money on their children at Christmas as they do not want them to suffer from the effects of poverty. But this value system – making things the most important part of life – is what we need to change. The much bigger problem for many children from 'deprived' backgrounds is that they often lack a home life which supports educational growth and provides a secure emotional base.

As we can see from the people of Baula, so much of what is good in life, and can make us feel happy, is not about material goods as such but about everyday happenings and relationships. If we look for these, and amplify our positive feelings about them, then we can experience positive feelings. These positive feelings can energise and so a virtuous circle is established. I am not suggesting that this approach is an alternative to tackling economic inequality or structural changes. I am merely pointing out that there is some room for immediate improvement for some individuals if they are able to take a more appreciative approach to life.

Dr. Harry Burns, Scotland's Chief Medical Officer, is also convinced that the absence of positive emotions, such as optimism and hope, contribute to Scotland's pronounced health inequalities. Pointing out that boys in Shettleston have only a fifty/fifty chance of reaching their 55th birthday he argues that what is killing these men is largely the diseases of old age which they are contracting twenty or more years before their time. Why should it be the case that men of 55 have the physiology of men twenty years older than them?

Dr. Burns explains that men from poor areas have effectively 'more miles on the clock'. In other words, their life experiences have been more stressful and this takes a toll on their physical health, accelerating the ageing process. Referring to large international research studies Dr. Burns explains how, on a daily basis, even a small elevation in stress hormones such as cortisol can lead to long-term health problems such as changes in arteries. He believes that feelings of pessimism and hopelessness play a part in the creation of ill-health.[48] Again there are large scale studies which suggest that whether people are optimistic or pessimistic may account for as much as seven years of life expectancy. [49]

Research by the Centre I run, on the optimism of young people in Scotland, suggests that it is low in poor areas of Glasgow, lower than our Scottish-wide figures which are also fairly low by international standards.[50] Pessimism has its place (and Scotland would have benefited from more pessimistic bankers) but there's little doubt that excessive pessimism undermines morale and motivation and de-energises people: why bother trying to improve anything about your life if you think the worst is bound to happen?

Gangs

In 2009 Dr. Ross Deuchar published some research on gangs. Deuchar reviews the international literature but mainly draws on his in-depth study of young people living in deprived areas of Glasgow. The picture he paints is bleak, yet sympathetic to these youngsters' plight. Many are aware that Glasgow is a city with an increasing cultural reputation but that this is not their reality. Their own lives are 'ravaged by the cumulative impact of poverty, alcoholism, drug abuse and violence'. [51] Gang culture in Glasgow is largely about 'territority' and this creates an additional problem for these young men: their freedom and mobility is restricted, sometimes to a few streets, as they fear what will happen if they are caught trespassing in a rival gang's territory. They often feel victims too of heavy surveillence and policing and 'frustrated by the way in which their voices were never heard and their identities. . . suppressed'. [52]

As we saw in Chapter 6, Glasgow has a long history of gang violence. Some gang rivalries have existed for decades, and some current members are involved in the same gangs as their fathers and even grandfathers. Originally Glasgow gangs had a strong sectarian feel but Deuchar argues that modern gangs are based on territory rather than religious attachment although some contain sectarian sub-groups and infighting can occur particularly on Old Firm match days. Deuchar does not attempt to quantify Glasgow's gang problem from his research but he does quote, uncritically, newspaper reports which estimate that '170 street gangs currently exist in Glasgow and that over half of Glasgow's teenagers consider themselves to be gang members and have inflicted serious violence against others.'[53] This estimate makes Glasgow's gang numbers the same as London's even though Glasgow is only a sixth of its size.

In an earlier chapter we saw evidence of a link between gang membership, inequality and a hard male culture. This too emerges from Deuchar's work. But we also hear how gangs are a way for youngsters, growing up in broken families where they get little emotional support, to make alliances and feel a sense of belonging. In other words, gangs give youngsters who feel cut adrift a sense of community, identity and belonging. One of the disturbing ideas which emerges from Deuchar's research, and which is corroborated by the police, is that gang membership does not only provide stimulation and something to do but also that many of the gang members are addicted to what they call 'the buzz' – the excitement gang warfare provides. It is easy to see how this can happen: fear releases hormones like adrenalin which help the body physically cope with the challenge of having to fight or run away. Some people come to enjoy the 'rush' of adrenaline so much that they feel normal life is boring without it. The temptation then is to seek activities that will not only keep giving this high but also give bigger and bigger highs. The problem is, however, that the body is not designed to cope with frequent emergencies and the continual release of adrenaline undermines health and can shorten life.

Tragically this process can also mean that people only feel alive and energised when they are involved in risk-taking, conflict-ridden or dramatic activities. So they get turned on to excessive drinking, drug-taking, arguing, confrontations and promiscuous sex. As they get older gang members turn away from street fighting but by then damage may have been done, not just to physical health but to their ideas that 'ordinary life' (without the stimulation of drink, drugs and cigarettes) is boring and unattractive.

A life worth living

Some doctors in Glasgow recount that if they outline to a patient, usually a man, how he could extend his life by ten years if he cuts down his drinking, takes exercise and loses weight, the patient often replies: 'and why would I want to do that?' In short, the patient feels he has nothing to live for and this is why many well-meaning health messages are destined to fall on deaf ears.

Many Glasgow housing schemes are beset by problems. Nonetheless there are still people in their midst who do not abuse substances, get involved in fights or die prematurely. We need to know more about them. International research suggests that they will have a good support structure – a spouse, parents, kindly neighbours, a sister, or work colleagues on whom they can rely. They are likely to work. They are likely to be optimistic (a key ingredient in resilience), count their blessings and appreciate the small things in life. They may well have a sense of meaning and purpose – looking after grandchildren; fetching messages for an elderly neighbour; belonging to the local church; taking part in community activities; or working to achieve a long-term goal. They may simply have a job which they think makes a difference. They probably pursue hobbies and interests – a yoga or dance class, games, puzzles, gardening, fishing, knitting, woodwork, playing a musical instrument, reading books. . . The chances are they are physically active – they may be part of a walking group, pursue a sport or lead an active life by climbing stairs or walking to the shops.

To help the man 'coughing his guts out in Shettleston' sizable shifts need to take place in society; we need more equality and inclusiveness. He needs the opportunity to work, earn a reasonable wage, and be part of a family. But he also needs to experience more love, hope, optimism and engagement in his life. Women in Glasgow's poorer communities need all this too but they also need to feel safe and protected in their own homes – not prey to the whims and punishments of drunken and violent men. Young people need to feel secure and loved by their parents and learn from them how to make good choices in life.

The life described above sounds sedate and old-fashioned yet, like it or not, it is in these mundanities that we find the resources to sustain hope and create a psychologically and physically healthy life. [54]

Chapter 16
The problems of self-esteem

> Though an overweening conceit of our own merit
> be vicious and disagreeable, nothing can be more
> laudable than to have a value for ourselves, where
> we really have qualities that are valuable. . . it is
> certain that nothing is more useful to us, in the
> conduct of life, than a due degree of pride, which
> makes us sensible of our own merit, and gives us a
> confidence and assurance in all our projects and
> enterprises.[1]

AS this quote from the great Scottish Enlightenment philosopher, David Hume, shows, the idea that it is important to value yourself is not new.

In various chapters of this book we have seen how historically the way people were treated in Glasgow often depended on whether they were judged to be worthy or worthless. But in the USA interest in feelings of self-worth has become, in recent decades, something of a national obsession. Proponents of self-esteem even argue that boosting it will not only improve how people feel about themselves but also cure all society's ills. With such extravagant claims, no wonder parents and teachers have changed their child-rearing practices. America has now exported these ideas to other countries via the mass media and even sceptical Scots have swallowed uncritically the notion that artificial self-esteem boosting is 'a good thing'. Unfortunately self-esteem building practices back-fire, paradoxically under-mining young people's achievements and resilience.[2]

Self-esteem is usually defined as the emotional judgement we make on our worth as an individual. Even critics of the importance of self-esteem believe that it exists and can be measured. Self-esteem is not a major ingredient of confidence as the latter is much more about what we think we can do and is more based on skills, experience and belief in our capacities than innate feelings of self-worth.

Psychology professor Roy Baumeister was once a fan of the self-esteem movement and wanted to help them find evidence to corroborate its importance. After copious study of inter-national research he announced that this work was 'the biggest disappointment' of his professional career: not only could he no longer support the idea of self-esteem as a panacea he concluded that while those with low self-esteem may damage themselves, high self-esteem was potentially a bigger social problem. The UK psychologist Professor Nicholas Emler came to similar conclusions.[3] So what's going on?

Contrary to what many people believe international research shows that research into self-esteem shows differing results. For example, low self-esteem is not a risk factor for drug and alcohol abuse. Those who abuse these substances may have low self-esteem but this may be the effect of their behaviour rather than the cause. Studies on whether people with low self-esteem are more likely to commit anti-social acts are contradictory. International research shows that there is no link between self-esteem and academic achievement. Research conducted recently at the Centre for Confidence and Well-being confirms this. Pupils at one of the top performing schools in Scotland score *lower* in self-esteem than the mean level of self-esteem for Scottish pupils as a whole. This makes common sense: gallus boys who are full of themselves often don't do well at school and shy, gauche girls can excel.

When it comes to aggression those who are at risk of being bullied often score low on self-esteem and bullies often score high. Indeed recent research in America shows that those who are most likely to bully are not the socially excluded youngsters but the most popular children who have a wide range of social skills. They bully to keep their place at the top of the pecking order.[4] People who are racist often score high on self-esteem as do those who are prone to aggression and violence or are leaders of gangs. Youngsters with high self-esteem often become involved in risky behaviour such as sexual experimentation as they believe that they will be able to cope with the consequences.

Turning to mental health, this is one area where self-esteem matters. Research shows that those with low self-esteem are more likely to feel depressed and rate their happiness as low. It is not difficult to see why, if you have low self-esteem, you could feel negative. One large study uses research on university students to show how the self-esteem mean of a country closely correlates with its suicide rate: the lower the self-esteem figure the higher the suicide.[5] The study does not use Scottish data but we can supply them and they suggest that the Scottish figures buck this trend. Scotland's male suicide figure is 7 per cent higher than England's and yet, according to the Centre's research, students' self-esteem in both countries is almost identical. It is possible than in the areas of the country, particularly some parts of Glasgow where suicides are excessively high, self-esteem is exceptionally low. This is indeed the finding in the Wellhouse study where the rate at the commencement of the study was the lowest average we have ever encountered in our research.[6] If this is the case it begs the question, why?

Low self-esteem is also a risk factor for teenage pregnancies though Nicholas Emler points out that it is only one risk factor among many, with poverty and whether the girl's father works being much more important variables. As we saw in Chapter 1, Glasgow's rate of teenage pregnancy in poor areas is twice Scotland's already high figure. Low self-esteem is also a risk factor for 'unemployment and low earnings in young men'. This overlaps with the group often referred to as NEET (not in employment, education or training) and again Glasgow has the highest rates in OECD countries.[7]

From this list we can see the complexity of the topic. Those who score high on self-esteem are a 'mixed bag' consisting of those who have 'authentic' self-esteem and who do not need to use others to feel good about themselves and those with 'inauthentic self-esteem' who really don't feel good about themselves and are intent on using others to prove their superiority. This echoes Wilkinson and Pickett's idea of the 'bicycling reaction' whereby people kick out at those lower in the hierarchy.[8]

The mixed bag idea is complicated further when we realise that people who can be classed as 'narcissists' also end up in the high self-esteem group. People with a narcissistic personality disorder lack empathy, crave attention and adulation from others and are often arrogant, manipulative and self-obsessed. Research shows that they can be very aggressive to people who win against them or do not show them adequate respect. It is the sheer complexity of the issue that encourages some psychologists to argue that general self-esteem building is dangerous.

The origins of self-esteem

Before looking at the pros and cons of self-esteem boosting let's look at where self-esteem comes from and why it varies from individual to individual.[9] It is commonly assumed that black people, or those from ethnic minorities, have lower self-esteem than white people given the supremacy of the latter in Western culture. However, the evidence does not support this view. In the United States, black people consistently report higher self-esteem than white people. A variety of reasons have been advanced for this finding including the idea that most people care about the approval of friends and family more than the views of others in the wider society. Social class is also commonly thought to be closely correlated to self-esteem but it is only 'modestly' so according to Emler. At the Centre for Confidence and Well-being we have collected data on over 5,000 young people in Scotland and while those in the highest socio-economic groups score higher on self-esteem than the lowest, the difference is only a few percentage points and not as large as people would anticipate.[10]

Gender is often seen as an important variable in self-esteem and here there is some evidence to support this view. Women, on average, have lower self-esteem than men but as Emler points out: 'The difference is highly consistent but it is also small. One factor influencing the size of the difference is age. The largest differences are apparent in late adolescence; they are smaller both before and after.'[11]

It is also commonly assumed that people who are successful in life will have high self-esteem and that those who suffer frequent failure low self-esteem. There is, according to Professor Emler, some evidence to support this view but it is not as strong a factor as people think. Emler argues that people who have high self-esteem are better at discounting or ignoring failure (eg they attribute it to bad luck or poor teaching) and so their self-esteem is less damaged by failure. On the contrary, those with low self-esteem tend to 'discount' success. 'Those blessed with high self-esteem', Professor Emler writes, 'ignore all the evidence of inadequacies. Those who lack self-esteem equally consistently deny that there is any positive evidence, using many of the same tactics in reverse.'[12]

So where does self-esteem mostly come from? Experts largely believe that an individual's self-esteem is partly determined by personality or genes (roughly one third) and the remainder largely determined by parenting style, with the following being the most important factors:

• the amount of acceptance, approval and affection parents show their children

• the degree to which parents make clear expected standards of behaviour

• the degree to which parents' discipline is based on explanation rather than punishment or coercion

• and the extent to which parents involve children in family decisions and value their contributions.

The importance of parents to a person's self-esteem does not end with childhood and continues not just into adolescence but adulthood.

Given the importance of self-esteem it is hardly surprising that a variety of studies have shown how neglect and physical/sexual abuse by parents have what Emler refers to as a 'devastating effect on self-esteem'. One study suggests that victims of child abuse are four times more likely than other people to have the lowest self-esteem scores. Family breakdown is another contributory factor in low self-esteem according to research.[13]

So self-esteem is something of a conundrum in Scotland: the problems which correlate with low self-esteem are a particular problem in Glasgow and yet the self-esteem figure for schools in poor areas of the city is not as low as we would expect. More research is needed and it would be helpful to compare Glasgow youngsters with other cities in the United Kingdom and other parts of Europe.

The dangers of artificial self-esteem building
In the meantime we must be very careful not to follow in the footsteps of the USA and try at every turn to artificially boost youngsters' self-esteem. Why? In a nutshell, as soon as teachers or parents think that young people's self-esteem is vitally important they lower their expectations and try to protect their feelings. This then leads to a series of actions which unwittingly undermine performance, resilience and well-being. For example, if the child is struggling with learning, adults lower their expectations of what they can achieve and give them easier work. They reduce challenges and opportunities to fail (everyone gets prizes at sports days); they avoid honest critical feedback and give praise for easy tasks. It is not difficult to see why these actions undermine academic performance and lead to a 'dumbing down'. In short, in this environment youngsters are less likely to be stretched and learn real skills. This is exactly what has happened in America. During the period that self-

esteem has held sway in their schools the standard of American education has declined dramatically in international league tables. America now spends huge sums on remedial education for those attending university.

Children who are neglected and live in what some term 'tough realities' are often remarkably resilient. They need to be. But talk to teachers in more leafy areas and they will tell you that parents are increasingly visiting schools to complain about their child's mental state: 'My son failed his spelling test and it's bad for his self-esteem'; 'my daughter didn't get the lead part in the pantomime and she is devastated'; 'my angelic daughter has fallen out with her friends and they are being cruel to her, so what is the school going to do about it?' One lovely primary head teacher recently complained: 'So many parents seem to think I'm trying to make their children's lives difficult that when I look in the mirror I expect to see Cruella de Ville.'

Teachers, as parents themselves, understand the problem: modern parents now believe that children's self-esteem and happiness matter so much that they must protect their offspring from bad experiences. However, teachers can see that this mentality is not beneficial as it is undermining resilience. Resilience is our psychological immune system – it's strengthened by being able to deal with life's inevitable adversities and weakened by overprotection.

The emphasis on good feelings has other unwanted side-effects. In the past, if a child came home and reported that he or she had a difficulty with friends or the teacher, parents commonly thought that the child must have contributed to the problem. Now youngsters routinely decline responsibility for any difficulty and parents automatically back them up. But how can we grow and develop as individuals if we reject responsibility for our errors and don't learn from them?

The emphasis on self-esteem is also impeding learning in other subtle ways. Internationally those working with young people report that more youngsters nowadays say that they can't do things before they've tried. For example, one Glasgow football coach recounts: 'Ten years ago lads would come to a training session to kick the ball and maybe learn something. Nowadays, they hang back in case they kick a duff shot and show they're not good at it.' Psychologists call this phenomenon 'self-worth protection'. People do this to protect their self-esteem but in doing so they sacrifice learning and the acquisition of skills, essential to the development of real confidence.

Young people commonly believe that success is about having natural talent, luck or self-belief – that's why they don't want to try something unless they think they are going to excel at it. The best antidote I have come across to the rise of young people believing they can't do things is the work of psychologist Professor Carol Dweck. Dweck's theory of 'fixed and growth mindsets' is based on extensive research.[14] It urges us to see that people are not born with a fixed amount of ability, intelligence or talent as these can all be developed. Of course, some people are born with more natural talent and ability but anyone can get better – much better – if they are motivated, work hard and learn good strategies for improvement. The idea of the growth mindset – that people can get better if they work hard – is supported by neuroscience.[15] Learning actually changes and develops the brain. Self-efficacy and mindset provide a much better focus for schools concerned to develop their young people. This is often best undertaken indirectly through physical activity and sport, the arts and music, outdoor learning and schemes such as the Duke of Edinburgh's Award. The emphasis should be on real challenge with support and encouragement.

I have given literally hundreds of talks on these themes largely to educational audiences in Scotland, England and elsewhere in Europe. Professionals everywhere recognise what I've described above and the vast majority agree with my conclusions. Many confirm that self-esteem boosting is the road they are now on. Many also report that they privately wonder about these practices but don't disagree publicly as it would seem 'politically incorrect'.

Glasgow often has the reputation for being resistant to change but it certainly has not been immune to the lure of self-esteem building. It is not difficult to see why. The idea of self-esteem has a positive, democratic, egalitarian ring about it: it urges us to see that everyone, irrespective of status in life, should be able to feel good about themselves. Indeed does it not echo Robert Burns and his famous line 'the rank is but the guinea's stamp/the man's the gowd for a' that'? In other words, if we see self-esteem as part of our birthright as individuals, how can we possibly disagree with the attempt to increase these good feelings, particularly for young people? If we are interested in the idea of universal self-worth it seems right to encourage self-esteem to rise across the board and not to attach these feelings to anything concrete that the youngster may have achieved.

Understanding that many young people come from very challenged backgrounds, it has also become commonplace in this city for genuinely well-meaning teachers, social workers, youth workers and politicians to lower their expectations, give copious praise for indifferent work or even negative behaviour, and steer clear of honest feedback. Preserve and boost the self-esteem at all costs and results will follow is what they believe. Unfortunately that's rarely true.

Self-esteem has become such a focus in Western societies in part because it is a victimless crime: it allows policy makers and practitioners to acknowledge problems and try to deal with them without pointing the finger and accusing anyone of causing them in the first place.[16] It is also tempting for governments, concerned about the well-being challenges many youngsters face as a result of rising inequality, family breakdown, sedentary lifestyles and the rise of materialist values, to want to take action by doing something practical in schools with a largely captive audience. Thus we get elaborate government-backed programmes to raise pupils' emotional literacy, for example, which are not only diversionary but often counterproductive.[17]

The value of Wilkinson and Pickett's book *The Spirit Level* is that it shows just how irrelevant many of these approaches are by linking mental health problems, violence, low educational attainment, teenage pregnancy and so forth to deep, structural inequality. The psychosocial factors which foster bad feelings are unlikely to be fixed by a few modules in a school programme or well-meaning teachers giving youngsters positive feedback. They need much bigger structural changes in society, the economy and our culture.

When I give talks on self-esteem, or psychological interventions of any kind, I am always aware of the complexity of the issues: people are different, contexts vary and often it is about striking a balance. For example, being empathetic and listening to people who have problems appears to have universal relevance but that is not true. Sometimes what people need is someone to challenge them and jolt them out of self-pity. Sometimes it is good to talk about problems, sometimes distraction is a better strategy. There are no hard and fast rules. This is why I am so opposed to centralised programmes and lists of learning outcomes.

I am also aware of the increasing polarisation within our culture. As a result of multiple social problems and the rise of alcohol and drug abuse, there is a growing number of children suffering from abuse and neglect. They need copious help and support. Some are acting as carers, and are remarkably resilient. What they often need is more practical help.

Undoubtedly there is also a growing number of young people in Scotland, as elsewhere, whose resilience has been undermined by overprotection and a lack of real challenge in their lives. These are the youngsters who are likely to blow out of all proportion every small setback in life, and who would benefit more from being told from time to time that the most important thing in life is not how they feel about themselves.

CHAPTER 17

Ringing the bell

This is the tree that never grew
This is the bird that never flew
This is the fish that never swam
This is the bell that never rang

What bloodless abortion silenced this unrung bell
split and cracked its gold;
and who can break the spell?

S O WRITES Neil McLellan in the first verse of his powerful poem on Glasgow 'This Unrung Bell'.[1] When researching Glasgow's history I've been continually perplexed by the city's motto and coat of arms which were approved by the Lord Lyon King at Arms in 1866. Each of the four symbols is associated with St. Mungo and his various miracles.

In Eastern and Western thought, action is generally labeled 'masculine'. So why would this busy, active, male-dominated city adopt a motto which suggests thwarted, ineffective action? Indeed why are its four subjects inactive? There is nothing in the stories about St. Mungo which suggest this interpretation: the wild robin flew and was then killed and brought back to life by the saint; the tree had grown; the fish had swum and the bell rang out over the city until the end of the sixteenth century.[2] Glasgow was once a city renowned for its spirituality, its beauty and the bounty of its orchards. Why did it not simply evolve into a big bustling industrial city rather than one which, as its motto suggests, saps energy, health and vigour?

In previous chapters of the book we have looked in depth at various aspects of Glasgow's story. In this concluding chapter I synthesise some of the most relevant parts of this story before looking at what needs to done to ring the bell and 'break the spell'.

Summarising the problem

In the eighteenth and nineteenth centuries, as a result of trading and manufacturing, Glasgow became a powerful industrial and commercial hub attracting large numbers of migrants from rural Scotland and Ireland. The city which evolved was one of huge contrasts: providing wealth and an elegant lifestyle for its industrial and commercial elite and the most squalid, over-crowded housing in Europe for its workers. Until the twentieth century, Glasgow was oversupplied with cheap labour and her heavy industries vulnerable to the vicissitudes of international markets, making jobs insecure. These factors retarded invest-ment in new industries, weakened workers' position and strengthened employers allowing them to act like autocrats. These conditions were ideal for the emergence of strong feelings of 'us' and 'them' and in the 1920s the city became the centre of left-wing radicalism.

The type of behaviour which Wilkinson and Pickett claim arises from extreme income inequality can be seen clearly in Glasgow's history: the rich saw the poor as a different type of human being and held them responsible for their appalling living conditions and the poor started to kick out at those even lower than them in the hierarchy. We can see the latter process at work in Glasgow's pronounced sectarian divide, particularly the prejudice against Irish Catholics; in the city's exceedingly male-dominated culture; in the long history of territorial gang warfare; and in the pronounced demarcation in the workplace which undermined the industries themselves. Women bonded together in communities to give each other support but even here there was a pronounced pecking order based on respectability and types of housing.

To help cope with the atrocious living and working conditions, and the dislocation from their previous (rural) culture, many used the pub as an escape and consumed large quantities of spirits. When extreme masculine values are mixed with alcohol they make a toxic brew and Glasgow was (and still is) a city scarred by excessive levels of serious domestic violence. Women in Glasgow were once noted for how much they sacrificed their lives and health for the sake of their families but not so their husbands. Glaswegian males commonly spent a large portion of their wages on their own pleasures and interests, particularly drinking, betting and football. Glasgow males felt threatened by the potential erosion of their already shaky position as the principal breadwinner and resented women's employment.

When the 'companionate' ideal for marriage began to take hold in the 1930s Glasgow men were neither interested nor able to embrace it, preferring instead to cleave to a more traditional idea of separate spheres of interest for men and women. This, and how men spent money, often led to bitter disagreements between husbands and wives. Women wanted more support and more money to improve their own, and their children's, standard of living. Given their poverty and poor living conditions, women placed great value on money and material goods and this was heightened further by Glasgow's status as 'cinema city' as they had ample opportunity to soak up American glamour and pronounced materialist values. These various developments, together with aspects of traditional Scottish values, and poor Glaswegians' negative school experience, led to a rather stultifying culture encouraging those who wanted something better for themselves and their families to emigrate.

The inherent aggression in Glasgow life was, and still is, demonstrated in the 'patter'. Glaswegian language excels at negative labeling, ridicule and abuse. This, together with the widespread domestic violence and excessive use of physical discipline, for example, created the type of domestic environ-ment which has now been shown to undermine people's later physical and mental heath, no matter how resilient they were as children. Verbal aggression and contempt also undermined marital relationships. By the 1960s fictional accounts of life in the west of Scotland reflected this negative family life and sense of general malaise and dysfunction.

This challenging family environment was destined to be strained further: from the 1950s on Glasgow Council embarked on wholesale demolition of many old communities. Many found themselves living in inhospitable tower blocks or in peripheral housing estates with virtually no facilities and far from extended family and friends. This created widespread feelings of disorient-ation and dislocation and territorial gang warfare became rife. Women's support networks crumbled. Unemployment figures slowly crept up as traditional industries closed or declined – a trend which accelerated after the election of the 1979 and 1984 Thatcher governments. Thousands of Glasgow employees lost their jobs, many of them men who had once been proud, skilled workers who had invested so much of themselves in work.

Family life was steadily eroded by the rise of divorce and single parent families. One of the main drivers here was unemployment as out-of-work men do not make attractive partners. But there may well be other reasons including the increasing financial independence of women who, given traditional hostilities, were only too eager to escape relationships with 'useless' or oppressive men. As marriage, especially a good one, has such an important role in physical and mental health, particularly for men, poor personal relationships may be one of the main reasons for the city's contemporary problems with well-being. The breakdown of the family, when taken together with unemployment, community disintegration and rising materialism, also helps us understand why more and more people turned to drink and drugs and why violence is so high.

Of course, none of this is unique to Glasgow – the city has no monopoly on capitalist exploitation, dislocation, drinking, domestic violence, gang warfare, single parent families, unemployment and the challenges of deindustrialisation. But there must be some explanation for why Glasgow's problems are more intense than other deindustrialised areas in Western and Eastern Europe.

At the end of Chapter 1, following an examination of the multiple social problems facing Glasgow and the thesis set out by Richard Wilkinson and Kate Pickett, I posed three questions:

- First, has dominance and inequality played an important part in Glasgow's history?

- Second, has Glasgow traditionally had strained relationships between the sexes and poor family relationships?

- And third, have Glaswegians traditionally been particularly drawn to addictive behaviour and to the feeling of oblivion?

My analysis suggests a resounding yes to all three questions.

The wider culture

In this book I have concentrated on what historians refer to as 'the lower orders' – workers, the poor, the socially excluded or deprived. However, the comparisons with Manchester and Liverpool show that people in Glasgow, even those from better-off backgrounds, are more likely to suffer worse health than their counterparts in these English cities. This is consistent with the analysis put forward by Wilkinson and Pickett. They show how in societies with profound inequality everyone suffers – even the better off. They explain this by saying that inequality leads to a breakdown of trust and social capital. Trust is important for well-being and so if it is eroded health suffers.

More importantly, what I've described in this book is unlikely to be confined to those at the bottom of the hierarchy. Much of what I have focussed on relates to culture, beliefs and values and permeates the whole society. In short, even middle-class Glasgow culture is dominated by masculine values; not enough attention is paid to relationships and family life; money dominates; and many people drink far too much. Those in public health would describe this as a 'population effect'. This idea was first advanced by Professor Geoffrey Rose in 1992 when he argued that the best way to prevent health problems in individuals is to reduce the whole population's level of risk.[3] In

Glasgow's case, rather than seeing the violence problem as mainly about gang fighting, it is better to look at how the whole culture marginalises women, glorifies traditional masculinity and makes it difficult for men to express tender emotions. In such a culture everyone's health suffers, though the worst victims will be those most struggling at the bottom of the hierarchy.

Taking an 'integral' perspective

I am not claiming that my analysis is the definitive answer to why Glasgow should be so plagued with violence, addictions and ill-health – there are other explanations with something to offer our understanding. The thinker who has done most to help encourage a broad and deep 'integral' perspective is the American philosopher Ken Wilber. One strand of his immense work shows the importance of perceiving the world in terms of the *individual* and the *collective*; the *interior* and the *exterior*.[4] (See Table IV) He points out that politicians on the left tend only to emphasise the importance of social, economic and political structures (exterior collective). On the other hand, politicians on the right often see the world in terms of the individual, particularly the individual's psychology and values (interior individual). For example, they believe the problem with the poor is not that they lack opportunities for work but that they do not have the right attitudes and values.

Wilber helps us to see that both these perspectives have something to offer as does an emphasis on cultural beliefs (exterior collective) and objective factors (exterior individual) such as physical health. In other words, he encourages us to see that 'it all matters'. Taking an integral approach which

Table IV: Ken Wilber's Four Quadrants

	Interior	Exterior
Individual	**I** (intentional) Psychology, art, spirituality	**IT** (behavioural) Physiology, neuroscience, nature, the built environment
Collective	**WE** (cultural) Beliefs, history, religion	**ITS** (social) Social/economic/ political factors and systems

emphasises the importance of the four quadrants is much more likely to help us solve problems.

The quadrant Scottish thinkers are most likely to favour is the bottom right and in this book I have continually analysed such factors including inequality and socio-economic forces affecting employment. However, I acknowledge that I could have addressed more of this quadrant's issues such as Glasgow's exceptionally high prison population. In numerous chapters of the book I have spent considerable time on the top left quadrant. For example, I have outlined the role of individual psychology and the need for autonomy, competence and relationships and the importance of optimism and hope. I have also given consid-erable attention to cultural issues in the form of collective beliefs and values. Thus, for example, I explain the effect of pursuing materialist values and try to decode the value system inherent in Glasgow speech.

I fully recognise that the quadrant which I do not give

adequate time to is the upper right. This includes human beings' physical existence. In earlier times those interested in improving Glasgow's health devoted a great deal of time, and rightly so, to this subject. Thus reformers were interested in rickets arising from children's poor diet and how overcrowding led to infant mortality. Nowadays, attention on this quadrant would mean looking for explanations for Glasgow's predicament in factors pertaining to genetics, neuroscience, nutrition, weather, physical activity, the physiological impact of addictions, contact with the green environment and building quality and design. I do not completely ignore these factors as I refer to aspects of infantile development and the impact of damp housing on health, for example, but there's little doubt that I do not do justice to this quadrant. Information on how these various areas affect well-being and violence in Glasgow is required to round out our understanding, help us focus on solutions and start involving a wider group of people in discussion.

It also goes without saying that we need to pay attention to the personal testimony and life experiences of people currently living in this city who, despite the odds, are either managing to live good lives, or who are struggling with some serious problems. It is important to hear and value their voices. Again this book does not claim to be definitive – it is simply trying to raise the importance of these issues and provide a historical and theoretical perspective which may help us frame better solutions.

Political responses

Before looking at potential solutions we need to consider politics 'Glasgow style'. In the historical sections we saw positive developments in the form of municipal provision but we also witnessed middle class opposition to increased rates to help poor people. We encountered the centralising, materialist and overly pragmatic approach of the Labour Party as well as the more empowering and spiritual vision of the Independent Labour Party. But above all we saw how politicians of all political views felt continually overwhelmed by the size of Glasgow's problems. For the ILP and the early Labour Party the major problems they faced were jobs for the unemployed; replacing thousands of slums; and finding ways to feed, clothe and look after the health of countless people living in incredible poverty. The ILPers were so convinced that Scotland could not deal with the sheer scale of the problem on its own that they effectively ditched their commtiment to home rule. The welfare state of the post-war years did improve many Glaswegians' lot. Nonetheless in a world where standards of living were improving, the state of Glasgow's housing stock continued to be a national disgrace. The Labour Council's approach came to be about numbers – demolitions and new build. They simply wanted to build as many new houses as quickly and cheaply as possible and effectively ignored the problems of facilities, bus routes, community decimation or rising damp.

Now the problems facing Glasgow Council are no longer about housing, as responsibility for this has been taken from them, and are much more about the challenges of poor health, drink, drugs, family breakdown and violence. These problems are not unique to Glasgow but, as in the past, the particular problem the city faces is *scale* – it is the sheer number of people who are classified as 'poor', on incapacity benefit, abuse drug and alcohol which is overwhelming. Those who are involved in social work feel that their services are stretched to breaking point. One woman I know organises volunteers to help poor families with children under five. 'If I am being honest,' she confessed, 'it is much easier to help the asylum seekers as their problems are largely practical. The white, Glaswegian families are mainly struggling with a host of problems which are much more difficult to resolve.' Those involved in drug or alcohol work report how terrified they are by the numbers abusing these substances. 'It isn't just the users that worry me,' they'll say, 'it is what it is doing to their children. That's another ticking time bomb.'

For perfectly understandable, yet nonetheless short-sighted reasons related to economic investment, tourism and civic pride, those running the city have always wanted to dwell on the more successful aspects of city life. In the past this positive story was about the might of its heavy industries, its transport system or the grandeur of middle class Glasgow. In recent years municipal leaders have trumpeted Glasgow's make-over from an ailing, industrial and working-class city to a vibrant new-look modern centre with a rich cultural scene. But airbrushing Glasgow's image does not eradicate the huge, real-life problems countless individuals face. If anything it makes the difficulty worse as it heightens feelings of exclusion and alienation for those not part of this new, successful Glasgow.

Alasdair Gray was right when he wrote in *Lanark* 'Let Glasgow flourish by telling the truth': we must be honest about the problems in our midst. We must face up to the fact that for a variety of historical reasons, many of them accidents and twists of fate, Glasgow has not been able to provide the conditions that are good for human health and flourishing. People endured hellish industrial conditions. Their lives were scarred and shaped not just by poverty but pronounced inequality and they managed as best they could – people may not have thrived but they generally survived. But, as the rhyme associated with the city's motto testifies, there is something stultifying and unhealthy about Glasgow's culture.

Glaswegians can be friendly and supportive of one another but nonetheless the culture has been too dominated by the values of macho men – drink focussed, territorial, sectarian and prejudiced. It is too easy in this city for people to shirrack and put down rather than show consideration and appreciation. We cannot hope to change this if we are blind to the fact that it is having a negative effect.

What is to be done?

This book has extensively analysed some of the reasons why Glasgow has such challenging problems. It would take another volume to debate the merits of how we might tackle these. Instead of doubling the book's length I have created web pages to post my own ideas, facilitate others to give information on their projects and experience and allow anyone to share their ideas and perspectives both on the analysis I've set out here and what we can do.[5] All I plan to do here by way of conclusion is outline a few key ideas and recommendations.

1. Take an integral approach

Glasgow's problems will only be solved *by taking an integral approach*. In short, what is required are the type of changes set out in Table V which is designed to be indicative, rather than exhaustive.

Some of these changes could be facilitated by Scottish Government or other agencies (eg devoting more resources to tackle domestic violence or provide relationship counselling) but some would require a change in individuals' attitudes.

2. Make the health, well-being and development of children the main Scottish priority

As there is good reason to believe that the well-being of Scottish children is the lowest in the industrialised world,[6] my second big recommendation is that the Scottish Government should replace its current 'Purpose' of increasing economic growth with one focussed on the health and well-being of Scotland's children.

Since the well-being of those from disadvantaged back-grounds must take priority, children in Glasgow and the west of Scotland would particularly benefit. My recommendation is not about a few new programmes here and there but a *funda-mental* restructuring of government spending and attention to prioritise maternity care and the under-fives.

Decades ago Sir Compton McKenzie wrote of Scotland's problems:

> Too many attempts at reformation have been made either in a spirit of hate and destructiveness or, what is ultimately more deadly, in a spirit of constructive utility. Desire the good of your fellow-men, but desire it because you love them, not

Table V:

Outline of an 'Integral Approach' to Glasgow's problems

A richer and healthier inner life	Improvements to physical health and infrastructure
• Increased feelings of hope and optimism about the possibility of change • More positive emotions • More people participating in spiritual practices such as meditation • Heightened feelings of transcendence, connection and purpose • More beauty in people's lives through contact with nature, classical music or art.	• Better care for the under-5s to improve physical, emotional and cognitive health • Enhanced opportunities for physical activity • Improved neighbourhoods – more green spaces • Better maintenance of social housing • Housing developments encompassing a greater range of social classes.
Cultural changes	**Socio-economic changes**
• More value placed on relationships, particularly committed relationships between men and women • More emphasis on the importance of family life and child rearing • More positive and appreciative interactions between individuals and groups • More willingness to embrace change and development • More tolerance of others who are different • Genuine respect for anyone irrespective of background.	• Getting people into work • Tackling inequality (particularly reducing gap between rich and poor through measures such as 'maximum' not just minimum wage and tackling poverty) • Reducing alcohol consumption through availability and pricing • More diversionary activities and youth work • Enhanced gender equality so that women play a more visible role in decision-making.

> because a well-fed, well-clad, well-housed creature
> will be an economic asset to the state. [7]

If you look south of the border at the centralised state planning, tick-the-box approach to child development and state nurseries to get mothers back to work or improve educational attainment, you find an approach which exceeds McKenzie's worst fears. I agree with McKenzie's sentiments: we should take action to ensure that children get the best start in life because it is the right and moral thing to do. Nonetheless we can embark on this radical change in public policy knowing that it is one of the best things we can do to tackle inequality and reduce the shadow this casts over people's lives. What's more, this type of approach is supported by three strong strands of evidence. The first is the neurobiological research which shows the link between early childhood experience and cognitive and emotional development. The second comes from international surveys which show that countries such as the Netherlands which invest heavily in maternal care and the early years have much higher child well-being, and fewer social problems, than countries which do not make this investment. The third source of evidence comes from longitudinal studies (some of them from the UK) which show that projects such as 'Nurse Family Partnerships', which seek to improve maternal care, or pre-school projects which enrich children's life experiences can make a dramatic difference to the life outcomes of those from poor backgrounds.[8] Some professionals working in Scotland are particularly taken by this evidence.

In 2008 Professor John Frank, a Canadian public health specialist, with a particular interest in inequality and health, became Director of a new Edinburgh-based Unit, funded by the

Medical Research Council and the Scottish Chief Scientist Office. This unit seeks to improve health in Scotland by developing and rigorously testing new public health policies and programmes. From his work in Scotland Professor Frank is convinced of the need for a radical change in how Scotland cares for its young. Indeed he argues that the country is unlikely to make serious improvements to the health challenges particularly presented by the west of Scotland unless we invest seriously in under fives from underprivileged backgrounds, especially their cognitive and social development before the age of four.

In recent times the person who has done a great deal to advance the child well-being agenda in Scotland is Alan Sinclair. At first glance, Alan is an unlikely campaigner for this cause: not only is his academic background economics but he also set up the employability organisation now called the Wise Group. He left there to become Head of Skills at Scottish Enterprise and in this capacity consulted widely with employers on the type of skills they wanted to see in school leavers and graduates. As we saw earlier, many stressed the importance of communication skills, team working and problem-solving which they generally thought were in short supply. Researching how people acquire these skills Alan quickly discovered that language skills and various aspects of future cognitive development are dependent on early years experience.[9] So too are social skills which depend to a large degree on empathy, essentially learned in the interaction between mother and baby. Despite this route into the promotion of early years policies, Alan too now believes that this agenda has to be pursued because it is morally the right thing to do for Scotland's children.

Another professional convinced of the importance of these

formative experiences is Detective Chief Superintendent John Carnochan, head of Scotland's Violence Reduction Unit. He believes that Glasgow's violence figures will be reduced by improving life for the under-fives and not through more jails or better policing, although the latter may be required in the short term. Indeed DCS Carnochan, and his Unit, have been ground breaking in promoting the idea of violence reduction as largely about public health.

So it is not difficult to see why international research suggests that money invested in maternal care or the early years leads to a reduction in later spending on health, social services, unemployment benefits, justice and prison services. I am not arguing that these economic benefits should be the main motivating factor for targetting child health and well-being – child health and development is an important moral issue in its own right – but nonetheless taking this approach is likely to be economically beneficial in the longer term by ensuring a healthier more productive population and by preventing problems rather than dealing with them years later.

We cannot, however, simply rely on Government to create a better environment for bringing up children. We all have a part to play in this. Emphatically this does not mean indulging children. It does mean giving them care and attention, and unqualified love and affection, while simultaneously being firm and setting clear rules and boundaries. If we are to raise parenting standards in Glasgow fathers have a large part to play. Men from European countries living in Glasgow are often struck by how fathers here spend little time with their families, appearing to care more about their jobs, football, mates, drink or watching the television than spending quality time with their children.

Indeed many lose total contact with their offspring. So we need more men challenging the traditional male stereotype of the independent man who pursues his own pleasures and suits himself. In short, we need more men who prioritise time with their children and partners.

3. Capitalise on existing knowledge

In Glasgow, and the surrounding area, there is a huge number of community workers, social workers, health practitioners and the like, who have worked in successful projects which have made a difference to the lives of those involved. Many have useful insights into what can work. There are also large numbers of community activists, particularly women like Cathy McCormack quoted in this book, who, against the odds, achieve things for their communities and who often feel they are marginalised and have little real voice. Unfortunately this wealth of experience and these important insights are continually lost. This is in part because innovative work is usually funded on a short-term, project basis. Even if a project is highly successful the funding comes to an end and the lessons are not disseminated within mainstream organisations. A new funding stream is established to tackle similar problems and so the cycle continues. In such a system a few individuals here and there are helped but mainstream practice is hardly changed and those involved in the successful projects become dispirited. This problem is widespread throughout the UK.

Professor John Frank, the Canadian public health specialist, is acutely aware of how the UK as a whole, unlike Canada, lacks organisations designed to capture the learning from innovative health research and disseminate it to policy makers and practitioners in the field. This problem is not confined to health but is also an issue across policy areas. The Scottish Government has set up Professor Frank's collaboration but it could do more to disseminate findings on approaches which really work. The emphasis should be on 'mainstreaming' effective practice not setting up pilot projects and looking internationally at what is effective particularly in tackling inequality or dealing with its effects.

4. Envisage ourselves as a community and take steps to reduce social problems and inequality

One of the worrying trends in Scotland is the rise in alcohol consumption. Recent research shows that over 40 per cent of men and 33 per cent of women drink twice the recommended level of alcohol on a daily basis. Enough alcohol is sold each year in Scotland to allow every adult over 16 to exceed weekly limits. This helps to account for why Scotland has one of the fastest growing Chronic Liver Disease mortality rates in the world at a time when rates in most Western European countries are falling.[10]

Given these stark facts, one of the most dispiriting aspects of the current debate on what to do to reduce Scotland's alcohol consumption is that the Scottish Government's desire to take action on pricing and availability has been met by disapproval in many quarters and the argument advanced that they are 'penalising those who aren't problem drinkers'. However, we face this problem as a society: it is our neighbours' health which is being destroyed by drink. It is also our taxes, social security and health systems which are being drained by this growing problem. We must understand that there is undoubtedly 'a population effect' at work here – Scottish culture as a whole is too focussed on drink and we must take steps collectively to remedy this.

History teaches us that what reduced drinking in Scotland in earlier times was making alcohol more difficult to buy and more expensive. If we are going to make headway again then everyone is going to be affected by higher prices or reduced availability. Surely this is a small price to pay to create a healthier society?

When it comes to the allocation of resources, better off Scots will also have to accept that more money needs to be spent on those who are most disadvantaged. Should wealthy areas, like Giffnock or Bearsden and Milngavie, which ring Glasgow, not pay for services in the city thus releasing money to be spent on some pressing social problems?

The Scottish Government does not have sizeable economic powers but it can set the tone for the country. It could take the lead with public sector pay and talk about a 'maximum wage' not just a minimum wage. It could help create a society where everyone feels that their contributions are valued and rewarded. Given how many people work for the public sector in Scotland the Scottish Government could make a difference to many people's lives if they did more to sidestep the target driven culture and create one that is genuinely more empowering and enabling. Evidence suggests that if they did this, performance is likely to go up, not down.[11]

As Scots we passionately believe in equality but we have certainly not created an egalitarian society and we have had a long history of judging some people 'worthless'. The time has now come to make Glasgow a more equal and less less class-divided society with much greater racial and gender equality.

'Breaking the spell'

When thinking about social change it is all too easy to over-emphasise the importance of government action but research increasingly shows that human beings are group animals. We are all influenced not just by the thoughts, feelings and actions of those we are closely connected to but even 'friends of friends of friends can start chain reactions that eventually reach us, likes waves from distant lands that wash up on our shores.'[12] As we can see from laughter, other people's emotions are contagious. We can start to shift Glasgow's problems if sizable numbers of people change their thinking and start to act differently.

Recently as I stood at the top of Buchanan Street and wondered what might begin to heal Glasgow's problems, a number of powerful words came to mind. The first is *hope*. As Helen Keller once said: 'Nothing can be done without hope and confidence'. We must believe that life can become better for people who are most struggling in this city and they must feel this too or they will give up.

The second is *spirituality*. Glasgow was once such a renowned spiritual centre that it attracted pilgrims – today it is one of the most secular, non-spiritual cities in the world. But if we are going to help improve the quality of life in the city people need to move away from materialism to values which stress the importance of beauty, nature, meaning and transcendence. Research shows that people who say they have a sense of connection to something bigger than themselves have higher life satisfaction and well-being than those who do not. Religion has played such a divisive part in this city's history that many will shy away from the idea of spirituality yet it has a part to play in the city's restoration. Spirituality matters and as individuals we would benefit from giving it a place in our lives.

Finally, in our day-to-day interactions with everyone – be they strangers, colleagues, friends, partners or children – we would do well to act with more *kindness, gentleness* and *love.* Indeed it is only when more Glaswegians feel loved, when they know that their lives have meaning, and when they have a sense of hope, that we shall 'break the spell' and let Glasgow and her people flourish.

AFTERWORD

THIS is an important book and a vital contribution to the debate about the causes of Glasgow's many health and social problems: but, it may not be popular.

Glasgow's political leaders need to present Glasgow as a success story to the outside world. At the same time they want to highlight Glasgow's health and social problems so that resources continue to flow into programmes that they need to present as 'successful' if funding is to continue. All of this is done for the best of motives but those responsible for managing Glasgow's image may find *The Tears that Made the Clyde* an uncomfortable read. Yet, the analogy that is most helpful here is that of a patient who, while he fears he is suffering from something serious, maintains a state of denial until he has a long and serious talk with his doctor. He leaves the consultation with his mood strangely lightened as he for the first time faces up to the true seriousness of his predicament. He is relieved to leave denial behind and face the truth. This book could have a similar energising effect on Glasgow and its leaders.

Nor may this book prove popular with some academics. For many academics the principles of reductionism (that mechanisms are best understood by reducing them to their component parts) command their highest loyalty. Their confidence is not misplaced. Reductionism allows the behaviour of clouds to be understood at the level of molecules; physical forces to explain the movement of planets; the growth of plants to be made manifest by the study of cells and the external characteristics displayed by plants and animals to be explained in terms of genes. However, despite its many successes, reductionism has failed in attempts to understand the full nature of Glasgow's problems. It has led to an overly narrow focus on single issues. The temptation for each specialist, schooled in the mindset of reductionism, is to claim that their take on the problem (material poverty, up-regulated inflammatory responses, family breakdown, lack of attachment in the early years or Vitamin D deficiency due to lack of sunlight – or what ever) is *the* mechanism that matters.

Carol Craig has undertaken a much broader analysis which combines the perspectives of many disciples, supported by data and information from several periods in Glasgow's history. The result is a truly convincing synthesis that reveals the roots and the multifaceted manifestations of Glasgow's challenges.

Central to her analyses are the ideas of Richard Wilkinson: that we all (rich and poor) suffer from inequality and the effects of flexible labour markets and the prioritisation of the needs of the economy over society. But it affects us differently. The poor and working class suffer the highest levels of insecurity, stress and exhaustion, but the middle classes are not immune. They too suffer from work insecurity, long hours and the stresses and strains of just about coping and just about keeping up appearances. Both groups want the same things in different ways – more time, respect and control over their lives.

This is also a hopeful book. It concludes by outlining Ken Wilber's integral model which combines the perspectives of the individual with the collective and the inner/subjective with the outer/objective. This integral model could spark the type thinking we need for a more creative response to Glasgow's current problems.

Finally, this book comes at an important time. Its historical analysis all too clearly demonstrates how material poverty is damaging to individual well-being and human relationships. Yet is also shows how in more recent times we have embraced a society of individualised consumerism which has caused more material 'things' to flow through our lives without addressing our need for intangibles like time, respect and a sense of control. Yet, the banking crisis, credit crunch and the unfolding threat of climate change are causing many to conclude that we 'just can't go on like this for much longer'. It is from insights like these that hope for something better can emerge.

Phil Hanlon
Professor of Public Health
University of Glasgow

REFERENCES

Please note that for brevity full publication details are mainly given the first time a work is cited. A full bibliography is available on the Centre for Confidence and Well-being's website (www.centreforconfidence.co.uk) in the section dedicated to *The Tears that Made the Clyde*.

Some important references give web addresses for where information can be retrieved. However, for practicality some of these are not included here but are available at the above web address. An asterisk * is included at the end of any notes where these URLs have been listed externally.

Introduction
1. See David L. Cooperrider and Diana Kaplin Whitney, *Appreciative Inquiry: a positive revolution in change* (San Francisco, 2005)
2. See Julian Baggini, *Complaint: from minor moans to major protests* (London, 2008)
3. 'Scotland: the official on-line gateway, 'Let Glasgow flourish'*
4. See speech by J. Carnochan to Children 1st 'Breaking the Cycle of Violence', 10 December 2008, p8*
5. For more information on Glasgow's violence rates, see Chapter 1
6. T.C. Smout, *Scottish Voices: 1745-1960* (London, 1990) p137
7. For an outline and commentary on the sources I have used in this book please go to the web address in the first paragraph above.

Chapter 1: Glasgow – No picture of health
1. P. Hanlon, D. Walsh and B. Whyte, 'Let Glasgow Flourish: A comprehensive report on health and its determinants in Glasgow and West Central Scotland' (Glasgow Centre for Population Health, 2006)

2. For information on the GCPH's work go to www.gcph.co.uk
3. Hanlon *et al.*, p11
4. All subsequent data in this chapter are drawn from Hanlon *et al.* unless otherwise stated. Any reference to 'Greater Glasgow' refers to 'the boundaries of NHS Health Scotland' (p21)
5. 'Community Health and Well-being Survey: baseline findings 2006, Summary' (GCPH, Gowell project), pp26-27*
6. Judith Brown *et al.*, 'Turning the Tap Off: incapacity benefit in Glasgow and Scotland – trends over five years' (GCPH, 2007)*
7. Hanlon *et al.*, p213
8. David Webster, 'Housing Implications of the 2001 Census Results' (Report to Glasgow City Council, Housing Development Committee)*
9. Hanlon *et al.*, p246
10. Daniel J. Exeter and Paul Boyle, 'Does young adult suicide cluster geographically in Scotland?, *Journal of Epidemiology and Community Health* (vol.61, 2007) 731-736
11. Hanlon *et al.*, p319
12. David Walsh, Martin Taulbut and Phil Hanlon, 'The Aftershock of Deindustrialisation: Trends in mortality in Scotland and other parts of post-industrial Europe (GCPH, 2008), p8
13. Walsh *et al.*, p62
14. See note 40 for this chapter
15. Lindsay Gray, 'Comparisons of health-related behaviours and health measures in Greater Glasgow with other regional areas in Europe' (GCPH, 2008)*
16. Walsh *et al.*, pp123-5
17. Walsh *et al.*, p116
18. See note 27 for Chapter 6
19. Information provided by the Violence Reduction Unit, Glasgow. Many documents are available on their website – http://www.actiononviolence.co.uk/aov/46.81.38.html
20. NFO Social Research, 'Sectarianism in Glasgow – Final Report' (Glasgow City Council, 2003)*
21. NFO Social Research, 'Sectarianism', p59
22. NFO Social Research, 'Sectarianism', p59
23. Glasgow's Single Outcome Agreement (Glasgow City Council, 2009), p25
24. Unicef, 'An Overview of Child Well-being in Rich

Countries', (Report from Unicef Innocenti Research Centre, Report Card 7, 2007), p23

25. Unicef, p24
26. Richard G. Wilkinson, *The Impact of Inequality: how to make sick societies healthier* (London, 2005)
27. Richard Wilkinson and Kate Pickett, *The Spirit Level: Why more equal societies almost always do better* (London, 2009)
28. Richard G. Wilkinson, p286
29. Richard G. Wilkinson, pp251-2
30. See Robin Dunbar, *Grooming, Gossip and the Evolution of Language* (London, 1996)
31. Willa Muir, *Mrs. Grundy in Scotland* (London, 1936), p25
32. Richard G. Wilkinson, p225
33. T.W. Adorno *et al.*, *The Authoritarian Personality* (New York, 1950)
34. See Richard G. Wilkinson, p227
35. Richard G. Wilkinson, pp217-9
36. Richard G. Wilkinson, p47
37. Richard G. Wilkinson, p148
38. Richard G. Wilkinson, p149
39. Richard G. Wilkinson, p110, figure 4.3
40. David Walsh, Neil Bendel, Richard Jones, and Phil Hanlon, 'It's not "just deprivation": why do equally deprived UK cities experience different health outcomes?' *In press*

Chapter 2: The making of industrial Glasgow

1. Robert Kent Thomas, 'Glasgow in the 18th Century'.
2. Both quotes from J. Cunnison and J.B.S. Gilfillan (eds), *The Third Statistical Account of Scotland: Glasgow* (Glasgow, 1958), p95
3. Quoted in Frank Wordsall, *The Tenement: A way of life* (Edinburgh, 1979), p69
4. Daniel Green (ed.), *Cobbett's Tour in Scotland*, (Aberdeen, 1984 edn), pp54-5
5. T.M. Devine, *The Scottish Nation,* p52
6. T.M. Devine, pp249-50
7. George Blake, *The Heart of Scotland* (London, 1934), p8
8. T.M. Devine, p153
9. Tom Johnston, *The History of the Scottish Working Classes* (Glasgow,1946), p321
10. William Bolitho, *Cancer of Empire* (London, 1924), p40

11. Quoted in Sean Damer, *Glasgow: Going for a song* (London, 1990), p61
12. T.C. Smout, *A Century of the Scottish People*, p151
13. Lewis Grassic Gibbon, 'Glasgow' in Lewis Grassic Gibbon and Hugh MacDiarmid, *Scottish Scene* (London, 1934), p 137
14. This may have been Neil Munro but it has not been possible to verify
15. Archie Hind, *The Dear Green Place* (London, 1966), p20
16. T.C. Smout, *Scottish Voices*, p207
17. Quoted in T.M. Devine, p346

Chapter 3: The tiers that made the Clyde

1.T.M. Devine, *The Transformation of Rural Scotland: Social change and the agrarian economy, 1660-1815* (Edinburgh, 1999 edn), p36
2. T.M. Devine *The Scottish Nation* p134
3. T.M. Devine, *The Transformation of Rural Scotland*, p62
4. Quoted in David Hackett Fisher, *Albion's Seed: four British folkways in America* (New York, 1989), p656
5. T.M. Devine, *The Transformation of Rural Scotland*, p62
6. The main exception to this is T.M. Devine whose work I have drawn on extensively in this section.
7. T.M. Devine, *Scotland's Empire 1600-1815* (London, 2003), p249
8. Quoted in Linda Colley, *Britons* (London, 1992), p121
9. Linda Colley, p139
10. T.M. Devine, *Scotland's Empire*, p247
11. Alfred Barnard, quoted in Glasgow Story on-line in section on F&J Smith and tobacco lords*
12. T.M. Devine, *The Scottish Nation,* p145
13. S.G. Checkland, *The Upas Tree* (Glasgow, 1981 ed), p 131
14. Willa Muir, *Mrs. Grundy in Scotland*, p26
15. T.C. Smout, *A Century of the Scottish People,* p2
16. T.M. Devine, 'The Urban Crisis' in T.M. Devine and Gordon Jackson (eds), *Glasgow Volume 1: Beginnings to 1830* (Manchester, 1995), p403
17. Edwin Muir, *Scottish Journey* (Surrey, 1935), p156
18. Quoted in Andrew Noble, 'Urbane Silence: Scottish writing in the nineteenth century city' in George Gordon (ed.), *Perspectives of the Scottish City* (Aberdeen, 1985), p87

19. M. Lindsay, 'I belong to Glasgow' in Maurice Lindsay (ed.), *As I Remember* (London, 1979)
20. S.G. Checkland, *The Upas Tree*, p22
21. Quoted in Andrew Noble, 'Urbane Silence', p93
22. Tom Johnston, *The History of the Scottish Working Classes*, p296
23. Enid Gauldie, 'The Middle Class and Working Class Housing in the Nineteenth Century' in A. Allan McLaren, *Social Class in Scotland: Past and present* (Edinburgh, 1976), p29
24. Stana Nenadic, 'The Middle Ranks and Modernisation' in T.M. Devine and Gordon Jackson (eds), *Glasgow Volume 1*, p296
25. Richard Rodger, 'Employment, Wages and Poverty' in George Gordon (ed.), *Perspectives of the Scottish City*, p28
26. T.M. Devine, 'The Urban Crisis', p414
27. See Hamish Fraser, 'Labour and the Changing City' in George Gordon (ed.), *Perspectives of the Scottish City*, p161
28. T.M. Devine, *The Scottish Nation*, p343
29. Quoted in Sean Damer, *Glasgow: Going for a song* (London, 1990), p114
30. Quoted in Tom Johnston, p290
31. For a brief outline of these ideas see T.M. Devine, *The Scottish Nation*, p85
32. Quoted in A. Alan McLaren, 'Bourgeois Ideology and Victorian Philanthropy: The contradictions of cholera' in A. Allan McLaren, *Social Class in Scotland: Past and present, p43*
33. A. Alan McLaren, 'Bourgeois Ideology', p49
34. Richard Rodger, 'Employment, Wages and Poverty', p53
35. For a discussion of this point see Enid Gauldie, p15
36. Richard G. Wilkinson, *The Impact of Inequality*, p38
37. Quoted in Hamish Fraser, p171
38. Meg Henderson, *Finding Peggy: A Glasgow childhood* (London, 1994), pp276-7
39. Brian Dicks, 'Choice and Constraint: Further perspectives of socio-residential segregation in nineteenth century Glasgow with particular reference to its west end' in George Gordon (ed.), *Perspectives of the Scottish City*, p98
40. See Moira Burgess, *Imagine a City: Glasgow in fiction* (Argyll, 1998)
41. George Blake, *The Shipbuilders (London, 1944)*, p146
42. Edwin Muir, *Scottish Journey*, p108

43. Maurice Lindsay, 'I belong to Glasgow' in *As I Remember*, p64
44. Sydney and Olive Checkland, *Industry and Ethos: Scotland 1832-1914* (London, 1984) p178
45. Richard Rodger, p53

Chapter 4: The twin track city
1. Quoted in Enid Gauldie, 'The Middle Class and Working Class Housing', p30
2. T.M. Devine *The Scottish Nation*, p261
3. T. M. Devine, p263
4. For more information on material in this section see Richard Rodger, 'Employment, Wages and Poverty'.
5. Richard Rodger, p46
6. Richard Rodger, p46
7. Piers Dudgeon, *Our Glasgow: Memories of life in disappearing Britain* (London, 2009), p106
8. Janice Galloway, *This is Not About Me* (London, 2008), p13
9. Meg Henderson, *Finding Peggy*, p17
10. Cliff Hanley, 'Snobs and Scruff' in Cliff Hanley (ed.) *Glasgow: A celebration* (Edinburgh, 1984), pp163-171
11. Cliff Hanley, p169
12 Enid Gauldie, p13
13. Ralph Glasser, *Growing Up in the Gorbals* (London, 1986), p46
14. Quoted in Ian MacDougal (ed.) *Essays in Scottish Labour History* (Edinburgh, 1978), p24
15. Quoted in John Foster and Charles Woolfson, *The Politics of the UCS Work-In* (London, 1986), p372
16. Sean Damer, *Glasgow: Going for a song*, p59
17. I.G.C. Hutchison, 'Glasgow Working-class Politics', in R.A. Cage, *The Working Class in Glasgow 1750-1914* (Kent, 1987) p134
18. T.M. Devine p503
19. T.M. Devine p319
20. Neal Ascherson, *Stone Voices* (London, 2003 edition), p69
21. Quoted in T.M. Devine and Gordon Jackson (eds), *Glasgow Volume 1: Beginnings to 1830*, p321
22. T.C. Smout, *A Century of the Scottish People*, p48
23. Hamish Fraser, 'Labour and the Changing City', p160
24. Richard Rodger, p31
25. S.G. Checkland, *The Upas Tree*, p59

26. Quoted in S.G. Checkland, p58
27. See, for example, Robert H. Frank, 'Does absolute income matter? In Luigino Bruni and Pier Luigi Porta (eds.), *Economics and Happiness* (Oxford, 2005)
28. S.G. Checkland, pp58-9
29. Carol Craig, *The Scots' Crisis of Confidence* (Glasgow, 2003)
30. Ralph Glasser, *Gorbals Boy at Oxford* (London, 1988), p158
31. Richard J. Finlay, *Modern Scotland 1914-2000* (London 2004), p127
32. Sean Damer, p161
33. Sean Damer, p169
34. Sean Damer, p170

Chapter 5: The demon drink

1. Bruce K. Alexander, *The Globalisation of Addiction: a study in the poverty of the spirit* (Oxford, 2008), p95
2. Bruce K. Alexander, p91
3. Bruce K. Alexander, p62
4. Quoted in Bruce K. Alexander, p130
5. Neal Ascherson, *Stone Voices*, p80
6. Quoted in T.C. Smout, *A Century of the Scottish People*, p134
7. Quoted in George Bruce and Paul H. Scott (eds*), A Scottish Postbag: Eight centuries of Scottish letters* (London, 1986), p106
8. Quoted in T.M. Devine *The Scottish Nation*, p351
9. T.C. Smout, *A Century of the Scottish People*, p136
10. T.M. Devine, *p353*
11. Quoted in T.C. Smout, *A History of the Scottish People 1560-1830* (Edinburgh, 1969) pp389-90
12. Quoted in Sean Damer, *Glasgow*, p82
13. See T.C. Smout, *A Century of the Scottish People*, p145
14. Daniel Paton, 'The Legend of Drunken Scotland' in Martin Plant, Bruce Ritson and Roy Robertson (eds), *Alcohol and Drugs: The Scottish experience* (Edinburgh, 1992), p12
15. T.M. Devine, p351
16. T.C. Smout, *A Century of the Scottish People*, p143
17. G. Gladstone Robertson, *Gorbals Doctor*, (London, 1970), p57
18. George Blake, *The Heart of Scotland* (London, 1934), p88
19. Quoted in T.C. Smout, *A Century of the Scottish People*, *p*139
20. Quoted in Kevin McCarra and Hamish Whyte (eds) *A Glasgow Collection: Essays in honour of Joe Fisher*

(Glasgow, 1990), p73

21. T.M. Devine, p355
22. T.M. Devine, p355
23. George Blake, *The Heart of Scotland*, p86
24. Sean Damer, p200
25. Hugh MacDiarmid, 'The Dour Drinkers of Glasgow' in Hugh MacDiarmid, *The Uncanny Scot* (London, 1968), pp93-4
26. Daniel Wight, *Workers Not Wasters: Masculine respectability, consumption & employment in central Scotland* (Edinburgh, 1993)
27. G. Gladstone Robertson, p62
28. Quoted in Martin Bellamy, *The Shipbuilders: An anthology of Scottish shipyard life* (Edinburgh, 2001), p106
29. Quoted in Piers Dudgeon, *Our Glasgow*, pp76-7
30. Quoted in Piers Dudgeon, p199
31. Quoted in J.A. Mack, 'The Changing City' in J. Cunnison and J.B.S. Gilfillan (eds), *The Third Statistical Account of Scotland: Glasgow*, p768
32. J.A. Mack, p769
33. Piers Dudgeon, p199
34. Daniel Wight, p116
35. Annmarie Hughes, 'Working Class Culture, Family Life and Domestic Violence on Clydeside', in *Scottish Tradition*, (vol. 27, 2002) p80*

Chapter 6: Macho city

1. Richard G. Wilkinson, *The Impact of Inequality*, p219
2. See the Wave Trust's report 'Violence and What to Do About It' (Surrey, 2005)*
3. Shadow, *Midnight Scenes and Social Photographs* (Glasgow, 1976)
4. Sean Damer, *Glasgow: Going for a song*, p150
5. Ralph Glasser, *Growing Up in the Gorbals*, p61
6. Ralph Glasser, *Gorbals Boy at Oxford*, p171
7. George Blake, *The Shipbuilders*, p147
8. George Blake, p135
9. Matt McGinn, *McGinn of the Calton* (Glasgow, 1987), p32
10. Piers Dudgeon, *Our East End: Memories of life in disappearing Britain*, p181
11. Piers Dudgeon, *Our Glasgow*, p201
12. Archie Hind, *The Dear Green Place*, p39
13. Ralph Glasser, *Gorbals Voices*, p37

14. Piers Dudgeon, *Our Glasgow*, p201.
15. Annmarie Hughes, 'Working Class Culture, Family Life and Domestic Violence', p63*
16. Quoted in T.C. Smout, *A Century of the Scottish People*, p138
17. J. Dee Higley, 'Individual differences in alcohol-induced aggression' in *Alcohol Research and Health* (vol 5, 2001)
18. Annmarie Hughes, p70*
19. G. Gladstone Roberston, *Gorbals Doctor*, p62
20. T.M. Devine, *Scottish Nation*, p309
21. Richard J. Finlay, *Modern Scotland*, p32
22. Richard J. Finlay, p120
23. Quoted in Martin Bellamy, *The Shipbuilders*, p106
24. News reports in *The Herald*, 20th and 26th March, 2009
25. J.A. Mack, 'Crime' in J. Cunnison and J.B.S. Gilfillan (eds), *The Third Statistical Account of Scotland: Glasgow*, pp 646-7
26. George Blake, p131
27. G. Gladstone Robertson, p63
28. For an interesting account of the novel *No Mean City* by Alexander McArthur and H. Kingsley Long and its impact see Sean Damer, 'No Mean Writer? The Curious Case of Alexander McArthur' in Kevin McCarra and Hamish Whyte (eds) *A Glasgow Collection* (Glasgow, 1990)
29. Richard G. Wilkinson, *The Impact of Inequality*, p218
30. Elspeth King, *The Hidden History of Glasgow's Women: The Thenew factor* (Edinburgh, 1993)
31. Ralph Glasser, *Gorbals Boy at Oxford*, p143
32. Richard J. Finlay, p120
33. R.A. *Cage, The Working Class in Glasgow 1750-1914* (Kent, 1987) p27
34. Sydney and Olive Checkland, *Industry and Ethos: Scotland 1832-1914* (London, 1984) p47
35. John Foster, 'The Twentieth Century, 1914-1979' in R.A. Houston and W.W.J. Knox (eds), *The New Penguin History of Scotland: From the earliest times to the present day* (London, 2001), p436
36. For a general overview of the southern states and a 'culture of honour' see Malcolm Gladwell, *Outliers* (London, 2008), pp161-76
37. Dov Cohen *et al.*, 'Insult, Aggression and the Southern *Culture of Honor*: an "Experimental Ethnography"' in *Journal of Personality and Social Psychology* (Vol 70, No 5, May 1996), 945-960
38. David Hackett Fisher, *Albion's Seed* p679

39. Quoted in Sean Damer, *Glasgow*, p75
40. S.G. Checkland, *The Upas Tree*, p86

Chapter 7: Women and children last
1. J.M. Gottman, 'A Theory of Marital Dissolution and Stability', *Journal of Family Psychology*, (vol 7, 1993), 57-75
2. Michael Munro, *The Patter: A guide to current Glasgow usage* (Glasgow, 2008 edition), p34
3. William Bolitho, *Cancer of Empire*, p35
4. Ralph Glasser, *Growing Up in the Gorbals*, p43
5. Richard J. Finlay, *Modern Scotland*, p118
6. Piers Dudgeon, *Our Glasgow*, p86
7. T.C. Smout, *A Century of the Scottish People*, p151
8. William McIlvanney, *The Papers of Tony Veitch* (London, 1983) p225
9. Annmarie Hughes, 'Working Class Culture, Family Life and Domestic Violence', p62
10. Richard J. Finlay, p146
11. T.C. Smout, p139
12. Richard J. Finlay, p22
13. George Blake, *The Shipbuilders*, p23
14. G. Gladstone Robertson, *Gorbals Doctor*, p56
15. G. Gladstone Robertson, p57
16. See, for example, the conversation between Ken Roy and Rikki Fulton in Kenneth Roy, *Conversations in a Small Country* (Ayr, 1989), p155
17. See, for example, Robert Douglas, *Night Song of the Last Tram* (London, 2005)
18. Cathy McCormack, *The Wee Yellow Butterfly* (Argyll, 2008), p37
19. George Blake, p26
20. Neil McMillan, 'Wilting, or the "Poor Wee Boy Syndrome": Kelman and masculinity' in *Edinburgh Review* (No 108), p49
21. William McIlvanney, *A Gift from Nessus* (London, 1968)
22. Beth Dickson, 'Class and Being in the Novels of William McIlvanney' in Gavin Wallace and Randall Stevenson (eds), *The Scottish Novel Since the Seventies* (Edinburgh, 1993), p60
23. Quoted in Richard J. Finlay, p102
24. T.M. Devine *The Scottish Nation*, p360
25. T.C. Smout, p158
26. Christopher Harvie, *No Gods and Precious Few Heroes* (London, 1981), p121

27 Jack House, 'Leisure Interests', in J. Cunnison and J.B.S. Gilfillan (eds), *The Third Statistical Account of Scotland: Glasgow*, p620

28. T.C. Smout, p158

29. Jack House, pp618-9

30. Quote from a full transcript of an interview with Janice Galloway which appeared in *The List*, 4 September, 2008*

31. Bawcutt, Patricia, Ed. *The Poems of William Dunbar* (2 vols), (Glasgow, 1999)

Chapter 8: Let Glasgow languish?

1. For an introduction to Self-Determination Theory's concept of human needs see Edward L. Deci and Richard M. Ryan, 'The "What" and "Why" of Goal Pursuits: Human needs and the self-determination of behaviour' in *Psychological Inquiry*, (vol 11, no 4, 2000), 227-268*

2. Edward L. Deci and Richard M. Ryan, p254

3. M.G. Marmot, *et al.,* 'Employment Grade and Coronary Heart Disease in British Civil Servants', *Journal of Epidemiology and Community Health* (vol 32: 1978), 244-249

4. James A. Mackay (ed.), *The Complete Letters of Robert Burns* (Ayrshire, 1990 edn), p207

5. Ralph Glasser, *Gorbals Boy at Oxford*, p12

6. Sean Damer, *Glasgow,* p89

7. Quoted in Sean Damer, p86

8. Edward L. Deci and Richard M. Ryan, p252

9. T.M. Devine, *The Scottish Nation*, p144

10. Fred M. Walker, *Song of the Clyde: A history of Clyde shipbuilding* (Cambridge, 1984), p205

11. Quoted in Martin Bellamy, *The Shipbuilders,* pp29-30

12. Quoted in Brian Lavery, *Maritime Scotland* (London, 2001), pp89-90

13. Anthony J.J. McNeill, *Images of Greenock* (Argyll, 1998), p36.

14. Quoted in T.M. Devine, p549

15. Ian Johnston, *Ships for a Nation: John Brown & Company Clydebank* (West Dunbartonshire, 2000), p14

16. Quoted in Martin Bellamy, p3

17. Ian Johnston, pp14-15

18. Quoted in Martin Bellamy, p12

19. Quoted in Martin Bellamy, p7

20. Quoted in Sean Damer, p40
21. Quoted in Fred M. Walker, p4
22. George Blake, *The Shipbuilders*, p155
23. George Blake, p151
24. T.C. Smout, *A Century of the Scottish People*, p87
25. See note 29 for Chapter 1
26. Quoted in T.C. Smout, *Scottish Voices*, p208
27. Robert Putnam, *Bowling Alone: The collapse and revival of American community* (New York, 2000). See pp19-28
28. Robert Crampsey, *The Scottish Footballer* (Edinburgh, 1978), pp66-7
29. See, for example, Ian Johnston, p15
30. Ian Spring, *The Phantom Village : The myth of the new Glasgow* (Edinburgh, 1990), p45
31. Quoted in Martin Bellamy, p127
32. Quoted in Martin Bellamy, pp25-6
33. Martin Bellamy, p154
34. Martin Bellamy, p154
35. William McIlvanney, *Surviving the Shipwreck* (Edinburgh, 1991), p167
36. William McIlvanney, p165

Chapter 9: Edification, elevation and dependency

1. Quoted in T.C. Smout, *A Century of the Scottish People*, p256
2. Harry McShane quoted in T.C. Smout, p262
3. Ralph Glasser, *Growing Up in the Gorbals*, pp88-9
4. T.C. Smout, pp270-1
5. C.R. Synder, *The Psychology of Hope* (New York, 2003)
6. John McNair, *James Maxton: The beloved rebel* (London, 1955), p28
7. Quoted in T.C. Smout, p272
8. Quoted in John McNair, p218
9. Quoted in John McNair, p279
10. Quoted in John McNair, pp222-3
11. John McNair, p14
12. John McNair, p87
13. Quoted in Gordon Brown, *Maxton* (Edinburgh, 1986), p315
14. Quoted in John McNair, p63
15 Quoted in John McNair, p328
16. For an outline of the concept of 'elevation' see Jonathan

Haidt, *The Happiness Hypothesis* (New York, 2006)

17. Quoted in T.M. Devine, *The Scottish Nation,* p399
18. Tom Johnston, *Memories* (London, 1952), p66
19. Lewis Grassic Gibbon, 'Glasgow' in Lewis Grassic Gibbon and Hugh MacDiarmid, *Scottish Scene*, p141
20. T.M. Devine, *The Scottish Nation,* p323
21. T.M. Devine, p325
22. T.C. Smout, p273
23. Quoted in Gordon Brown, p309
24. Christopher Harvie, *No Gods and Precious Few Heroes*, p106
25. Sean Damer, *Glasgow,* pp172-3
26. Sean Damer, p168
27. Richard Rodger, 'Urbanisation in Twentieth-Century Scotland' in T.M. Devine and R.J. Finlay (eds), *Scotland in the 20th Century* (Edinburgh 1996), p138
28. Richard Rodger, p139
29. Richard Rodger, p136
30. T.C. Smout, p274

Chapter 10: The three Bs

1. Mary Rose Liverani, *Winter Sparrows: Growing up in Scotland and Australia* (London, 2000), pp88-9
2. George Davie, *The Democratic Intellect: Scotland and her Universities in the 19th Century* (Edinburgh, 1961)
3. For a commentary on Davie's work and some of the myths that surround it see Jean Barr, *The Stranger Within: On the idea of an educated public* (Rotterdam, 2008)
4. For much of the material used in this chapter see Robert Anderson, 'Education and Society in Modern Scotland' in *History of Education Quarterly*, (Vol 25, No 4, Winter, 1985), 459-481 and Robert Anderson, 'In Search of the "Lad of Parts": the Mythical History of Scottish Education' in *History Workshop*, (No 19, Spring, 1985), 82-104
5. See Robert Anderson, 'In Search of the "Lad of Parts"', p91
6. Quoted in T.C. Smout, *A Century of the Scottish People,* p220
7. Quoted in T.C. Smout, p225
8. Quoted in Robert Anderson, 'Education and Society in Modern Scotland', p474
9. T.M. Devine, *The Scottish Nation,* p406
10. Richard J. Finlay, *Modern Scotland*, p125
11. Richard J. Finlay, p124
12. Quoted in Piers Dudgeon, *Our Glasgow,* p156
13. Janice Galloway, *This is Not About Me* (London, 2008), p238

14. Quoted in Piers Dudgeon, *p157*
15. Quoted in Richard J. Finlay, p124
16. Quoted in T.C. Smout, *Scottish Voices*, p79
17. William McIlvanney, *Docherty* (London, 1975)
18. R.K.S. Macaulay, *Language, Social Class and Education: A Glasgow study* (Edinburgh, 1977)
19. See Richard Wilkinson and Kate Pickett, *The Spirit Level*.
20 See, for example, C.M. Steele *et al.*, 'Contending with group image: The psychology of stereotype and social identity threat' in M. Zanna (ed.), *Advances in Experimental Social Psychology* (Vol 37, 2002)
21. This research is outlined in Richard Wilkinson and Kate Pickett, *The Spirit Level*
22. See Scottish Government, 'Literature Review of the NEET Group'*

Chapter 11: Glasgow limited

1. Archie Hind, *The Dear Green Place*, p228
2. Moira Burgess, *Imagine a City: Glasgow in fiction*, p200
3. Archie Hind, p40
4. Maxwell MacLeod, 'Archie Hind: Author of *The Dear Green Place*' obituary in *The Independent* (23 February, 2008)
5. Archie Hind, pp79-81
6. Archie Hind, p94
7. Archie Hind, p228
8. Archie Hind, p100
9. Archie Hind, pp173-4
10. Archie Hind, p65
11. Douglas Gifford, *The Dear Green Place: the novel in the West of Scotland* (Glasgow, 1885), p8
12. T.C. Smout, *A Century of the Scottish People*, p229
13. Richard J. Finlay, *Modern Scotland*, p279
14. Archie Hind, p97
15. Willie Gall and Cliff Hanley, *The Sheer Gall of it: The wit of Glasgow* (Edinburgh, 1988)
16. Janice Galloway, *This is Not About Me*.
17. Quote from a full transcript of an interview with Janice Galloway which appeared in *The List*, 4 September, 2008*
18. Cathy McCormack, *The Wee Yellow Butterfly*, (Argyll, 2009) p148
19. 'The Scottish Diaspora and Diaspora Strategy', Scottish Government Report, May, 2009*

Chapter 12: Love actually

1. George Albee interview entitled 'Focus on the Growing Efficacy of Prevention Programs' in *Lifelines*, Journal of Centre for Study of Health Disparities (Vol 1, Fall 1999)*

2. J. Bowlby, *Attachment* (London, 1969). There has now been extensive research on this topic. Two websites contain considerable information: www.attachmentnetwork.org and also www.richardatkins.co.uk For an outline of differences between Scottish thinkers' views and those of Bowlby and other attachment theorists see Gavin Miller, 'Why Scottish "Personal Relations Theory" Matter Politically' in *Scottish Affairs* (No 2, winter 2008)*

3. See Sue Gerhardt, *Why Love Matters* (East Sussex, 2004)

4. Patrick O. McGowan, 'Epigenetic regulation of the glucocorticoid receptor in human brain associates with childhood abuse' in *Nature Neuroscience* (12, 2009) 342-348

5. Frances A. Champagne *et al.*, 'Maternal Care Associated with Methylation of the Estrogen Receptor-1b Promoter and Estrogen Receptor-Expression in the Medial Preoptic Area of Female Offspring' in *Endocrinology* (Vol 147, No 6, 2006)

6. For a good overview of this literature see Alan Sinclair's report for the Work Foundation, '0-5 How Small Children Can Make A Big Difference', (2007)*

7. See Jeremy D. Coplan *et al.*, 'Persistent elevations of cerebrosinal fluid concentrations of corticotropin-releasing factor in adult nonhuman primates exposed to early life stressors' in *Proc. Natl. Acad. Sci. USA* (Vol 93, Feb 1996), 1619-1623

8. See Centers for Disease Control and Prevention's report on ACE Study and the prevalence rates at www.cdc.gov/nccdphp/ace/prevalence.htm*

9. Vincent J.A. Felitti *et al*, 'Relationship of Childhood Abuse and Household Dysfunction to Many of the Leading Causes of Deaths in Adults; The Adverse Childhood Experiences (ACE) Study' in *American Journal of Preventive Medicine*, (vol. 14, issue 4) 245-258*

10. Vincent J. Felitti, 'The Relationship of Adverse Childhood Experience to Adult Health: Turning gold into lead', retrieved from ACE Study website: www.acestudy.org/aboutus.html*

11. See Centers for Disease Control and Prevention's report

on ACE Study and the prevalence rates at www.cdc.gov/nccdphp/ace/prevalence.htm*

12 The ACE questionnaires for males and females can be retrieved from: www.acestudy.org/aboutus.html*

13. Michael Munro, *The Patter: A guide to current Glasgow usage* (Glasgow, 2008 edn)

14. See Moira Burgess, *Imagine a City*, p281

15. Michael Munro, *The Patter*, p4

16. Mary Rose Liverani, *The Winter Sparrows*, p84

17. Robert Douglas, *Night Song of the Last Tram* (London, 2005), p161

18. Mary Rose Liverani, p68

19. Gordon Williams, *From Scenes Like These* (Glasgow, 1996)

20. Quoted in Moira Burgess, *Imagine a City*, p216

21. Cathy McCormack, *The Wee Yellow Butterfly* (Argyll, 2008), p20

22. See research conducted in 2002 in Cranhill/Ruchazie by 'Communities that Care' and 'Schools Health and Wellbeing Survey: A summary report for Glasgow City Schools (Greater Glasgow and Clyde NHS, 2007), p23

23. Meg Henderson, *Finding Peggy*, p141

24. See Nicholas Emler, *The Costs and Causes of Low Self-worth* (York, 2001)

25. Robert Anda, 'The Health and Social Impact of Growing Up with Adverse Childhood Experiences: The human and economic costs of the status quo', retrieved from www.acestudy.org/aboutus.html*

26. Bonnie Benard, *Fostering Resiliency in Kids: Protective factors in the family, school, and community* (San Francisco, 1991)

27. Vincent J. Felitti, p6

28. Robert Anda, p12

29. See the Scottish Government's website on how 'Scotland Performs'*

30. Vincent J. Felitti, p6

Chapter 13: Lanark on the couch

1. Edwin Morgan, 'Tradition and experiment in the Scottish novel' in Gavin Wallace and Randall Stevenson (eds) *The Scottish Novel Since the Seventies* (Edinburgh, 1993), p87

2. For a summary of the idea of division in Scottish culture and my critique of it see Carol Craig, *The Scots' Crisis of Confidence*

3. Gavin Wallace, 'The Novel of Damaged Identity' in *The Scottish Novel Since the Seventies*

4. Edwin Muir, *Scott and Scotland* (London, 1936 edn), p21

5. Edwin Muir, pp25-6

6. Quoted in Gavin Wallace, 'The Novel of Damaged Identity', p222

7. Cairns Craig, *Out of History: Narrative paradigms in Scottish and British Culture* (Edinburgh, 1996), p13

8. Alasdair Gray's 'Personal Curriculum Vitae' p2*

9. Rodge Glass, *Alasdair Gray: A secretary's biography* (London, 2008), p34. For Alasdair Gray's reaction to the biography see Alasdair Gray, 'Be My Boswell' in *The Guardian* (20 Sept., 2008)

10. Alasdair Gray, *Lanark* (Edinburgh, 1981), p123

11. Alasdair Gray, *Lanark*, p129

12. Alasdair Gray, *Lanark*, p486

13. Quoted in Rodge Glass, p34

14. Alasdair Gray, *Lanark*, p124

15. Alasdair Gray, *Old Negatives: 4 verse sequences* by Alasdair Gray (London, 1989), p25

16. Quoted in Rodge Glass, p32

17. Colin Manlove, *Scottish Fantasy Literature: A critical survey*, (Edinburgh, 1994), p198

18. Alasdair Gray, *Lanark*, p501

19. Alasdair Gray, *Lanark*, p456

20. Alasdair Gray, *Lanark*, p527

21. Janice Galloway, 'Glasgow Belongs to Us' in *The Guardian* (12 October, 2002)

22. Alasdair Gray, *Lanark*, p559

23. Alasdair Gray, *Old Negatives*, p45

24. Quote from Alasdair Gray in an interview with Mark Axlerod in *The Review of Contemporary Fiction* (Illinois, Summer, 1995)*

25. Alasdair Gray used this quote from Chekhov in an interview with Lidia Vianu in 2000*

26. Alasdair Gray, *Lanark*, p6

27. See Rodge Glass, p34
28. Janice Galloway, *The Trick is to Keep Breathing* (Edinburgh, 1989)
29. Gavin Wallace, p224
20. Janice Galloway, *This is Not About Me*, p39
31. Janice Galloway, *This is Not About Me*, p86
32. Janice Galloway, *This is Not About Me*, p102
33. Quote from a full transcript of an interview with J. Galloway, *The List*, 4 September, 2008*
34. Gavin Wallace, 'The Novel of Damaged Identity', p217
35. Douglas Gifford *et al.*, (eds), *Scottish Literature* (Edinburgh, 2002), p726
36. Doulgas Gifford *et al.*
37. Peter Zenzinger, 'Contemporary Scottish fiction' in Peter Zenzinger (ed.), *Scotland: Literature, Culture, Politics* (Heidelberg, 1989), p228
38. Pete Zenzinger, p232
39. Manfred Malzahn, 'The Industrial Novel' in Cairns Craig (ed.), *The History of Scottish Literature: Volume 4 Twentieth Century* (Aberdeen, 1989 edn), p237

Chapter 14: Dislocation, dislocation, dislocation

1. See, for example, 'Report on the State of Public Health in Canada 2008', Public Health Agency for Canada (July, 2008)
2. Meg Henderson, *Finding Peggy*, p92
3. Piers Dudgeon, *Our Glasgow*, pp297-8
4. Quoted in Chris Arnot, 'New exhibition reappraises the career of architect Sir Basil Spence' in *Society Guardian* (11 June, 2008)
5. Lynsey Hanley, *Estates: An intimate history* (London, 2006), p122
6. Cathy McCormack, *The Wee Yellow Butterfly*
7. Cathy McCormack, p61
8. For a report linking damp houses with physical health in Glasgow see E.L. Lloyd et al, 'The effect of improving the thermal quality of cold housing on blood pressure and general health: a research note' in *Journal of Epidemiology and Community Health* (vol 62, 2008), 793-797
9. Cathy McCormack, p76
10. Cathy McCormack, p47
11. Cathy McCormack, p101

12. Tibor Scitovsky, *The Joyless Economy: The psychology of human satisfaction* (New York, 1992 edn), p vii
13. 'Disarming Britain: The Truth About Street Weapons', Channel 4, July 3 2008
14. James Q. Wilson and George L. Kelling, 'Broken Windows: The policy and neighbourhood safety' in *The Atlantic Monthly*, March 1982*
15. James Q. Wilson and George L. Kelling, p2
15. James Q. Wilson and George L. Kelling, p2
17. Lynsey Hanley, p82
18. Lynsey Hanley, p181
19. William Julius Wilson, *More than Just Race: Being black and poor in the inner city* (New York, 2009)
20. Quoted in John Foster and Charles Woolfson, *The Politics of the UCS Work-In*, p200
21. Quoted in Jimmy Reid, *As I Please* (Edinburgh, 1984), p124
22. See David Torrance *'We in Scotland' – Thatcherism in a cold climate*, (Edinburgh, 2009)
23. Richard J. Finlay, *Modern Scotland*, p343
24. Richard J. Finlay, p347
25. See Richard Wilkinson and Kate Pickett, *The Spirit Level*, p235
26. Quoted in Ian Spring, *The Phantom Village*, pp41-2
27. William McIlvanney, *Surviving the Shipwreck* (Edinburgh, 1991), p248
28. Richard J. Finlay, *Modern Scotland*, p375
29. William McIlvanney, *Surviving the Shipwreck,* pp248-9
30. See C. Warhurst *et al.*, 'Aesthetic labour in interactive service work: Some case study evidence from the "new" Glasgow' in *The Services Industries Journal*, (vol 20 [3], 2000), 1-18
31. Cathy McCormack, p152
32. William Julius Wilson, *More than Just Race*
33. Cathy McCormack, p108
34. Cathy McCormack, p138
35. Cathy McCormack, p96
37. Cathy McCormack, p226
38. Christopher Harvie, *No Gods and Precious Few Heroes*, p125 My emphasis

Chapter 15: Straws in the wind

1. See Greg Easterbrook, *The Progress Paradox: How life gets better while people feel worse* (New York, 2003)

2. The main report is 'Dame Carol Black's review of the health of Britain's working age population' published in 2008 as 'Working for a healthier tomorrow'.* Other reports and responses from the Westminster and Scottish Governments and other organisations are also available.

3. Futureskills Scotland, Employers' Survey, 2004

4. 'Quality and Equity in Schooling in Scotland', OECD Reviews of National Policies for Education Examiners' Report', (OECD, 2007), p6*

5. OECD report, p6

6. OECD report, p7

7. OECD report, p37

8. For a summary see Richard Layard, *Happiness: Lessons from a new science* (London, 2005)

9. 'Breakthough Glasgow: Ending the costs of social breakdown', (The Centre for Social Justice, 2008), p10

10. For a detailed overview of the impact of living in a one parent family without a father see Rebecca O'Neill, 'Experiments in Living: The fatherless family', (Civitas, 2002)*

11. See, for example, Kathy Sylva *et al.*, (eds) *Early Childhood Matters: Evidence from the Effective Pre-school and Primary Education Project* (London, 2009)

12. Robert Rowthorn and David Webster, 'Male Worklessness and the Rise of Lone Parenthood in Britain', (Oxford Centre for Population Research, working paper no. 30, 2007), p3

13. David Webster, 'Scotland's Family Structures', paper presented at a Public Health Information Network for Scotland Seminar, (September, 2006), p2*

14. David Webster, 'Scotland's Family Structures', p2

15. Unicef, 'An Overview of Child Well-being in Rich Countries', (Report from Unicef Innocenti Research Centre, Report Card 7, 2007), gives comparative data on lone parent families. For unemployment figures for European countries and cities check the URLs listed externally*

16. Information supplied by General Registrar Office, Scotland and Office for National Statistics

17. The UK economist who had undertaken most research on the benefits of marriage to individuals is Professor Andrew J. Oswald at the University of Warwick and he has written a number of relevant papers. The two I have drawn on most in this section are: Chris M. Wilson and Andrew J. Oswald, 'How Does Marriage Affect Physical and Psychological Health?: A survey of the longitudinal evidence' * and Jonathan Gardner and Andrew Oswald, 'Is it Money or Marriage that Keeps People Alive?' (2002)*

18. These various pieces of research are quoted in David Servan-Schreiber, *Healing Without Freud or Prozac* (London, 2005 edn), pp178-9

19. Quoted in Sally Wyke and Graeme Ford, 'Competing Explanations for Associations Between Marital Status and Health' in *Social Science & Medicine*, (vol 34, no 5, 1992), p524

20. Sally Wyke and Graeme Ford, p528

21. Sally Wyke and Graeme Ford, p530

22. Debra Umberson *et al.*, 'You Make Me Sick: Marital quality and health over the life course' in *Journal of Health and Social Behaviour*, (vol 247, March, 2006), 1-16

23. Debra Umberson *et al.*, 'You Make Me Sick'

24. David Walsh, Martin Taulbut and Phil Hanlon, 'The Aftershock of Deindustrialisation'

25. Sally Wyke and Graeme Ford, p530

26. David G. Myers, *The Pursuit of Happiness: Who is Happy, and Why?* (New York, 1993)

27. Andrea Nove, 'Towards a Better Understanding of Happiness and Its Correlates in Glasgow', (MSc dissertation, University of Southampton, 2007), p11

28. Andrea Nove, p96

29. Andrea Nove, p97

30. Andrea Nove, p110

31. Richard Layard, *Happiness*

32. For an overview of the link between money and happiness and economists' pursuit of economic growth see Richard Layard, *Happiness*

33. For a general introduction to the ideas behind 'positive psychology' see Martin E.P. Seligman, *Authentic Happiness* (London, 2003)

34. Andrew Oswald, 'The Hippies were Right all Along about Happiness' in *The Financial Times*, 19 January, 2006

35. Tim Kasser, *The High Price of Materialism* (Massachusetts, 2002), p22
36. Tim Kasser, p111
37. For a summary of this research see Oliver James, *Britain on the Couch* (London, 1998) and Richard Layard, *Happiness*
38. Tim Kasser, p35
39. For international figures see OFcom International Communications Market report 2009*; the figures on Glasgow are cited in 'A Social Capital Framework and Assessment for Glasgow: Final report, (GCPH, 2006)' p15*
40. See Mihaly Csìkszentmihlyi, *Flow: The Psychology of Optimal Experience* (New York, 1990)
41. For a full account of Putnam's analysis and the role he thinks television has had in the decline of social capital see Robert Putnam *Bowling Alone,* (New York, 2000)
42. Jean M. Twenge and W. Keith Campbell, *The Narcissism Epidemic: Living in the age of entitlement* (New York, 2009)
43. 'Being Young in Scotland 2007', (MRUK report for YouthLink Scotland)*
44. Bill Hunter, report on 'Baula-Ruchazie Partnership' in local church magazine
45. For some information on the project see Andrew Denholm, 'Drop out pupils put to work in an Ecuador slum' in *The Herald*, 7 May 2007
46. See Martin E.P. Seligman, *Authentic Happiness*
47. Elaine Duncan, 'Final Report on Positive Psychology Interventions in the Community of Wellhouse, Scotland', 2009*
48. You can listen to Dr. Harry Burns outline what he sees as the link between hopelessness and ill-health and view his slides on-line. *
49. For a summary of the literature see Martin E.P. Seligman, *Authentic Happiness*
50. This is based on unpublished empirical research conducted by the Centre for Confidence and Well-being involving more than 5,000 young people and iavailable at* www.centreforconfidence.co.uk
51. Ross Deuchar, *Gangs, Marginalised Youth and Social Capital* (Staffordshire, 2009), p51
52. Ross Deuchar, p52
53. Ross Deuchar, p13
54. The Centre for Confidence and Well-being is collecting evidence on what makes for a good life in its web-based

'Flourishing Lives' project. This includes summaries of evidence supporting the conclusions in this chapter: www.centreforconfidence.co.uk/flourishing-lives.php

Chapter 16: The problems of self-esteem

1. David Hume, *Treatise of Human Nature*, vol 2 (London, 1985)
2. Much of the material in this section is covered in depth in Carol Craig, *Creating Confidence: A handbook for professionals working with young people* (Glasgow, 2006)
3. The summary in this and following pages on the correlations between self-esteem and various outcomes in life come mainly from Roy Baumeister *et al.*, 'Does high self-esteem cause better performance, interpersonal success, happiness or healthier lifestyles? in *Psychological Science in the Public Interest*, (vol 4. no 1, May, 2003)* and Nicholas Emler, *The Costs and Causes of Low Self-worth* (York, 2001)
4. Research quoted by Po Bronson and Ashley Merryman, *NurtureShock: New thinking about children* (New York, 2009)
5. A. Chatard *et al.*, 'Self-esteem and suicide rates in 55 nations' in *European Journal of Personality* (23: 2009), 19-32
6. See note 50 in Chapter 15
7. See note 22 Chapter 10
8. Richard Wilkinson and Kate Pickett, *The Spirit Level*
9. This material is mainly drawn from Nicholas Emler, *The Costs and Causes of Low Self-worth*
10. See note 50 in Chapter 15
11. Nicholas Emler, p38
12. Nicholas Emler, p40
13. See, for example, Shan A. Jumper, 'A meta-analysis of the relationship of child sexual abuse to adult psychological adjustment' in *Child Abuse & Neglect (*vol 19, issue 6, June 1995) 715-728
14. Carol S. Dweck, *Mindset: The new psychology of success* (New York, 2006)
15. See Norman Doidge, *The Brain that Changes Itself* (London, 2007)

16. For an elaboration of this argument see Frank Ferudi, *Therapy Culture* (London, 2004)
17. See my critique of the UK Government's initiative on emotional literacy in schools: 'The potential dangers of a systematic, explicit approach to teaching social and emotional skills (SEAL)'*

Chapter 17: Ringing the bell

1. Neil McLellan, 'This Unrung Bell' in Hamish Whyte (ed.), *Noise and Smoky Breath* (Mass., 1988)
2. See Jocelinus of Furness, 'The Life of St. Kentigern' in Brian D. Osborne and Ronald Armstrong (eds), *St. Mungo's City* (Edinburgh, 1999)
3. G. Rose, 'Sick individuals and sick populations' in *International Journal of Epidemiology* (vol 14: 1985), 32-38
4. See Ken Wilber, *A Theory of Everything* (Boston, 2000)
5. For more ideas on solutions and to post your comments please go to: http://www.centreforconfidence.co.uk/information.php?p=cGlkPTIzMA==
6. John McLaren, 'Index of Wellbeing for Children in Scotland', (Barnardo's, 2007)
7. Compton McKenzie, 'Safety Last' in David Cleghorn Thomas, *Scotland in Quest of Her Youth* (Edinburgh, 1932), p64
8. David L. Olds, 'The Nurse-Family Partnership: An evidence-based preventive intervention' in *Infant Mental Health Journal* (vol 27 (1), 2006), 5-25. For a reference for EPPE see note 18 in Chapter 10
9. Alan Sinclair, '0-5 How Small Children Can Make A Big Difference'*
10 Health in Scotland 2007: Report by the Chief Medical Officer (Scottish Government, 2008)*
11. See, for example, John Seddon, *Systems Thinking in the Public Sector* (Axminster, 2008)
12 Nicholas A. Christakis and James H. Fowler, *Connected* (New York, 2009), p7

INDEX

W

Z